1927 Charles Lindbergh – flying the Spirit of St. Louis, a Ryan NYP monoplane – takes off from Roosevelt Field on the morning of May 20 in the first successful nonstop solo flight from the New World to Paris. Lucky Lindy makes the trip in 33½ hours.

1929 Army Lt. Jimmy Doolittle makes the world's first "blind" flight over Mitchel Field. Flying under a hood, Doolittle navigates his Consolidated NY-2 biplane through a 15-mile course using new gyroscopic instruments.

1931 Taking off from Roosevelt Field, Wiley Post flies his Lockheed Vega, Winnie Mae, around the globe with Harold Gatty. In 1933, Post flies the same plane around the world by himself, this time taking off from Floyd Bennett Field in Brooklyn; and in 1935, the pilot is killed with humorist Will Rogers in an air crash in Alaska.

1936 In October, TWA launches Air Express service with its Ford Tri-Motor aircraft from Glenn Curtiss Airport, which later becomes North Beach Airport and today is known as LaGuardia Airport.

1939 Pan American Airways' Dixie Clipper, a Boeing B-314, takes off from Port Washington on the first regularly scheduled transatlantic commercial passenger service. The June 28 flight sets down in the Azores, then Lisbon and Marseilles, France.

1946 Republic begins producing the RC-3 Seabee, an amphibian that the Farmingdale company hopes will become a family leisure aircraft. But the plane's high price – $4,495 – and the recession that grips the nation hurt sales.

The nation's first regularly scheduled airmail began in 1918 on Long Island, between Belmont Park and Washington, D.C. Seven years earlier, Earle Ovington flew a sack of cards and letters from Garden City to Mineola in the first-ever air transport of the U.S. mail.

Philip Dionisio

Newsday
B·O·O·K·S

TAKEOFF!

How Long Island
Inspired America to Fly

Stories and photographs of the men and women
who took us from the farm fields to the moon

Foreword by Nelson DeMille

ISBN 1-885134-26-6

Printed in Brentwood, N.Y.

Other books in this series:
"Long Island: Our Story"
"Hometown Long Island"

Earle Ovington takes off from Garden City in 1911 in the nation's first air-mail delivery.

Growing Up In the Shadows Of Winged Wonders

BY NELSON DEMILLE

From where I sit in my writing office, I can see the Garden City Hotel, where Charles Lindbergh slept the night of May 19, 1927. The following morning, Lindbergh got into a car and was driven the few miles to Roosevelt Field. He climbed into the cockpit of the Spirit of St. Louis, and the rest, as they say, is history.

Unfortunately, the old Garden City Hotel was torn down in 1973, replaced by a new one, and Roosevelt Field is now a shopping mall with the same name. In fact, many of Long Island's associations with early aviation no longer exist, victims, for the most part, of suburban development.

But the spirit of these places and people lives on in historical markers, monuments, photographs, books such as this one, and in the memories of men and women who were there at the beginning.

As memories fade, and as the participants and pioneers of Long Island aviation move away or pass away, it becomes more important to preserve this rich and unique heritage, and to pass it on to our children and grandchildren.

I'm not sure why the Wright brothers from Ohio chose Kitty Hawk, North Carolina, to attempt their first flight; probably it had to do with the strong winds, which were crucial in lifting their flying machine off the ground. Certainly it wasn't proximity to the news media that went into their decision.

But soon afterward, Long Island, with its flat, open fields and proximity to New York City became, if not the birthplace of flight, the cradle of aviation.

Growing up on Long Island, I recall a school field trip to Mitchel Air Force Base. My class of about 30 fifth-graders from Elmont was treated to a day of absolute magic. We had lunch in the officers' mess hall; we watched jet fighters taking off; we were allowed to climb into the cockpits of various aircraft; and we saw the flight crew ready rooms where men slept and waited for the order to scramble.

This was the height of the Cold War, and most of us, I think, imagined those pilots running toward their fighters to defend us against Russian bombers headed our way. Probably most of the boys in our class and maybe even some of the girls that day resolved to become fighter pilots. And maybe some of them did.

The point is that aviation on Long Island in those days was part of the fabric of our society. There were many airfields, some military, most civilian; there was Grumman Aircraft, Republic Aviation, Sperry Gyroscope, and smaller aviation-oriented industries where many of our parents earned their livelihoods.

A dominant local industry usually begets many generations of people who gravitate toward that industry — automobile makers in Detroit, coal miners in western Pennsylvania, fishermen in Gloucester and so forth. And I always thought that if a survey were ever done of the hometown origins of military and commercial pilots, aeronautical and space engineers, Long Island would have a disproportionate number of such men and women.

But these days, most of the aeronautic and space industry has moved away, many of the civilian airfields have been developed for housing or shopping, and the military airfields are all closed. What was once an active and living part of Long Island is now history.

Probably as a result of my field trip to Mitchel Air Force Base, I took my first flying lesson at age 17 at Zahns Airport in Amityville, now a housing development. After logging 25 hours of dual instruction, plus a few cross-country trips to Massachusetts, Maine, and New Jersey, I discovered that those men I'd seen in the cockpits of those jet fighters had more of the right stuff than I did. Some people are born to fly, like the men and women on the following pages, and some, like me, are not.

But I count my flying lessons as one of the more interesting things I've done in my life. And I wonder if I'd even have attempted it if I hadn't been born and raised in the cradle of aviation.

Every writer has a dream book or two that he or she would like to write. I have two — a murder mystery set in Rome during the Dark Ages, which I may actually write, and a multigenerational novel set on Long Island, which I may never get to. This novel has aviation as its background, and begins during World War I, goes through the Roaring Twenties, the Depression, World War II, the Korean War, the Cold War, the Space Age, and ends in the present.

Aside from my fictional characters, this novel would have cameo appearances by people such as Glenn Curtiss, Harriet Quimby, Charles Lindbergh, Amelia Earhart, Alicia Patterson, Elinor Smith, Henry Walden, Paul Rizzo, George Dade, and dozens of others.

I began a research folder on this project about 12 years ago, which has now grown to a hefty box of materials. The project is daunting in its scope and would probably take two volumes to complete the story. I noticed, when I began the research a dozen years ago, that history was still being made, and I wondered if I'd ever catch up to the present. But in the past decade or so, Long Island's aviation history began to slow up and finally, I believe, it has stopped. From the perspective of a novelist engaged in research, it has become obvious that the story is finished and awaits my commitment of time and energy.

I have no doubt that many volumes of history will be written about Long Island aviation, and maybe film documentaries will be made, but as for the great Long Island aviation novel, if I don't do it, perhaps someone else will.

Much of this history has finally been assembled in Long Island's Cradle of Aviation Museum, a world-class facility where this rich and important heritage will be viewed, experienced, and marveled at for generations to come.

Meanwhile, we have "Takeoff! How Long Island Inspired America to Fly," which goes into my research box.

Enjoy,

Nelson DeMille

Nelson DeMille

Best-selling novelist Nelson DeMille grew up in Elmont and still lives on Long Island.

Airports of Long Island

*Some 80 airfields have served Long Island in the last century. Here is a sampling of
major and minor fields from Brooklyn to the East End.*

1 Belmont Park Racetrack, Elmont
When the state banned horse racing and wagering in 1910, Belmont Park hosted the 1910 International Aviation Tournament. It was used for airmail deliveries from 1918 to 1920.

2 Nassau Boulevard Aerodrome, Garden City
Located west of Nassau Boulevard between the modern-day Merillon Avenue and Nassau Boulevard railroad stations, the aerodrome was the site of the 1911 International Aviation Tournament. At this tournament, Earle Ovington made the first U.S. airmail flight.

3 Hempstead Plains Aerodrome, Mineola (1911-1917)
The original parcel of land – bordered on the east by Clinton Road, Old Country Road on the north and Hempstead Turnpike on the south – would be renamed several times. In May, 1917, the airfield became **Hazelhurst Field,** named for Army Lt. Leighton Hazelhurst, killed in a flying accident. Also in 1917, the Army opened **Field No. 2,** south of Hazelhurst. It was named **Mitchel Field** a year later for John Purroy Mitchel, a former New York City mayor killed while training for the Army Air Service in Louisiana. Later in 1918, the eastern part of Hazelhurst Field was renamed **Roosevelt Field,** in honor of Theodore Roosevelt's youngest son, Quentin, an Army flier shot down and killed over France in WWI. After Glenn Curtiss' company bought Hazelhurst Field in 1920, the area reopened in 1921 as **Curtiss Field.** In 1929 it was incorporated into Roosevelt Field. Flying ceased in 1951 when plans were drawn for the Roosevelt Field Shopping Center, built in 1956.

4 Republic Airport, Farmingdale (opened 1928)
Fairchild Aviation Corp. opened a new plant and airfield in 1928. Fairchild Republic Co. closed in 1987, but the airfield remained Republic Airport.

5 Curtiss Field, Valley Stream (1929-1933)
The "new" Curtiss Field opened after Roosevelt Field incorporated the old Curtiss Field in Garden City. Later, this Curtiss Field became the Green Acres Shopping Center.

6 Floyd Bennett Field, Brooklyn (1931-1971)
New York City's first municipal airport was dedicated in 1931. By 1936 part of the field was leased to the Coast Guard and in 1941, it became a Naval air station. It was made part of the Gateway National Recreation Area in 1975.

7 Francis S. Gabreski Airport, Westhampton Beach (opened 1931)
Westhampton Beach Airport, established as a civilian field in 1931, became **Suffolk Army Air Base** during WWII and was turned over to the county in 1970. **Suffolk County Airport** became **Gabreski Airport** in 1991, named for the Long Island resident and decorated aviator.

8 LaGuardia Airport, Flushing, Queens (opened 1937)
Mayor Fiorello LaGuardia arranged for the city to buy **North Beach Airport** – formerly **Glenn Curtiss Airport** – from Curtiss-Wright Corp. in 1937. In 1939 it opened to commercial traffic and became **New York Municipal Airport-LaGuardia Field.** The field was renamed **LaGuardia Airport** in 1947.

9 John F. Kennedy International Airport, Queens (opened 1942)
Acres of marshland were filled in at Idlewild Golf Course in 1942 when the city began building **New York International Airport,** dedicated in 1948. In 1963, the airport was renamed to honor the slain president.

10 Long Island MacArthur Airport, Ronkonkoma (opened 1942)
With a federal grant of $500,000, the airport began as a defense-plane landing area in 1942. In 1945, Sperry Gyroscope Co. moved flight operations there. Later that year, the Town of Islip bought the airport. In 1968, the Douglas MacArthur terminal was completed.

11 Bayport Aerodrome, Bayport (opened 1947)
Owned by the Town of Islip, the aerodrome is one of a few grass airfields on Long Island. The Bayport Aerodrome Society flies vintage aircraft there.

12 Calverton Naval Weapons Industrial Reserve Plant (1953-1995)
Built by the Navy for $22 million in 1953, and leased by Grumman Corp., the field was closed when Northrop Grumman Corp. reduced local operations in 1995. The Town of Riverhead took over the facility in 1998 and named it Enterprise Park at Calverton.

13 East Hampton Airport (opened 1936)
Was built by the Works Progress Administration for Suffolk County. It was sold to the Town of East Hampton for $1 in 1942.

14 Zahns Airport, North Amityville (1945-1980)
David Kaplan flew the first successful quadrotor here in 1956. In 1980, the Town of Babylon bought the airport for use as an industrial park.

15 Brookhaven Calabro Airport, Shirley (opened 1942)
Known during WWII as **Mastic Flight Strip,** the airport served military aircraft protecting the East Coast. By 1961, the state transferred title to the Town of Brookhaven. The airport was renamed for prominent local physician and pilot Frank Calabro, killed in a plane crash with his wife, Ruth, in 1991.

Drawing, Philip Dionisio: Research, Kevin Amorim

Operating in 2000
Closed

vi

They Inspired America to Fly

══

T hey taxi along the runways of the past — daring men and women in leather boots and goggles and shirtsleeves and knickerbockers perched behind the whirring propellers of flying machines made of silk and bamboo. And then, as a world watches in wonder, they soar into the sky and a new age.

Just think of it. They were farmers and tinkerers and motorcycle racers and some of them were little more than children and they flew across plains and cities and battlefields and oceans and into a future that would carry humankind onto the moon.

Oh what a time it was.

It was a time of derring-do and dreams, of courage and romance. It's backdrop was a flat and sandy expanse called the Hempstead Plains that in the annals of American history was once known as the largest prairie east of the Mississippi. Just six years after Orville Wright had flown for 59 seconds and 852 feet in a powered aircraft, a motorcycle racer named Glenn Curtiss kept his rickety Golden Flyer aloft for 25 miles and turned Long Island into the cradle of aviation.

Over the years, the cradle would rock the world.

"Takeoff! How Long Island Inspired America to Fly" examines the enduring role Long Island played in shaping America's passion to conquer the air. It includes more than 200 photographs, some of them never before published, and a list of aviation milestones that range from balloon ascents to space flights. But it is above all a human story, and our intent is to convey the spirit and the history of aviation on Long Island by telling the stories of some of its most colorful figures — men and women who flew larger-than-life across a new frontier.

They are not the most recognizable names to flash across the sky. Although he is mentioned in the pages that follow, Charles Lindbergh, whose transatlantic flight from Long Island transfixed the world, is not the subject of one of the 11 chapters that constitute the heart and soul of this book. Nor is Amelia Earhart. Their stories do not require retelling. But the protagonists of this book all had the right stuff. And all were chosen because they had ties to Long Island. Some were born on Long Island, some learned to fly here, some built their worlds in its skies. All of them made memorable contributions to aviation. The book's subtitle sums up their standing: They inspired America to fly.

They are people like Harriet Quimby, who for one short and shining year personified fame and glamor as the first American woman to get a pilot's license and the first woman to fly across the English Channel — only to fall to her death from a plunging monoplane a few weeks later. Bert Acosta, the wild-living "Bad Boy of the Air" who said he could fly a barn door if it had wings. Elinor Smith, who was just 16 when she flew beneath four bridges of New York City.

And they include some of the people who found fame at Grumman Aircraft, which helped shape the face of Long Island for more than 50 years and put humans on the moon. Founders Leroy Grumman and Jake Swirbul, and Teddy Kenyon, one of the first women test pilots employed by the company. And Tom Kelly, the propulsion expert who headed the company's space-exploration operations and became known as the father of the lunar lander called the LEM.

We'd also like to note that "Takeoff! How Long Island Inspired America to Fly" is the third volume in a series of Newsday books that includes "Long Island: Our Story," the Island's history from the Ice Age to the Space Age, and "Hometown Long Island," a close-up look at the region's hundreds of communities.

And it's appropriate to mention that the founders of Newsday, Harry Guggenheim and Alicia Patterson, both played key roles in the story of aviation on Long Island. Both saw tomorrow in the airways. Guggenheim was a patron of Lindbergh and sponsored rocketry pioneer Robert Goddard. Miss Patterson was the first glider pilot to receive instructions aloft by radio. Captain Harry and Miss P. — as they were known — would have enjoyed this book.

We hope you do, too.

Harvey Aronson

Harvey Aronson, editor

Contents

Glenn Curtiss, a speed demon who loved to tinker, came to Long Island to build aircraft and set records.

The World's First Great Birdman

BY JAMES KINDALL

They arrived at daybreak in cars and on horseback. No one wanted to be late.

Glenn Curtiss, already known as the "fastest man in the World," had promised to do something many people in 1909 flatly thought was impossible. In a single moment, he would rise above the Hempstead Plains and transform himself into a golden bird. This wasn't going to be some fairgrounds show with a hapless human suspended from a homemade balloon. No, Curtiss had pledged to circle more than 15 miles in his silk and bamboo aircraft, a feat of controlled flight unheard of at this stage in American aviation. For his effort, he would collect prize money and have his name

*Peter McLaughlin's Gold Bug Hotel on Old Country Road in Mineola
became Curtiss' Long Island headquarters.*

engraved on a silver trophy. Or, he could plunge to an instant death.

At 5:15 a.m. on July 17, the thin, intense daredevil tugged on a black topcoat, borrowed a mechanic's cap and slipped into the blue. The crowd gasped as the Golden Flyer rose in the air. It was true. Humans actually could ride the sky.

Maneuvering like a graceful hawk, Curtiss dipped and banked around the marked circuit. Below, a woman held up placards numbering each completed pass. By the 12th circuit, the required distance had been met. With a wave, he acknowledged the cheering field, then tapped his gas tank to gauge its volume and kept going. After an astounding 25 miles he settled to Earth.

It was another milestone in a miraculous age, one that would make Long Island a focal point for a succession of historic flights by famous birdmen. Over a two-decade period beginning at the start of the century, Curtiss would break records and create airplanes at breathtaking speed. Immediately after completing the Hempstead flight, he made history again with the first commercial sale of an aircraft in the United States. Later, as aeronautics roared into high gear, he would move to Garden City to establish three airfields as well as set up the industry's premier aircraft experimental site.

But watching him rise that day in the Golden Flyer was a moment spectators would never forget.

"I have lived 88 years to see one of those curious flying machines," an elderly man said, "and I now feel satisfied."

All manner of flying machines, monstrous motorcycles, a succession of powerful new engines, giant winged boats and other creations sprang from Glenn Curtiss' imagination. An acquaintance once described his brain as "always going a hundred miles an hour."

His air triumphs — the Long Island flight, a win at Europe's most prestigious air show, a record-setting trip from Albany to New York City and others — rank him close to the Wright brothers in aviation history. But he also was that rare individual who exactly fit his times, a garage inventor endowed with the era's technological faith that all problems required only a little thought and some elbow grease.

"He had that quality of ingenuity about him, the Yankee tinker who made things work," says Tom Crouch, senior curator for the aeronautics division at the Smithsonian Institution's National Air and Space Museum in Washington, D.C. "Not to say that was all there was to him. He was a very complex guy."

Pictures show Curtiss as a brooding presence, although friends claimed that was because he was always thinking of some engineering problem. He was a man who sought recognition, but was uneasy with acclaim — his patented response at ceremonies was, "The parrot can talk but not fly. I can fly but not talk." Later, even though he became the first large-scale producer of planes, he developed no love

for big business. He was amiable and sometimes prickly, a sharp man with a dollar who could be surprisingly generous (he once sent a man who had helped him with his fledgling motorcycle business a stock certificate worth $10,000). A thrill-seeker himself, he later tried to restrain his show pilots from their increasingly risky stunts. Although a shrewd operator, he proved to be naïve in judging character, a trait reflected in his choice of a flimflam business partner who became the bane of his life.

Above all, he was driven by his fascination for things mechanical.

When working on a problem, he was known to bang on the door of friends staying at his house at 3 a.m. to discuss his latest inspiration. Once, while talking to a workman and idly twisting a piece of rubber, he looked at his hands and rushed inside to in-

On July 17, 1909, Curtiss circled the Mineola Fairgrounds in his Golden Flyer, and won the Scientific American's $10,000 prize.

Straddling his motorcycle, Curtiss set a world's record speed for the mile — 26 ²/₅ seconds — in Ormond Beach, Fla., in 1907.

vent the motorcycle handle throttle. Tinkering may have been the only time he was truly happy.

"As long as we were experimenting," he wrote of his workshop days with the cronies who sometimes labored with him through the night, "we never grew tired."

Little in his background promised that the lanky, blue-eyed boy born May 21, 1878, in upstate Hammondsport, N.Y., would become a pioneer of the air. His father was an alcoholic harness maker who died early, his mother a flighty artist. This left a stern grandmother and a deaf sister to guide his upbringing. Money was tight, perhaps the reason he regarded aviation as both a business and an adventure. As a young man, he sold harness and sewing machines, installed acetylene lamp systems and raised rabbits. At one point, he worked for what became the Eastman Kodak Co. and studied photography.

"He did everything he could to make a buck," says Kirk House, director of the museum bearing the aviator's name in his picturesque hometown located at the tip of Lake Keuka, near Buffalo.

One day during a long bicycle ride, he stopped to ask for a drink at a farmhouse. A shy, brown-haired girl named Lena Neff brought him a bucket of spring water. The two became lifelong partners and confidants. On the marriage license, Curtiss stated he was 21 (he was 19) and listed his occupation as "photographer."

Like the Wright brothers, bicycles were his first passion.

After a stint at a photography factory, Curtiss began zipping through the streets as a Western Union bike messenger. Later, he joined a bike club and began dominating local competitions. Eventually, he opened his own bike shop, where he constantly tinkered with improving the vehicles. It wasn't just the nuts and bolts of the sport that drew him. Curtiss lusted for speed.

"He had a passion for it," says House. "He may have been one of those people for whom things never went fast enough until they were going really, really fast."

The advent of motorcycles was perfect timing.

Here was something that enabled him to combine his aptitude for engines with his need to go faster. During his first attempt to build a motorcycle, he discovered the engine parts he received by mail were so primitive that they came without a carburetor. No problem. Quickly, he assembled one from a piece of screen and a tomato can, added it to the engine and pointed the creation downhill. When it suddenly roared into life, Curtiss didn't know how to stop and ditched it before hitting the lake.

Immediately, he began making lighter and faster engines (his ingenuity became so famous that he reputedly was a model for "Tom Swift"). Soon, Curtiss motorbikes were breaking all speed records. Then he did something so extraordinary, it captured the attention of the world.

While working on eight-cylinder engines, he began wondering how fast one would go if strapped to a motorcycle. He set to work with his crew. The result was a 7-foot-long monstrosity supported by a rear car tire and a seat positioned toward the back — the massive engine made it too large to straddle in the middle. In 1907, the inventor rolled out the black, ominous-looking vehicle at a "Speed Carnival" in Florida. The judges were hesitant. Since it wasn't an official entry, it couldn't be entered in the contest. Curtiss talked them into a timed run anyway. Then, he flattened himself to the frame, took a 2-mile head start along the beach and flashed past the finish line at more than 136 mph.

Newspapers immediately dubbed him the "fastest man in the world." It was a record that stood for seven years before finally being broken by an auto racer.

Curtiss built speedboats for his personal use and experimentation, but never for production.

Motorcycles remained his love for years and only a concurrence of circumstances brought his attention to flight.

Like many doubters of the time, he was unimpressed by "balloonatics," and labeled other types of aviators "cranks." His first exposure to the field came when Thomas Scott Baldwin, a famous lighter-than-air devotee who became a lifelong friend, asked him to make a two-cylinder, air-cooled engine to power his airship (the two later built the Army's first dirigible). At one point, Curtiss rode the Baldwin balloon into the sky and proclaimed it "delightful." Overall, he was underwhelmed, remarking, "There is no place to go."

One man he couldn't dismiss as a crank was Alexander Graham Bell. The legendary inventor had long pondered flight using giant kites. An avuncular man who cultivated young adventurers, Bell admired Curtiss' mechanical aptitude. When he formed the Aerial Experiment Association, a group of air enthusiasts who pooled their knowledge to create an aircraft, he brought in Curtiss as the engine expert.

Soon, the Hammondsport workshop became the group's focal point and the frozen lake its testing ground. The local paper reported that during Bell's stay at Curtiss' house, he put a pillow over the ringing phone, saying, "Little did I think when I invented this thing that it would rise up to mock and annoy me!"

By this time, people had heard of the Wright brothers' accomplishments, including their historic first flight in 1903. Air pioneers were still a clubby group, competitive, but mostly wrapped up in the enthusiasm of invention and usually willing to share general knowledge. One of Bell's men wrote the brothers asking for advice. Curtiss himself visited in Dayton, Ohio, and peppered them with questions. Although the Wrights responded amicably, they later suspected their ideas had been stolen. The animosity turned into a long-running patent battle.

At first, "Bell's Boys" had trouble getting off the ground at all.

The bearded patriarch provided most of the funds for their efforts and pushed his kite concept of flight. After those experiments failed, the association turned to gliders. When prototypes began making successful leaps into the air, the group became convinced they were on the right track. A Canadian member took their first effort, the Red Wing, for a short hop before a small crowd in 1908. Newspapers called it "the first public flight by an airplane in the United States." This infuriated the Wrights, who said they had been flying in plain view beside a Dayton trolley line for years.

The brothers became increasingly annoyed at the Bell outfit. Orville Wright, in a letter to Wilbur, noted that the group was offering its machines for sale. "They have got good cheek," he wrote.

The association's third model, the June Bug, was an exciting advance for the time.

Not only was Curtiss responsible for much of its design, he also equipped it with one of his engines. Later, the angry Wrights said that the craft's introduction of ailerons, wing components, was a direct borrowing of their "wing-warping" concept.

The restless inventor's opinion of aviation had increased considerably. Here was something that not only promised to satisfy his craving for speed, but also had business potential. He and others realized that his athleticism along with the balance and control learned from his days as a bicycle competitor made him a natural pilot. Now, the world's fastest man was ready to test his wings.

As he told friends, "There is a fascination about flying that is unnecessary to explain and difficult to resist."

In 1907, a publication dedicated to advancing technology, the Scientific American, offered a massive trophy (the silver alone was worth $2,500) to coax innovators into the sky. Scientific American's proposal was for a series of three air accomplishments, the first being a documented flight of more than a kilometer — about two-thirds of a mile. The other two involved staying aloft during a controlled maneuver and a distance run. The winner of each leg got his name inscribed on the trophy. If the same person completed all three, he got to keep it.

The Aerial Experiment Association decided to go for the first challenge. Curtiss was chosen as the pilot.

The date was to be July 4, 1908. Curtiss notified the newspapers, told Hammondsport citizens to invite everyone they knew and made sure chartered trains brought in crowds. The inventor urged townspeople to spread the news, so that they could "prove to the world that we can really fly."

On the appointed day, a course, which extended through a local vineyard, was measured off. Spectators flocked into town carrying picnic baskets and staking out viewing areas. Reporters and photographers climbed from the train. Everything was ready. After a false start, the strange-looking contraption of crossed sticks and wires jumped into the air, soared around the vineyard and continued for a mile. People could hardly believe their eyes. Some wept outright.

Curtiss flies the June Bug upstate in 1908. The Wright brothers accused Curtiss of "borrowing" their "wing-warping" design for the plane's ailerons.

One woman became so rapt she suffered two broken ribs after being struck by a slow-moving train.

A film crew recorded the flight, which had a hit run in Manhattan.

Everyone, even Bell's son-in-law, David Fairchild, was flabbergasted.

"The thing is done," he said. "Man flies."

Others were shocked, too.

For the Wrights, who had predicted that no one would have a "practical" plane like theirs for at least five years, it was staggering news.

Glenn Curtiss may have been famous before. Now, he was making history.

"It [the June Bug] was probably the most famous airplane in the U.S. until the Spirit of St. Louis came along," says House.

After the Aerial Experiment Association was dissolved, Curtiss began pushing the aviation envelope with a series of new planes and more efficient engines. By the time he was through with the Golden Flyer, it was the fastest and most maneuverable ship of its time. Its introduction came when the Aero Club of America coaxed Curtiss to an exhibition in Morris Park in the Bronx to prove to New Yorkers that airplanes weren't a joke. Other craft displayed included a man-carrying kite, a foot-powered helicopter and a preposterous craft with eight propellers as well as a "wind wagon." At first wowing spectators with short jaunts over the tight field, Curtiss later was jeered by a crowd of 10,000 when wind kept him on the ground. His reluctance to fly under windy conditions led to questions about his courage, an issue that dogged him in later episodes.

Curtiss didn't like flying at Morris Park, but he remembered a locale that seemed promising. The spot was a flat, sandy section in the middle of Long Island known as the Hempstead Plains. He had attended car races there once and told the Scientific American he thought it was an ideal place for its second challenge. Here again, wind became an enemy. During a preparation flight, a gust tipped his plane to the point that a wing tip brushed the tall grass, almost leading to a crash. But a few days later, he piloted the plane into fog and came back exhilarated, describing it as like flying through the clouds.

After his spectacular 1909 Hempstead showing, he turned the Golden Flyer over to the Aeronautic Society of New York for a price of $5,000. It was the first airplane sale in America. Then, he cabled news of the triumphant flight to his mentor Alexander Graham Bell, who promptly wired back congratulations.

The day also had an element of comedy. Along with delivering the plane, Curtiss was under contract with the society to teach two of its members to fly. The first man did fine with a short flight and acceptable landing. The second, fortified by alcohol taken on an empty stomach, took a turn too sharply, lost speed and landed upside down with the engine still throbbing. He was pulled from the plane unconscious and retired from flying on the spot.

A few days before making his Long Island flight, Curtiss had been talked into entering an international air meet taking place the next month in Rheims, France. Competition between the United States and Europe was a matter of fierce patriotic pride, but odds were against him. European aviation was the most sophisticated in the world since governments there, anticipating war, had been investing heavily in air machines. The meet's jewel, the Gordon Bennett trophy, awarded for the fastest flight, had drawn the cream of the continent's fliers. Some brought along five planes for spares. Curtiss had built a small, unimpressive-looking craft with a special eight-cylinder motor for the contest. Its appearance raised no eyebrows. Comments were made that it looked like a boy's hobby craft.

Newspapers already had reported speeds by Europe's fliers well beyond any recorded by the Hammondsport man. The favorite was Louis Blériot, a flamboyant French pilot who had been the first to cross the English Channel. Getting wind of Curtiss' new engine, he had a similar one built for himself that supposedly produced superior speeds.

The contest day arrived. Curtiss climbed into his toy plane. Using racing tricks learned from his bicycle days, he took a run at the start line and banked sharply on the turns. The crowd was dazzled. When it was over, he landed to find that he had reached an average speed of 46½ mph, a record. Other entrants tried for the mark and failed. Finally, Blériot shot into the sky and set a fast pace that looked like a winner. Curtiss waited glumly for the decision. When the judges were through with their calculations, they found the Frenchman trailed "l'Américain" by six seconds. Curtiss had won.

"The Wright brothers didn't go," says the Smithsonian's Crouch. "For awhile, it looked like America wasn't even going to be in attendance. But Curtiss decides to go and darned if he didn't walk away with the biggest prize."

The victory made Americans swell with pride, but for the quiet inventor its glow was short lived.

Plans had been made in New York at the end of the year for a commemoration of Hudson River history. One star event was an exhibition of flying machines at Governors Island with appearances by both Glenn Curtiss and Wilbur Wright. Newspapers tacitly painted it as a face-off, predicting the two would rise over the skyscrapers and chase each other "down the river and over the rooftops."

For Curtiss, the meeting was a disaster.

Once again, skittish about using a new plane in blustery conditions (his nettlesome partner had tied up the Rheims flyer by putting it on display for a fee at a department store), he made two short flights around the small island and quit. The trips were witnessed by so few that some questioned whether he had flown at all. Wilbur, on the other hand, delighted the public by circling the Statue of Liberty. On another day with American flags fluttering from his plane, he passed over Grant's Tomb.

The inventor had a chance for redemption in 1910 and took it.

As part of the Hudson River celebration, a $10,000 challenge had been issued by the New York World for a long-distance Albany-to-Manhattan flight. Curtiss was attracted by the money, but he also realized this would give him another chance to prove his courage to New Yorkers. Its completion also promised permanent possession of the Scientific American trophy.

Still, this was no small feat. At 152 miles, the distance would be an American cross-country record. An Englishman already had established a world distance record of 182 miles abroad, but over a two-day period. This time, two landings were allowed en route and the flight had to be accomplished in 24 hours.

Dangers were obvious. Emergency landing fields were limited. Curtiss had equipped his plane with a rudimentary pontoon, but knew crashing in the river could be fatal. Early air experimenters had died trying far less risky ventures. Considering the dangerous winds that whipped along the Hudson River Valley, some doubted it could be done at all.

Weather delays brought mumbling from the press. Some reporters, remembering Curtiss' last failure, called the event a "pain in the neck." At one point, the airman threw himself on the ground in frustra-tion. Finally, at 7:02 on a calm Sunday morning, he lofted above the field and headed down river.

On a chartered train racing below, a news photographer snapped pictures hanging out of a baggage car window. Telegraph wires ticked out the news. In New York, people crowded onto Riverside Drive rooftops and waited.

The air was smooth at first. Curtiss landed at a midpoint, borrowed five gallons of gas from spectators and took off again. His most dangerous moment came near Poughkeepsie, where the topography created a natural wind tunnel. Surprised by a fierce downward draft, Curtiss dropped 100 feet and was nearly tossed out of his plane. It was the worst dip he ever took, he said. He regained control, leveled out at 40 feet above the water and located calm air currents. Oil was low by the time he made an impromptu touchdown on a Harlem estate. Technically, he had won the contest, but he remembered his humiliation. Curtiss borrowed more oil and gas from the estate owner and returned to the sky. Finally, in a total of a little less than three hours from Albany, he passed by the cheering city, circled the Statue of Liberty and came down on Governors Island.

"Certainly, it was one of the most important flights in aviation history," says Joshua Stoff, curator of the Cradle of Aviation Museum in Garden City.

Securely in the record books, Curtiss turned his interests elsewhere.

Mounting prize money being offered by cities throughout the airplane-mad nation seemed a fine way to make a buck. Curtiss responded by organizing and training a group of exhibition pilots. They quickly became the stars of the air, some earning up to $5,000 a day. All were colorful ranging to eccentric. Many, pushing their planes beyond their limits, lived high and died young. As airplanes improved and speeds increased, Curtiss urged his pilots to stay within their planes' limits. Some, such as Lincoln Beachey of Toledo, Ohio, ignored him completely.

Beachey was famous for his "death dip" and once dropped 2,000 feet into the mists of Niagara Falls before leveling out. Another time, apparently miffed by the governor of California, who tried to shake his hand after a performance, Beachey took off again and disrobed in the air, dropping his clothes onto the field. He died later in another incident when his wings folded during a death dive over San Francisco Bay.

Curtiss also helped — reluctantly — women avia-

Glenn Curtiss, in his Golden Flyer at Mineola, was issued airplane license No. 1 in the United States in 1910 by the Aero Club of America.

tors into the air. His first pupil, 18-year-old Blanche Scott of Rochester, possessed a bit of showmanship herself. Since swirling skirts were a problem in open airplanes, she daringly switched to bloomers. His second woman pilot, Julia Clarke, came to him for lessons after being turned down by the Wrights. He, too, refused to give her instructions. The young woman purchased a plane. Finally, after realizing she was going to fly anyway, he taught her to fly. Two years later while performing at a state fair, she died in a crash when her plane clipped a tree.

In 1914, Curtiss became engaged in a remarkable experiment to revise history.

Samuel Langley, secretary of the Smithsonian and a famed scientist, had built a craft that flew successfully as a model in 1896. He and his longtime friend, Bell, watched it sail over the Potomac River together. Langley followed with a full-sized "aerodrome" which, because of an accident not connected to its design, crashed into the river in 1903 — nine days before the Wright brothers' first flight at Kitty Hawk, N.C. The press made so much fun of Langley's attempt that the scientist abandoned further attempts and died a bitter man.

Advocates wanted his reputation restored. Curtiss,

knowing a successful demonstration would help his court fight against the Wrights by showing they weren't the first to come up with a flying machine, volunteered to rebuild it. The bizarre, birdlike contraption was restored at Hammondsport. Afterward, Curtiss climbed into the seat located beneath the front wing and soared for 150 feet before landing softly.

This and later flights with the same craft — one was for 10 miles — were later disputed mostly because Curtiss had added pontoons, but others saw it as Langley's long overdue redemption. Bell sent him a telegram saying it was the "crowning achievement of your career." Later, a plaque at the Smithsonian next to the restored aerodrome called it, "The first man-carrying aeroplane in the history of the world capable of sustained free flight."

In addition to his talent for invention, Curtiss was a visionary foreseeing the airplane as a major form of transportation and a deadly form of warfare.

The point that planes could be useful as weapons had been driven home to him during his Albany-to-New York flight. Passing over West Point, he noticed how vulnerable it was from above. Upon landing, he predicted, "All the great battles

A plane is displayed in front of the Gold Bug Hotel in 1910.

of the future will be fought in the air."

Convincing the military was another matter.

In 1910, he dropped oranges instead of bombs near Atlantic City to demonstrate the use of airplanes in combat. Another time, he piloted his plane over a Brooklyn racetrack while a marksman put two bullets into a target from 100 feet in the air. These and other experiments intrigued observing officers, but it was war that developed this aspect of aviation. And it was war that catapulted Curtiss into the ranks of big-time airplane production.

The advent of World War I flooded his Buffalo plant with orders from around the world. Someone at the British Embassy reportedly told Curtiss his government wanted him to "build all the planes you can as fast as you can." Production of the JN model, nicknamed the Jenny, was an immediate hit. Its trusty performance and tandem cockpit made it ideal for training military pilots. After the war, the low-priced Jennys became the favorite of barnstormers throughout the United States.

"Curtiss built airplanes in larger numbers than anyone else in America and he was the only one here who sold in large numbers to European governments," says Crouch.

Some of his greatest air triumphs were associated with the sea.

The idea of planes landing in water had always fascinated Curtiss. In 1908, he mounted the famous June Bug with floats and unsuccessfully attempted to fly off the surface at Lake Keuka, the first trial of this kind ever made. Realizing the value of a craft that could use water as an airfield, he began experimenting in San Diego. There, his pilot, Eugene Ely, landed on a shipboard platform rigged with a series of ropes attached to sandbags to slow his plane. Then, he took off again, a feat that foreshadowed aircraft carriers.

Still, Curtiss wanted a plane that could operate on liquid. He designed a plane with a hull that could float, but suction kept it from rising in the air. Finally, in 1911, he hit on the idea of redesigning the hull with a "step" to break free. Shortly thereafter, he had the brilliant stroke of adding retractable landing gear, making it a vehicle for land, air and sea — a Triad. Later, he created a craft with a true hull, the first actual flying boat. In 1919, one of his products, the huge NC-4, became the first airplane ever to cross the Atlantic. For a time, seaplanes were the world's major form of long-distance transportation.

Curtiss' sojourn on Long Island was one of the most contented times in his life. It also was the site of another of his far-sighted concepts.

For years, Curtiss dreamed of building the ultimate tinker's workshop. In 1917, the Curtiss Engineering Corp., one of a number of companies Curtiss started and controlled, was born in Garden City, the first facility devoted to research and development and a forerunner of fantastical R & D sites such as the Skunkworks. He added the largest and most elaborate wind tunnel in the United States, 10 feet in diameter. Here, prototypes were assembled and tested, then sent to the Buffalo plant for production.

"People know of Grumman and Republic aircraft, but before they existed, Glenn Curtiss was a world aviation leader here on Long Island," says Stoff of the Cradle of Aviation Museum.

The factory shell still exists in Garden City, including a smokestack with the Curtiss name on it, at the corner of Clinton Road and Stewart Avenue.

By this point in his life, the airman had cut back on his personal flying (he conceded that air travel had progressed so fast that he would have to learn all over again) and made a conscious effort to relax.

The Garden City home he purchased had a formal garden, a greenhouse, a swimming pool, several practice golf holes and a bowling green. He began riding bikes again and took jaunts with his wife and their son, Glenn Jr. He made a serious study of archery and took family and friends to the beach. Even relaxing, he never stopped experimenting.

An acquaintance discovered him barefoot on his lawn, his feet pushing against an oversized bow while he drew back a particularly long arrow. Sixty feet away was a target full of arrows.

He was just "studying flight," he explained.

No one doubts the Wrights' pre-eminence in the pantheon of flight, but Curtiss' achievements spanned several decades, included a wide range of inventions and took the airplane from its fabric and wire beginnings into modern aviation.

"He produced some of most famous planes of the 1920s in terms of military fighters, bombers, trainers, sport planes, racing planes," says Stoff. "Curtiss racers won every speed race in the 1920s."

The Wrights' legal battle with Curtiss and other aviation builders eventually was settled with a compromise that allowed others use of the Wright inventions.

It may have been a measure of some satisfaction to Curtiss that when the two factions merged in 1929, the name settled upon was the Curtiss-Wright Corp.

"The Wrights produced a very small number of planes and by World War I were out of the business. Curtiss became the largest manufacturer of airplanes in the world," says Stoff. "So the Wrights won the battle but lost the war."

In his last years, Curtiss began investing in Florida real estate with amazing success. At one point, he and his partners sold a million dollars worth of lots in a 10-day period. During this period, he developed Hialeah, as well as Opa-locka, a city he built on the theme of the Arabian Nights.

History granted him one last triumph.

Twenty years after the event, the Aeronautical Chamber of Commerce of America persuaded Curtiss to re-enact his famous Albany to Manhattan flight. This time he rode with 80 passengers in a new airliner, the Curtiss Condor, escorted by four other planes in what amounted to an air parade. At cruising altitude, the pilot gave him the controls. After reaching New York, he circled Governors Island, then handed the controls back.

It was his last moment in the sky.

At the time of his death at age 52, he had been credited with more than 500 inventions, including such things as a wind propeller-driven boat (the forerunner of swamp boats) and a streamlined trailer for luxury camping. His Wright brother rivals retained their reputation as premier air inventors, but Curtiss' water experiments gave him historical credit as the "father of naval aviation."

"He was the king of the flying boat," says Crouch.

Two months after his re-created Albany trip, Curtiss was taken to a Buffalo hospital with acute appendicitis. True to his spirit, his mind was busy to the end. The day before his death of complications from his operation, a secretary found him propped up in his bed sketching a glider.

Glenn Curtiss died on July 23, 1930.

At his funeral in Hammondsport, 10 planes circled the air, then dipped low and, one by one, dropped flowers on his grave. ●

Harriet Quimby, seen with her Blériot monoplane, became interested in flying at the 1910 aviation tournament at Long Island's Belmont Park.

America's Flying Sweetheart

BY LAURA MUHA

I n May, 1911, a mysterious veiled figure was spotted taking flying lessons at the Moisant Aviation School on the Hempstead Plains. Rumor had it that the unidentified flier was a woman.

In an era in which women weren't considered capable of driving cars, never mind the dangerous new contraptions called airplanes, that was big news, and curiosity-seekers soon began showing up at the field at 4:30 a.m., eager to see for themselves what was happening.

Sure enough, there was the flier: a slender, youthful figure of indeterminate sex, clad in knickerbockers, goggles and a helmet with a heavy veil attached to the brim. Without a word to the crowd, the aviator climbed into an airplane, took off and circled the field at an altitude of 50 feet.

The performance was repeated the next day, and the next, with still no hint as to the identity of the person at the controls.

It wasn't until May 10 that the mystery was solved, when a breeze blew the pilot's veil aside just long enough for someone in the crowd to recognize her: It was Harriet Quimby, a New York theater critic and photojournalist, who was already well-known not only for her intrepid reporting and riveting feature stories, but for a beauty so striking that nearly a century later, it would still be a subject of conversation.

"Woman In Trousers Daring Aviator," The New York Times headlined the next morning, going on to quote Quimby as saying that she'd taken up flying "just because I thought I should enjoy the sensation."

"Motoring is all right, and I have done a lot of that," she added, "but after seeing monoplanes in the air, I couldn't resist the desire to try the air lanes, where there are neither speed laws nor traffic policemen, and where one needn't go all the way around Central Park to get across Times Square."

For 14 months after her identity was discovered, Quimby would continue to make headlines and history as the first licensed woman pilot in America and the second in the world, after the French flier Baroness Raymonde de la Roche. She was the first American woman to pilot a monoplane — an aircraft with one set of wings instead of two — as well as the first woman to fly at night, the first woman to fly over Mexico City and the first woman to pilot a plane across the English Channel.

For not quite a year, she was a star on an international stage — the daring and glamorous figure she may have always dreamed of being. Quimby's flying career was cut short when she was thrown from her plunging plane and fell to her death in a crash in

Quimby's beauty only added to her celebrity as an aviator. "I think she was the prettiest girl I've ever seen," said her friend Matilde Moisant, standing next to Quimby, below.

Quimby was the first American woman to pilot a monoplane, as well as the first woman to fly at night.

Dorchester Bay, Mass., on July 1, 1912. But, her legend lives on in more than a half-dozen biographies and children's books, exhibits in aviation museums around the country, an annual research conference and a 50-cent airmail stamp emblazoned with her picture and the words "Harriet Quimby, Pioneer Pilot."

Perhaps more significant, Quimby's achievements opened doors for the many more famous female pilots, such as Elinor Smith, Amelia Earhart and Teddy Kenyon, who would follow in her footsteps in the years to come.

"Harriet wasn't just a 'girl' pilot — she could actually fly at a time when aircraft were very, very dangerous and difficult to operate," says Peter Jakab, curator of early aviation at the Smithsonian Institution's National Air and Space Museum in Washington, D.C. "Male or female, she was not an insignificant pilot in this period — but the fact that she was a woman made what she did even more of an accomplishment."

In 1911, when Quimby took her first flight, women were still nearly a decade away from being allowed to vote, and weren't permitted to serve on juries in most states. They rarely worked outside the home, and the few who drove automobiles were considered wildly adventurous — not to mention unladylike.

The idea that a woman might want to pilot a contraption as dangerous as an airplane — back then crashes were an everyday occurrence — was, to most people, ludicrous.

Still, very few women had made a mark in aviation, among them Bessica Medlar Raiche, a Mineola resident credited with being the first American woman to fly solo. One of the "new" breed of women, who drove a car and wore trousers while playing sports, Raiche had become fascinated with aviation while studying in France in the early 1900s — so much so that when she and her husband, Francoise, returned to the United States, they built a silk-and-bamboo biplane in their living room.

The couple transported the finished aircraft to the Hempstead Plains, and on Sept. 26, 1910, Raiche climbed aboard and took off. The flight lasted only a few minutes and, according to some accounts, ended in a crash. (Other reports say the crash occurred during Raiche's fifth flight in the fragile aircraft.)

Either way, one newspaper described the aftermath of the wreck this way: "She scrambled to her feet and before any one of the mechanicians and others who had witnessed the fall of the biplane could reach her, she had shut off the engine and stopped the propeller. She calmly said she was not injured to those who ran to her aid, and then she directed the men to drag the wrecked plane back to the shed."

For Raiche's efforts, the Aeronautic Society presented her with a gold-and-diamond medal inscribed "First Woman Aviator of America," although in fact, Rochester native Blanche Stuart Scott, a student of famed aviator Glenn Curtiss, had flown two weeks earlier, on Sept. 2.

The circumstances under which Scott's flight occurred, however, were ruled questionable by the Aeronautic Society, with some members speculating that a gust of strong wind lifted the plane off the ground as Scott taxied across the field. So the official honor of being America's first female pilot went to Raiche — who ironically quit flying soon thereafter and became a physician, leaving the aviation stage to other pioneering women such as Quimby.

When it comes to Quimby's early life, it is sometimes difficult to separate fact from fiction, because much of what is known is based on interviews she gave after becoming famous — and because Quimby wasn't above stretching the truth to create the impression that she wanted.

"She was very conscious of her image, and knew how to use it," says the Smithsonian's Jakab. "The fact that she kind of fabricated some things about her life, and hid her humble beginnings — I'm speculating here, but I don't think it was because she was

ashamed of where she came from; I think it was to help her gain access to places that otherwise would have been closed to her, places where she could do what she was capable of doing."

Among other things, Quimby insinuated that she was born in 1884 to wealthy parents who owned a California orange plantation. In fact, she appears to have been born on May 11, 1875, in Coldwater, Mich. Her father, William, had served in the Union Army, but was apparently discharged because of poor health; her mother, Ursula, was reportedly a skilled herbalist who nursed him through his illness. Quimby also had an older sister, Kittie.

The 1880 census lists the family as living in Arcadia, Mich., but after their farm failed at the end of that decade, they joined the westward movement. Their first stop appears to have been Arroyo Grande, about 100 miles north of Santa Barbara, Calif., where some reports have William Quimby operating a grocery store, and others, working in a dairy.

By the 1890s, however, the family had moved to San Francisco, where Ursula Quimby reportedly supported them by making prune sacks for a fruit-packing factory and by manufacturing herbal medicines.

The business prospered, and as the family grew wealthier, Ursula apparently decided that her daughters should enter San Francisco society. According to some reports, it was she who encouraged the girls to

Quimby, at left in a Blériot, may have been the nation's first licensed woman pilot, but Mineola's Bessica Raiche, below, was officially recognized as the first American woman to fly solo.

In the male-dominated world of aviation, Harriet Quimby never masked her femininity. She opened the door for future women of flight.

create an air of mystery about themselves, by hinting that they'd grown up wealthy and been educated abroad in private finishing schools. In fact, none of Quimby's school records have been found, although her abilities as a writer do suggest that she was well educated.

In their efforts to break into San Francisco society, both Quimby sisters were aided by their head-turning good looks. Harriet, in particular, was striking, with dark hair and fine features that would later earn her the nickname "Dresden Doll Aviatrix."

"I think she was the prettiest girl I've ever seen," her friend Matilde Moisant, whose brother ran the school where Quimby learned to fly, reportedly said years later. "She had the most beautiful green eyes — oh, what eyes she had! And she was tall and willowy."

Quimby's portrait is said to have hung in the all-male Bohemian Club until it was destroyed in the 1906 earthquake, and a series of early photographs show her posing in flowing hats, romantic long dresses and gloves. "She runs strong to overhung bonnets and antique ornaments such as basil-

isks, amulet scarabs and the like, so that even in business attire her individuality is very distinctive," a journalist of the era wrote in World magazine after interviewing her.

In fact, Quimby's femininity is part of her enduring appeal. "A lot of guys studying early aviation are just in love with her," says Jakab. "Many of the women that got involved in flying in that era were tomboy types, or wanted to be taken seriously, so they downplayed their femininity. Harriet never did. She broke a lot of barriers and taboos for professional women, but still she was very much a female, and reveled in that as well."

While Quimby's charm and good looks undoubtedly would have made it easy for her to land a husband and settle into the life of a society lady, there is no indication that she ever considered doing so.

Instead, she appears to have reveled in flouting convention whenever possible. Between 1897 and 1903, she and her father are listed separately in San Francisco street directories, suggesting that she may have lived on her own. She also tooled about town in a yellow roadster, and in an era in which well-bred young ladies were expected to marry and devote themselves to home and family, Quimby announced that she wanted a career.

In the 1900 census, she listed her occupation as "actress," but not long after that, began writing articles for the San Francisco Dramatic Review, and later for the Call-Bulletin and Chronicle.

In 1903, she was hired by Leslie's Illustrated Weekly, a New York magazine that catered to the fashionable and sophisticated set. Heading east, she moved into the Victoria Hotel, her parents in tow. (They eventually moved into their own home, but Quimby continued to reside at the hotel in Manhattan.)

While Quimby is often referred to simply as the magazine's drama critic — and she did review plays — she also was a photojournalist whose career took her to Europe, Cuba, Iceland and Mexico. She wrote on a wide range of subjects, from her life as a single woman in New York City ("A chafing dish, a tea-caddy, and a genial friend who . . . is glad over your little successes and silent over your failures, goes a long way toward real contentment") to the importance of wildlife preservation ("If killing [wild birds] goes on as it now is going, our grandchildren will see a gameless continent").

She reportedly wrote a number of screenplays, which were purchased by friends who made silent films for the Biograph Co. in New York, making her one of America's first female screenwriters.

In 1910, perhaps looking for a novel feature story, Quimby attended the International Aviation Tournament at Belmont Park, where she was much impressed with the performance of an American pilot named John Moisant, a dashing former soldier of fortune who flew with a tabby kitten as a mascot.

That evening, while having dinner with friends at the Astor Hotel, Quimby spied Moisant at a nearby table. "I went directly over to him and told him I wished to learn to fly," she recalled later.

Moisant invited her to join a flying school he intended to open on the Hempstead Plains, but was killed in a crash two months later. The school opened anyway, under the direction of his brother Alfred and French flying instructor A.J. Houpert; in the next few years, it would become one of the most famous flying schools in the country.

It was at the Moisant school that, in April, 1911, Quimby had her first lesson — the only female pupil among the six original students.

Years later, Matilde Moisant, who began taking lessons at her brother's school shortly after Quimby did, described the process of learning to fly: "We were all taught the same way. We just had little single-seat machines. The first step was a heavy machine not designed to leave the ground. That was called Saint Genevieve. She was the patron saint of fliers in France. After learning to keep straight, our next machine was the Grasshopper, which would go up to 5 or 6 feet, then come down again. That was to get the feeling of being in the air."

Because the sport was so male-dominated, Quimby apparently felt she had to disguise her identity when she started lessons. But when she was quickly found out, she didn't seem terribly concerned about it.

"Miss Quimby laughed when she found she was discovered for, in the two weeks that she has been here making daily morning flights . . . she has managed to keep her identity a secret," wrote a New York Times reporter at the scene. "For more than a week it was not even suspected that she was not a man, for her costume, in every detail is that of any expert aviator."

It is hard to fathom what the reporter meant by that, for an earlier sentence in the story referred to Quimby's "aviation jacket and trousers of wool-backed satin" — hardly the typical flying costume of the era. In fact, Quimby had designed the plum-colored suit herself, and it quickly became a part of her trademark; the satin knickerbockers tucked into high, pointy lace-up boots, and the enormous hood converted into a walking skirt; she also liked to set the suit off with jewelry.

But there was little doubt that she intended to be more than a fashion plate in the air. In the same story, the reporter asked Quimby if she liked flying. Her reply: "Well, I'm out here at 4 o'clock every morning. That ought to be answer enough."

Then she added, "I thought it would be nice to be the first American woman to win a pilot's license and I shall get one soon. I have not found it very difficult to learn to control my monoplane in short flights and there is no reason why I soon shouldn't make longer ones."

Ironically, only two days later, Quimby had her first known mishap, while trying to take off at full speed.

"In turning, the wheels of the running gear were wrenched off, and in a twinkling the forks and one of the wings were broken," according to one news re-

Harriet Quimby, a theater critic, took wing and began flying in May, 1911. She was the first American woman to earn a pilot's license.

port. "The plucky girl, however, retained her seat, shut off the power and jumped from the machine."

Undeterred, Quimby continued her flying instruction, and on July 31, 1911, after 33 lessons, she took her licensing exam. The test, administered by the Aero Club of America, required her to demonstrate skills in takeoff and altitude, perform a series of figure eights around pylons, and land within 100 feet of a specified mark.

At first, everything went well. "Miss Quimby . . . gave a beautiful exhibition, banking on the curves and handling the Moisant monoplane with an ease and smoothness which elicited warm praise from the other aviators," The New York Times reported.

But when Quimby landed, she forgot to shut off the motor, and after touching down well within the specified circle, was carried 40 feet beyond it by the engine.

"Miss Quimby was almost in tears because of her failure," the paper reported. "She declared, however, that she would repeat the attempt at 4:30 o'clock this morning."

When she arrived at the airfield, however, it was shrouded in fog, and the Aero Club's official observers wanted to leave. "Miss Quimby insisted that the sun would burn the haze away, and finally persuaded everyone to wait," The New York Times reported. "Her skill as a weather prophet was vindicated at 6 o'clock when the sun managed to work through the mist, and there was every promise of a speedy clearing. Miss Quimby had her monoplane wheeled from the hangar and it was not much after 6 o'clock when she gave the word to release her craft."

After takeoff, Quimby quickly climbed to an altitude of 100 feet, and made the required five circuits of the pylons, alternating right and left turns.

"She banked her craft prettily at the turns and

Bad weather kept Quimby grounded in April, 1912, when she wanted to cross the English Channel alone. Here, she prepares for her big flight.

soon had accomplished the first test, the one which she had performed last night," the Times reported. "Then, she had tried immediately to land beside the mark. This time, warned by her failure of last night, she came to earth, let her motor cool and then ascending again, dropped within seven feet nine inches of the mark" — a near record for accuracy.

Next, to complete the altitude requirements for the test, Quimby "swung aloft in a series of spirals, and then dropped easily to earth after her barograph had recorded 220 feet."

When she climbed from the plane, she was obviously elated. Reported the Times, "Her face was covered with grease and dirt, but her . . . eyes flashed happily as she greeted the official observers with the remark: 'Well, I guess I get that license.'

" 'I guess you do,' was the response, and without waiting for further congratulations, Miss Quimby

hurried off to change into her usual garments."

Only a month later, on Sept. 4, Quimby was back in the headlines when she became the first woman to fly at night, in a demonstration that drew 15,000 people to the Staten Island Fair. "Harriet Quimby Darts About in the Moonshine Above an Admiring Crowd," The New York Times headlined the next morning, before going on to elaborate:

"It was almost dark when Miss Quimby's monoplane was wheeled out. The field was overrun by anxious spectators, and Miss Quimby . . . appealingly asked the crowd to stand back lest someone be hurt."

When she was finally able to take off, Quimby circled the track first at a high altitude, then a lower one.

"On the third time around she passed within a few feet of the judges' stand and waved a handkerchief vigorously at friends in the paddock," the Times reported. "She seemed to be enjoying her spin, and the motor worked without a hitch."

After Quimby's landing — "a bouncing affair, the monoplane once rising ten feet into the air when it hit a rut," the paper said — her mother rushed over to her and kissed her repeatedly.

"You were up just seven minutes, Harriet, and I think that I would have come up after you if you had remained in the air any longer."

"Oh! mother," Quimby replied. "You'll get used to it all right. It was grand. I didn't feel like ever coming to earth again."

To reporters she said: "It was a great temptation not to keep right on flying until I got to New York. The funny thing about it was that I was so hot up there. I think it was the effect of the applause which made my blood rise. I never had so much applause before."

For her performance, Quimby was presented with a check for $1,500 by the president of the fair's board of directors. Around the same time, she earned another $600 for beating famed French aviator Hélène Dutrieu in a race at the Staten Island Fair. The two were also scheduled to compete for the women's endurance record, which Quimby held at the time. But when she discovered the contest was to take place on a Sunday, she refused to participate.

"Miss Quimby announced that she had promised her mother that she would not fly on Sunday, and would not think of doing so," reported the Times. "From a hangar she watched her opponent soar aloft until her own record had been broken by many minutes. She said she didn't care, as a record won on Sunday would be to her not worth while."

In December, 1911, Quimby and Matilde Moisant, who received her pilot's license shortly after Quimby, joined the Moisant International Flyers, an exhibition team that was heading for Mexico. There, Quimby performed at the inauguration of President Francisco Madero, becoming the first woman to fly over Mexico City.

But the trip was even more notable for another reason: While there, she wrote later, "an ambition to be the first woman to cross the English Channel alone entered my mind."

Although the first such trip had been made by pioneering French aviator Louis Blériot in 1909, and repeated by several other male pilots since then, it had never been attempted by a woman. To be the first to accomplish such a feat, Quimby knew, would bring her worldwide attention.

"The more I thought about it, the less formidable the feat seemed to be," she wrote.

When she returned to New York, she hired well-known balloon designer A. Leo Stevens as her manager and secured a letter of introduction to Blériot, who by then owned an airplane manufacturing company in Paris.

On March 7, 1912, she and Stevens set sail for Europe with the letter in hand. Landing in London, they first pitched Quimby's idea to, as she put it, "the wide-awake editor of the London Mirror."

He quickly offered her "a handsome inducement" if she would make the trip on behalf of the paper, and also gave her a small bronze idol for good luck.

"The next thing necessary was to get a monoplane," Quimby wrote. "I went to Paris, saw Mr.

Quimby designed her trademark plum-colored suit: satin knickerbockers tucked into high, lace-up boots.

Blériot and . . . arranged for the loan of a fifty-horse-power monoplane of the type I had been accustomed to in the United States."

Fearful that some other female aviator might learn of her plans and make the trip before she could do so, Quimby arranged for her plane to be shipped secretly to the Dover aerodrome, which sat about three miles from the channel, not far from Dover Castle.

"I saw at once that I had only to rise in my machine, fix my eyes upon the castle, fly over it and

America's pioneer woman aviator gets ready for her channel flight on April 16, 1912. She flew safely in the fog to France.

speed directly across to the French coast," Quimby wrote. "It seemed so easy that it looked like a cross-country flight."

Then, on April 2, 1912, Quimby's worst fear seemed to come true when newspapers reported that an Englishwoman, Eleanor Trehawke Davies, had flown the channel — although only as a passenger in a plane flown by British pilot Gustav Hamel.

Although Quimby still had the opportunity to become the first female pilot to fly the channel, it is apparent that she felt some bitterness at what Hamel had done. Writing later in World magazine, she insinuated that she'd told a pilot she refused to identify about her channel-crossing plans, and that two days later he'd made the same flight with a female passenger, "robbing me of the distinction of being the first woman across."

At the time, however, Quimby simply asked Hamel to join her team, and he agreed. However, he had grave reservations about her flight, and even went so far as to offer to fly across for her, dressed in her purple satin costume. Once in France, he suggested, he would land on some remote beach, where Quimby could meet him, change places and take credit for the trip.

Quimby's response: "I adamantly refused his offer, and if he had not been such a dear friend I would have been very angry."

She did, however, accept his offer to teach her to navigate using a watch and compass, while waiting for several days of stormy weather to clear.

Finally, on April 14, the wind died down. "The sun was bright and warm. The air was so clear that by straining our eyes a little we could see the French coast dimly outlined across the channel. Everyone said, 'Start now. This is your chance. We may have high winds tomorrow and they may last two weeks.' "

Unfortunately, it was Sunday, and Quimby, remembering her promise to her mother, refused to leave; by the next morning, more bad weather moved in.

"After all our patient waiting and hoping against hope that the wind would go down toward evening, there was no abatement in its strength," Quimby wrote. "We went back to our hotel at seven p.m., tired, chilled and disgusted."

At 3:30 a.m. Tuesday, the storm finally died out. "We were called, had our hot tea, got into our automobiles and at four o'clock were on the flying grounds. There was no wind. Scarcely a breath of air was stirring. The monoplane was turned out of the hangar. We knew that we must hasten, for it was almost certain that the wind would rise again within an hour."

The only problem was that the channel was shrouded in fog — something that worried Quimby's crew, but didn't deter her. "I felt impatient to realize the project on which I was determined, despite the protest of my best friends," she wrote.

The only known newsreel footage taken of her on that day shows Quimby powdering her nose, then climbing into the wicker seat of the flimsy plane, which had an open cockpit, no windshield and controls consisting of only a joystick and rudder bars.

On the film clip, she signals the ground crew to let go, waves once, and the plane rolls forward, jouncing on its rubber tires.

"In a moment I was in the air, climbing steadily in a long circle," Quimby wrote. "I was up fifteen hundred feet in thirty seconds."

From that vantage point, she could easily see Dover Castle, perched on the cliffs ahead. "It was half hidden in a fog bank. I felt that trouble was coming, but I made directly for the flagstaff of the castle, as I had promised the waiting Mirror photographers and the moving-picture men I should do.

"In an instant I was beyond the cliffs and over the channel. Far beneath me I saw the Mirror's tug, with its stream of black smoke. It was trying to keep ahead of me, but I passed it in a jiffy. Then the thickening fog obscured my view . . . I could not see ahead of me at all, nor could I see the water below. There was only one thing for me to do and that was to keep my eyes fixed on the compass."

Two thousand feet in the air, traveling at about a mile a minute, Quimby soon felt chilled, even though she wore two pairs of silk long underwear under her satin flying suit; over it she wore a woolen coat, a raincoat and a sealskin stole, as well as a hot water bottle that Hamel had tied around her waist just before takeoff.

"My hands were covered with long, Scotch woolen gloves which gave me good protection from the cold and fog, but the machine was wet and my face was so covered with dampness that I had to push my goggles up on my forehead."

At one point, the plane tilted, flooding the engine and causing it to skip. "I figured on pancaking down to strike the water with the plane in a floating position," Quimby wrote. But "to my great relief the gasoline quickly burned away and my engine resumed an even purr."

It was only about 22 miles across the channel, and when Quimby had been airborne just over 20 minutes, she knew she had to be approaching the French coast.

Unable to see it through the fog, she descended to 1,000 feet. "The sunlight struck upon my face and my eyes lit upon the white and sandy shores of France. I felt happy, but I could not find Calais."

She decided to land anyway, so she brought her plane down on the beach; later, she discovered she was in Hardelot, about 30 miles from Calais.

"I jumped from my machine and was alone upon the shore. But it was only for a few moments. A crowd of fishermen — men, women and children each carrying a pail of sand worms — came rushing from all directions toward me. They were chattering in French, of which I comprehended sufficient to discover that they knew I had crossed the channel. These humble fisherfolk knew what had happened. They were congratulating themselves that the first woman to cross in an aeroplane had landed on their fishing beach."

Pictures taken at the time show a beaming Quimby being borne into town on the shoulders of the locals. There, one woman insisted on serving Quimby "a very welcome" cup of tea along with bread and cheese. "The tea was served in a cup fully six times as large as an ordinary teacup and was so old and quaint that I could not conceal my admiration of it," Quimby wrote. "The good hearted woman insisted upon giving it to me, and no cup that I have ever won or ever shall win as an aero trophy will be prized more than this."

Although she had no change of clothes, reporters had brought her long seal coat across the channel with them, and she put it on over her flying suit.

"Then I got into an automobile and motored to Calais . . . in time to catch a fast train that took me into Paris at seven p.m., a very tired but a very happy woman."

Quimby's feat should have been on the front pages of newspapers around the world the next morning — and undoubtedly would have been, if not for another, far bigger piece of news: the sinking of the Titanic. The magnitude of that tragedy relegated Quimby's channel crossing to a small article on the inside pages of most newspapers — if they covered it at all.

What Quimby thought of this is not known. But when she arrived back in New York on May 12, she quickly busied herself with plans for more feats in the air. Among other things, she announced, she would attempt to beat an earlier speed record set by male pilot Claude Grahame-White, and would transport a sack of mail between Massachusetts and New York.

But first, she was scheduled to appear at the Third Annual Boston Aviation Meet, flying her new, pure-white, two-seat monoplane, which she'd purchased from Blériot while in France. The fee for her appearance reportedly was $100,000.

When Quimby arrived in Boston, she decided to take a trial flight, and agreed to take with her air-show manager William Willard as a passenger.

Willard was a heavy-set man, and according to some reports, was cautioned that he would have to stay still to avoid throwing the aircraft, which was quite unstable, off balance.

Before they took off, The New York Times reported, someone asked Quimby about what would happen if the plane's engine failed while over water. She reportedly explained that if the plane landed "pancake" on the water, the wings would float it for at least two hours.

"Then, with a brilliant smile, she made this significant remark: 'But I am a cat and I don't like cold water,'" the Times reported. "These were among the last words Miss Quimby said before leaving the starting line on her last flight."

Twenty minutes later, after looping around Dorchester Bay, Quimby's dragonfly-shaped airplane reappeared on the horizon. As 5,000 spectators watched, she began to descend at an estimated speed of 85 mph.

The Times described what happened next: "There was an upward flash of the tail and the machine was seen to stand almost on end in the air. For an instant it poised there and then began a swift plunge downward.

"Sharply outlined against the setting sun, Willard's body was thrown clear of the chassis, followed almost immediately by Miss Quimby's body in her dark aviation suit. Hurtling over and over the two bodies shot downward, striking the water 200 feet from shore. They splashed out of sight a second before the monoplane plunged down 300 feet away."

It was low tide, and the water where the two victims landed was only 5 feet deep; when men from a nearby yacht club reached the spot in motorboats, they found both bodies deeply embedded in the mud.

The magnitude of fame that Quimby had sought in life was finally realized at her death, which was front-page news around the country.

Many papers speculated as to the cause of the accident; some wondered whether Willard had shifted in his seat, throwing the plane off balance. Others thought the aircraft had hit turbulent air, while still others wondered whether Quimby had fainted, lost her grip or was attempting to descend too quickly. Many newspapers pointed out that if the two had been wearing seat belts — which at the time were uncommon in aircraft — they might have been saved.

On July 4, 1912, three days after her death, Quimby was buried in Woodlawn Cemetery in the Bronx. But a year later, her remains were moved to Kensico Cemetery in upstate Valhalla, where she lies beneath a large monument engraved with the picture of an airplane.

In the years since, thousands of words have been written about Quimby and her legacy. But perhaps she herself summed it up best in an article she wrote for Good Housekeeping magazine; she finished it the day before she left for Boston, and it was published after her death.

"In my opinion there is no reason why the aeroplane should not open up a fruitful occupation for women," Quimby wrote. "I see no reason why they cannot realize handsome incomes by carrying passengers between adjacent towns, why they cannot derive incomes from parcel delivery, from taking photographs from above, or from conducting school for flying . . . Any of these things it is now possible to do." ●

After crossing the English Channel and landing on the beach at Hardelot, France — about 30 miles away from her intended destination at Calais — Quimby was carried into town by a group of happy locals. Once in town, she was served a breakfast of tea, bread and cheese.

The Pilots: Daredevils Who Defied Gravity

PILOT PROJECT

John J. Frisbie of Rochester, N.Y., in his Curtiss aircraft in August, 1910. Frisbie received his aviator's certificate after flying from Garden City to Belmont Park, Long Island in 1910. He would die in an aircraft accident in Norton, Kan., in 1911.

They stand out as skywriters of history — going where no man or woman had gone before. Pilots such as stunt flyer Lincoln Beachey, who did aerial acrobatics in a plane that looked like a tricycle with wings. Matilde Moisant, who ascended to the amazing height of 1,200 feet in a 50-horsepower monoplane. Or Bessie Coleman, the world's first black pilot, who had to get her license in France. Their feats and faces fill this photo gallery.

DAREDEVIL   *Lincoln Beachey was a pioneering stunt flier. Above, he demonstrates his "Rubber Cow" blimp at Jamaica Oval Ball Field in Queens in 1908. Beachey became the first pilot to complete a loop-the-loop in his Curtiss Pusher, below, circa 1912.*

Lincoln Beachey and his Aeroplane

HOP, SKIP AND A JUMP *Clarence Chamberlin, pictured at right, gave Garden City residents a thrill when he took off in his Sperry Messenger, above, and immediately touched down and took off again on a road beside Curtiss Field at the start of a 30,000-mile air tour. The event took place during the late 1920s.*

SOUND SUCCESS *In 1912, Beckwith Havens made a dangerous night flight across L.I. Sound. This shows "Becky" on a photo mission in Texas in a Curtiss Pusher.*

HEINRICH MANEUVERS

Arthur Heinrich sits in the rear cockpit of a Heinrich Model D with Mary Simms, later his sister-in-law, wearing typical period flying garb. The picture was taken in Mineola in 1914. Albert Heinrich, right, and his brother, Arthur, began building an aircraft of their own design in a chicken coop on their Baldwin farm. That plane, the Model A, first flew in May, 1910 and was the first American monoplane powered by an American engine. Both brothers flew the aircraft without ever having had the benefit of a flying lesson.

CURTISS FLYING SERVICE
PHOTO DIVISION

FAY AND HER FLEDGLING
*Fay Gillis, the first airplane saleswoman for Curtiss Flying Service, stands with
her Curtiss Fledgling at Curtiss Field in Valley Stream in August, 1929.*

THE NINETY-NINES
The first meeting of the Ninety-Nines — an international women's pilot association so named because it initially boasted 99 members — was held in 1929 during the Women's Air Derby at Curtiss Field in Valley Stream. From left, Mona Holmes, Mary Samson, Elvy Kalep, Ruth Elder, Mrs. John Reiney, Amelia Earhart, Elinor Smith and Viola Gentry.

FLYING NURSE
Betty Gillies began flying in 1928 while a student nurse in New York City. Here, she stands with a moth airplane at Long Island's Aviation Country Club in early 1930.

LATE BLOOMER
Blanche Stuart Scott, later a member of the Ninety-Nines, almost made history with a solo flight Sept. 2, 1910, in Hammondsport, N.Y. However, the designation as the first American woman to solo was given to another because Scott's plane had accidentally been lifted by a gust of wind while she taxiied on a runway.

DEVOTED DESIGNER
Native Sicilian Giuseppe M. Bellanca, a leading designer of modern aircraft, operated his own flying school at Hempstead Plains Field and built his first aircraft there. A Bellanca plane, the Miss Veedol, made the first nonstop flight across the Pacific Ocean in 1931.

RECORD BREAKER
Stunt pilot Jack O'Meara of New York performed a record series of 46 loops in his glider in 1933. He started from 12,000 feet and straightened out only when he was within 500 feet of the ground. O'Meara began his flight at Roosevelt Field.

ILL-FATED MISSION
The research plane American Nurse was lost at sea after it left Brooklyn for Italy in 1932. Three people were aboard: Edna Newcomer, 28, a pilot and student nurse, right; physician Leon Pisculli, 53, and pilot William Ulbrich, 31, of Mineola, thought to be the man at far right.

INSTRUMENTAL PIONEER
In September, 1929, Jimmy H. Doolittle, above, used the Sperry gyro-horizon and directional gyro, both developed on Long Island, to make the world's first "blind" flight. These instruments made flying at night and in bad weather possible, and within three years, all commercial airliners were fitted with the technology. At left, Doolittle stands aside his Curtiss Hawk, circa 1929-'30. With funding from Long Islander Harry Guggenheim, Doolittle carried out aviation safety experiments at the Full Flight Laboratory at Mitchel Field. During World War II, he led a surprise air attack on Tokyo in 1942.

MATILDE MOISANT
AND HER
MONOPLANE

Matilde Moisant, the second woman in the country to earn a pilot's license, learned to fly at the Long Island aviation school run by her brother Alfred. In 1911, she won the Rodman-Wanamaker altitude trophy by flying her 50-hp. Moisant monoplane to 1,200 feet. She gave up flying after an accident in Texas in 1912. Below, Shakir Jerwan, an instructor at the Moisant Aviation School on the Hempstead Plains, sits aboard a Blériot aircraft with his dog, Monoplane. Below left, another brother, John Moisant, took part in an air race from Belmont Park around the Statue of Liberty in October, 1910. He died in an air crash later that year.

LION MASCOT *Roscoe Turner was a renowned air racer who typically traveled with a pet lion cub, Gilmore. In this photo, he and Gilmore are about to depart Roosevelt Field in an attempt to establish a new east-west flight record between Long Island and Los Angeles. They accomplished their goal over 18 hours and 43 minutes in this Lockheed Vega on May 27, 1930.*

RACIAL PIONEER *Pilot Bessie Coleman, daughter of an African-American mother and a Choctaw father, learned to fly in France and Germany after World War I. She went overseas after being rejected by U.S. aviation schools, which were inhospitable to both blacks and women. Her first flight over American soil was at an exhibition at Long Island's Curtiss Field on Sept. 3, 1922. Coleman, the first licensed black pilot in the world, died in a Florida plane crash in 1926.*

ADVENTURER LANDS   *Polar explorer Richard E. Byrd stops at Roosevelt Field on
June 25, 1928. Byrd made history with a North Pole flyover and six Antarctic expeditions.*

MASTER OF ALL TRADES
A World War I combat pilot, aircraft designer and industry advocate, Maj. Alexander P. de Seversky spent his entire life in some aspect of the aviation industry. De Seversky played a role in developing the foundation for all gyroscopically stabilized flight instruments, thus making the automatic pilot possible. His Seversky Aircraft Corp. ultimately became Republic Aviation in Farmingdale.

AVIATOR, JOURNALIST
Aviator Alicia Patterson Simpson was the first glider pilot to receive instructions in the air by radio when she took off from Roosevelt Field on March 16, 1930. Ten years later she would co-found Newsday.

READY TO SOAR *Pilot Troy W. Newkirke, right, is congratulated after a test at Roosevelt Field. He earned a commercial license in June, 1940. Working as an instructor, he died in a crash in West Virginia in August, 1940.*

FIGHTER ACE
Lt. Col. Francis S. Gabreski, below right, is greeted by a fellow aviator. During World War II, the P-47 Thunderbolt pilot had 28 confirmed kills and destroyed three more German planes on the ground, making him the top ace in the European Theater. He also was one of a handful of fighter pilots who took to the sky against the Japanese at Pearl Harbor. During the Korean War, Gabreski downed six enemy pilots. Gabreski was a commander of the U.S. Air Force Base in Westhampton, and in 1992 the Suffolk County Airport there was renamed in his honor.

*Henry Walden in his model X, particpating
in an air meet in St. Louis in 1911.*

The Dentist Who Yearned To Fly

BY LAURA MUHA

awn tinged the sky over the Hempstead Plains as Henry Walden, cigar clamped between his teeth, climbed into his homemade airplane and opened the throttle.

The three-cylinder motor roared and the mahogany propeller, mounted just behind the pilot's seat, whirled furiously. Walden's two assistants, gripping the tail to prevent the plane from shooting forward, grimaced as they were hit in the face with a high-pressure spray of engine-lubricating castor oil. Their hair and dusters, caught in the propeller wash, streamed behind them. A boy standing nearby made the sign of the cross.

It was Aug. 3, 1910, and Walden, a 26-year-old New York dentist with a passion for airplanes, was about to make what he hoped would be one of the most important test flights of his career.

He'd already had some success with the wood-and-linen airship he called the Walden III: During a test run in December, 1909, it climbed a few feet off the ground and traveled about 300 feet, becoming the first American monoplane — an aircraft with one set of wings instead of two — to fly.

But on that flight and numerous subsequent ones, Walden had been unable to stay aloft more than a minute before the plane's 1-gallon gas tank ran dry. Only a handful of people witnessed the flights, and when he described them, not everyone believed he was telling the truth. Some even dismissed him as a crackpot, the common perception of aviators of that era.

On this day, with a new 10-gallon tank mounted on the wing above the pilot's seat, Walden was determined to prove them wrong. "This was to mark some sort of semi-officially recognized flight . . . a record flight of the First American Monoplane," he would write later in an unpublished 117-page autobiography now in the collection of the Cradle of Aviation Museum at Mitchel Field.

With a thrust of his arm, Walden signaled his assistants to let go of the tail. The plane hurtled across the grass, shaking violently as it picked up speed. The embankment of the Long Island Motor Parkway loomed ahead; beyond it lay the vast field that pilots would later dub "the graveyard" because downward air currents caused so many crashes there. "If I could clear that menace, I had the entire island at my disposal," Walden wrote.

Glancing at his pants legs, he noted that the fabric flapped stiffly from his calves — a sign he'd reached flying speed. He pulled the steering wheel toward him. The shrubbery blurred into a smooth green carpet as the Earth dropped away.

"I never was that high before," he wrote.

Walden was soaring over the parkway when suddenly, unexpectedly, the plane seemed to stop moving. His pants legs went limp. A downdraft! Frantically, he clutched the steering wheel as the horizon came up to meet him.

Then everything went black.

How much time passed, Walden couldn't say. But gradually, he became aware of voices — fuzzy at first, then louder and clearer. "A feeble throbbing in my temples grew more distinct," he wrote. "A heavy weight seemed lying on my chest. My head, hands and feet seemed fastened to the ground on which I lay . . . I wanted to talk but couldn't bring a syllable out."

He'd fractured his ankle and collarbone, torn several ligaments, broken three ribs, punctured a lung and totaled the Walden III — in the process earning the dubious distinction of becoming the first person seriously injured in a plane crash on Long Island. But to his joy, news of the wreck appeared on the front page of the New York Evening Journal under the headline "Walden Airship Falls." Now people would *have* to believe he'd flown.

"I had a harrowing experience and I was in pain, but . . . [It] turned

Nassau County quickly became an aviation center around 1909. The hangars below were part of the Walden-Dyott Aeronautic Co., formed in 1910.

Walden went on to build nine more planes after the Walden III. Here the flying dentist is in the pilot's seat of a Walden IV, around 1910.

out to be the happiest day in my youthful life," he wrote. "My 'failure' turned into a complete success."

In the next decade, Walden would go on to build nine more planes, survive at least 15 more crashes, perform at numerous air shows and establish three airplane manufacturing companies. And while none of his inventions revolutionized the aeronautics industry, his courage and determination were indisputable.

"Today, we think of airplane-flying as relatively routine, but to do it at the time he did — not only was it challenging and dangerous, but his peers and friends would have looked askance at him," said Peter Jakab, curator of early aviation at the Smithsonian Institution's National Air and Space Museum in Washington, D.C., where a model of the Walden III and a photo of its inventor are on display.

In those early days of aviation, courage and creativity were far more important than an engineering degree when it came to building and flying airplanes. Yes, there were professionals out there laying the foundation for what would become the aviation industry. But for every Orville Wright or Glenn Curtiss, there were dozens of people like Henry Walden: backyard tinkerers who cobbled together airplanes using nothing more than their wits and parts from

the local hardware store — and doing it simply because they yearned to fly. And they were willing to take their life in their hands every time they did it.

"Weren't you frightened when you were up there?" Walden's son, Dr. Richard Walden, a retired plastic surgeon, once asked him.

"Frightened, hell — every time I went up, I practically peed in my pants!" Walden replied.

Born Nov. 10, 1883, in a small town in Massachusetts, Walden spent part of his childhood in Romania, where his father, a builder, had a contract to lay out a series of roads.

While there, the boy saw a demonstration of a hot-air balloon in a park, a demonstration that ended in tragedy when a gust of wind slammed the balloon into a wall on liftoff, killing the balloonist.

Despite the disaster, Walden would recall the event as one of the formative experiences of his life. "The sailing through space fascinated me," he wrote. "It stroke a cord within me, probably inborn, which I can definitely trace to tendencies, experiences and developments in my later life."

Walden and his best friend, Emmet, soon began crafting 10-foot tissue-paper balloons of their own, following directions they found in a magazine. Using a kerosene stove as a heat source, they managed to get the balloons to inflate, but none would fly; they were too heavy.

The solution inadvertently presented itself after Walden's mother confiscated the stove, saying it was too dangerous to play with fire near the barn. Undeterred, the boys soaked a length of wick in kerosene and suspended it from cross wires attached to a hoop at the base of the balloon. To their joy, they discovered that the wick burned hotter — and therefore provided more lift — than the stove.

"What a flame," Walden wrote. "In the blink of an eye the bag began to take its form . . . ten feet high . . . What a bulk of roaring heat that was . . . Then it began to tug . . . It really tugged. The mooring released, we let go . . . And off went the balloon, hoop, wick, kerosene and all . . . Our work was a complete success."

Eager to show off, the boys built a new balloon and organized a demonstration for their friends, charging pen-tips and buttons as an entry fee. Sure enough, the second balloon also flew away, and was such a hit that the boys tried to set off another the next afternoon. This one, however, refused to fly. As they tried to coax it into the air with a pole, a friend dashed into the yard, yelling "Run . . . run . . . the cops . . . the cops."

"Forgetting all about the balloon, we dropped the pole and ran," wrote Walden. "We jumped the fence back of the barn eluding our pursuers, ran to the rear of Emmet's house, ran into it and made for the bedroom. There, we sneaked into the shelter of their large twin bed, or rather under it and there we lay."

As it turned out, the previous day's balloon had landed in a lumberyard in a nearby town and burned it down. To make matters worse, in their haste to escape the police, the boys forgot about the balloon they'd been about to set off. It had settled on the family's wooden well — and burned that down, too.

"What a mess . . . what a mess," wrote Walden. His father received a bill for the lumberyard damages, Walden received a spanking and his youthful career as a balloonist came to an end. But his dreams of flying did not. "Riding my bike in open spaces, I imagined to have wings on and wished it was true."

Around the turn of the century, however, a crisis temporarily drove thoughts of flight from Walden's head. His father had badly underestimated expenses for the Romanian project, and lost his fortune as a result. The family moved to Vienna, where to help support them, Walden took a job as an assistant to an American dentist attending the kaiser; upon returning to the United States a few years later, he solidified his career choice by enrolling in Columbia University's dental school.

While Walden was there, an event occurred that would change the world forever: Brothers Orville and Wilbur Wright made the first machine-powered flight at Kitty Hawk, N.C. Although their 1903 accomplishment was at first largely ignored by the public — probably, Wilbur speculated, because no one believed it was true — by 1908, a growing number of people were trying to duplicate the brothers' success.

By then, Walden had graduated from dental school and set up a practice in Manhattan. That summer, he read a newspaper article about the newly formed Aeronautic Society of New York, a motley group of scientists, mechanics, millionaires — or, as Walden put it, "dreamers bound by one great object and moved by one great ideal . . . to achieve practical flight." He paid $10 and joined the club.

The society provided members with work space at the old Morris Park racetrack in the Bronx. Arriving there for the first time, Walden was astonished by the array of strange-looking contraptions members were working on: a bicycle with a propeller mounted on its rear; a triplane, which had three sets of wings; a machine called an ornithopter, which beat the air with its wings like a bird.

Looking at them, Walden would say later, he felt as if he'd finally found his calling. "It all became part of me, and I became part of all. I was not conscious of any definite plans but plans were being built up within me. That was the beginning of my aviation career."

Before long, Walden was devoting more time to building planes than to cleaning teeth. He hired an elderly dentist to cover his practice, appearing only when patients insisted on his personal services. The rest of the time, he studied what little information he could find on aerodynamics and attempted to apply it to airplanes of his own design.

His first two models, both biplanes, were failures. So for the third, Walden decided to try something different: a plane with one set of wings instead of two. Similar monoplanes had been flown in Europe on several occasions, but most people believed them to be dangerous. Walden, however, said he became convinced of the soundness of the design by studying

Walden at the controls of his model IX, which had an engine, he said, that made "the sweetest humming tone."

birds. "I'd think, 'God only gave it [a bird] two wings. He must know what He's doing.'"

To avoid the three-hour round-trip to Morris Park, Walden rented a loft a block from his dental office and, with the help of his cousin Henry and a mechanic named Radu Tatu, he began building the new plane.

"As it was usual with me, there was no time to be lost," he wrote. "We really went to it. There was no rest until late at nights and there was little sleep until the early morning hours. We even gulped our meals while we were at work."

Six months later, when the monoplane was finally ready for testing, a new problem arose: how to get it out of the loft. Eventually, Walden and his helpers decided to disassemble the airship and lower the parts through the window to a waiting truck. All went well until they got to the wings. "They were about one half of an inch too wide to pass them through. We had miscalculated the thickness of the window frame."

Obviously, there was only one solution: Hack out the window and worry about damages later.

It took five hours for Walden to transport the plane to a vast field adjacent to the Mineola Fair Grounds. Pioneer aviator Glenn Curtiss had moved his base of operations there from Hammondsport, N.Y., in July, 1909; the Aeronautic Society, whose lease at Morris Park was about to expire, had soon followed. In a matter of months, the grasslands of central Nassau County had become a center of aviation — albeit a primitive one.

"We housed our disassembled plane in [a] creaky shanty . . . about thirty by forty feet in size," Walden wrote. "A few panneled windows faced the Old Country Road and a very large door opened to the fields. A few broken panes and a little round coal stove were to keep us warm for the rental of $7 per month . . . A frozen water outlet was the sole additional accommodation. The wide and apparently endless field was there and that was what we wanted."

At daybreak on Dec. 9, 1909, after a week's work reassembling the plane, Walden and his assistants rolled it from the shed and stood back to admire it.

Compared to today's sleek jets, the Walden III was little more than a motorized box kite. But to Walden, the sight of the plane sitting on the frozen ground was so awe-inspiring that, more than half a century later, he could recall every detail: the gray-ish-white wings, the bright red struts, the gleam of the aluminum-painted motor and nickel-plated wheels. "With its thirty foot wing spread and over twenty foot length . . . it looked nimble and ready to sprint into the air."

Sprinting skyward was not something Walden planned to attempt that day, however. First, he had to do what pilots called "grass-cutting" — driving the plane along the ground to check the engine, the steering, the thrust of the propeller.

The initial trial didn't go well. When Walden opened the throttle to test the motor, his assistant, who was supposed to hold onto the tail, accidentally let go and the plane shot forward. Walden tried to stop it by releasing the throttle pedal, but it was stuck, and he dared not take his hands off the wheel long enough to flip the electrical cut-off switch.

Gaining speed, the out-of-control airship hurtled down the field. With the embankment to the Motor Parkway looming, Walden frantically made a U-turn: "Momentarily my right wheel was off the ground . . . The plane dipped on its side as the turn began, the left wing approaching the ground."

Then, just as he thought he was safe, he looked up — and realized that the shed loomed ahead. "I [was] headed straight for it . . . when, without warning, the motor suddenly stopped."

The plane had run out of gas.

"I had learned a lot about taxiing in jigtime," Walden wrote in an aviation magazine years later. "When my knees stopped shaking, I figured the progress was worth the fright."

After fixing the throttle and moving the electrical cutoff to the steering wheel so he could reach it easily, Walden climbed aboard for another test run. Again he raced down the field and made a U-turn at the Motor Parkway embankment.

But this time, something unexpected happened on the return trip: The plane suddenly took off. "I do not know exactly how it happened but . . . [It] was a wonderful sensation," Walden wrote.

That is, until he realized the shed lay dead ahead.

"Quickly I pushed the tail into the positive angle . . . The wheels were on the ground again as I slapped the foot brake into it and stopped short a few feet before I reached the shed. Henry almost fainted while Radu had closed his eyes at

what looked like an unavoidable crash."

Thus ended the maiden voyage of the first American monoplane.

Walden made a series of brief but successful flights in the little airship over the next eight months, until it was destroyed in his August, 1910, crash. His injuries that day bothered him less than the damages to his plane — especially because the final payment on the engine was due the next day, and he had no money with which to make it. In fact, he wrote, the reason he'd selected that particular day for his "big flight" was because, "I felt that somehow or other, a successful flight in the nick of time might save the situation," although how, he didn't specify.

Fortunately, a friend came up with the solution: String a tarp around the wreckage and charge admission to the curiosity-seekers who thronged to the field to ogle it. "The idea got me solvent again," Walden recalled.

Until the accident, Walden had been planning to participate in the International Aviation Tournament, scheduled for Oct. 22-31, 1910, at Belmont Park Racetrack. Such meets were becoming an increasingly popular form of entertainment for the public and this one was expected to be the biggest ever, drawing fliers from all over the United States and Europe. Walden was bitterly disappointed when he realized that neither his body nor his plane would be in any shape to compete.

Still, he managed to attend every day, joining an estimated 10,000 people who crammed the bleachers and cheered the daredevil pilots in their flimsy flying machines as they raced around pylons, performed stunts and set records for altitude (9,714 feet) and speed (70 mph).

"This was a great event in . . . early aviation," Walden wrote, adding that there was only one downside: "The foreigners were there with their monoplanes and the Americans were there with their biplanes. America's only monoplane lay in a heap."

Shortly after the meet, Walden — whose reputation as a legitimate aviator had been sealed by his crash — teamed up with an Englishman named Capt. George Dyott to form the Walden-Dyott Aeronautic Co.

They erected a corrugated iron hangar at the Hempstead Plains field, bought two new engines and, with a third salvaged from Walden's earlier

At his short-lived Walden Aircraft, above, Walden, far left, and his test group set up a test rig to optimize propeller location on multiengine aircraft. Years earlier, it was evident that the dentist was spending less time cleaning teeth and more time flying. Below, his aviator's license and its cover from 1911.

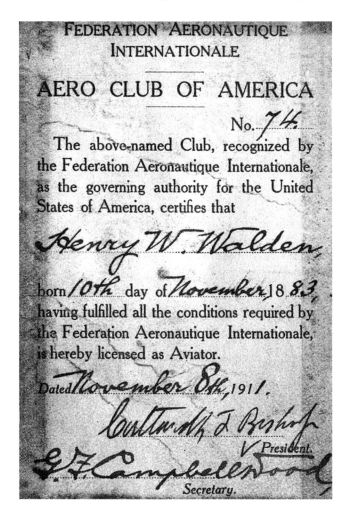

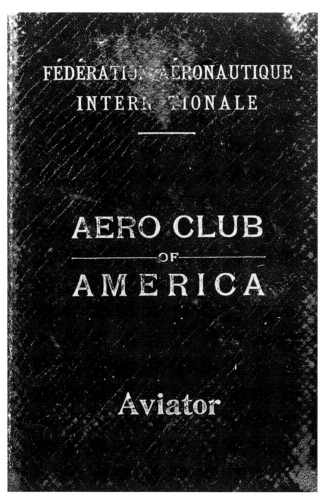

wreck, began building monoplanes, which soon attracted widespread attention.

On one occasion, the United Dressed Beef Co. paid Walden and Dyott $300 to hang one of their monoplanes at a convention. "A large basket had to replace the usual aviator's seat and various parts of beef were to hang from it. It was intended to prophesize a futuristic delivery of perishable victuals . . . The exhibit was a great success, but no sales were made."

On another occasion, shaving-equipment magnate King Gillette visited the airfield and accepted a ride across the field in a Walden-Dyott monoplane — on the condition that it not take off with him aboard. (That was a stroke of luck, Walden noted wryly, since Gillette would have had to lose at least 150 pounds before the plane's little engine could have gotten him off the ground.) Still, Gillette "was delighted with his grass cutting experience," Walden wrote, "and shortly thereafter we received 2 gold (or were they gold-plated?) razors, beautifully engraved with our initials."

Unfortunately, gold-plated razors didn't pay the bills, and by the spring of 1911, the financially strapped partners decided to disband their company. Dyott received two of the monoplanes, which he later sold in South America; Walden, who had decided to keep the business going on his own, got the hangar and the third plane, which wasn't quite complete.

Money remained his most pressing problem. There was no corporate backing for aviation in that era, so pilots scraped together cash in any way they could to build and maintain their planes. The Aeronautic Society helped by erecting bleachers at the airfield and charging a 25-cent admission fee to watch the planes; the take was then divided among the pilots. But the most Walden ever got at one time was $14, not nearly enough to cover the piano wire, motorcycle parts and Irish linen from which he constructed his planes.

Instead, he financed his love of flying by working from 10 a.m. to 8 p.m. daily in his dental office; after closing up for the evening, he'd hop on his motorcycle for the hour-long trip to Hempstead Plains.

"We worked nightly at the field at the light of kerosene lamps until about 1 a.m. and were ready at the starting line for trials before the air stirred at 5 a.m.," he recalled, adding rather unnecessarily: "That left little time for rest and sleep."

Particularly exciting to Walden was the news of a new, four-cylinder, 50-hp. engine that had just come on the market. He secured one on a trial basis, installed it in his latest plane, the Walden VIII, and took off. He was 100 feet in the air when the engine began missing and the little airship plummeted.

"They picked me up fully conscious lying on my back, the plane, nose-down and tail pointing at the sky, pinning me helplessly to the ground . . . Gas was dripping freely on to my grimmaced face, thoroughly soaking a lit cigar I held firmly between my teeth."

As usual, Walden's injuries — two broken ribs — failed to slow him down. Before long, he'd constructed a new plane, the Walden IX, which he described as "a beautifully finished job" made of steel struts and second-growth hickory, with an engine that made "the sweetest humming tone."

On July 25, 1911, Walden was aloft in the plane when it started to pour. At first he was alarmed, since to his knowledge no one had ever flown in the rain before. "[B]ut I soon discovered that it did not hamper my flight. I was soaked to the skin but that did not bother me. I flew on."

When he returned to the hangar an hour later, he was surprised to find it empty; given the weather and how long he'd been gone, his ground crew assumed he'd crashed and fanned out to search for his remains.

"We had a happy reunion later on that day . . . [And] the following morning, I was the hero of the day," Walden wrote. "All the newspapers acclaimed me and the feat accomplished by America's First Monoplane. It was the first recorded flight in the rain and the longest flight my plane had ever made."

Unfortunately, fame was one thing; fortune was another. "Money, the little there was, ran out and debts increased at an alarming rate," Walden recalled. "Aviation had to be made to pay for itself or I had to abandon the path I chose for my life's work. The dreams of my youth threatened to crumble into dust and failure at the height of my so-called success."

He gave flying lessons to help make ends meet, but the venture turned out to have the opposite effect; none of his students paid what they owed, and their mishaps left his planes in need of expensive repairs.

To make matters worse, Walden had recently suf-

The Walden IX was "a beautifully finished job," the inventor said.
The plane was made of steel struts and second-growth hickory.

fered yet another mishap of his own: "[M]y rebuilt No. VIII stalled in midair because of a faulty tail surface and dropped me into a pair of accommodating trees near Hempstead, L.I. They broke the fall but smashed the plane and added to my troubles. Something had to be done again quickly."

Then he heard about an air meet that was to be held at Brighton Beach the weekend of Sept. 16-17, 1911. Renowned aviators from as far away as England were to appear, earning as much $1,000 for each day they performed.

Walden had no experience flying in such events, which required taking off and landing within a fenced-in racetrack. When he tried to sign up, the organizer, a Mr. Davies, merely snorted.

"Walden, this is a small track," Davies said. "You couldn't fly there and there is not enough grass to cut."

Walden was stung. "Those few words surely hurt," he wrote later. "He actually knew of me as a 'grass cutter' . . . So that was the degree of 'success' I had reached."

But unwilling to give up the prospect of a cash infu-sion, he "begged and prayed and even insisted" until Davies relented. The deal: Walden would earn $1,000 if he could stay aloft for 15 minutes the first day, and another $1,000 if he could repeat the feat on the second.

"But take my advice and stay on the ground, hug it and don't try to fly," Davies told him. "You can't get away with it."

"Thanks . . . I will be here on time," was all Walden said.

That Saturday, looking out at the field, Walden felt his first pangs of worry. "Davies was right. It did look small and cramped when compared to our spacious fields at Mineola . . . Trees lined about three quarters of the track's circling length. Telephone poles and wires were abundantly in evidence. The large grandstand was towering over the field on one of its broader sides. There were smaller stands, stables, fences, pylons and many other what-nots. And there was . . . a real ditch [that] ran clear across the infield."

But there was no time to reconsider, as Walden heard his name announced through the megaphone.

Hopping into the pilot's seat, he opened the throttle and rolled forward. After one false start, he managed to get off the ground, but couldn't gain enough height to clear the trees at the end of the field. Instead, he did laps within the confines of the track, with the plane in a sharply banked position. "It was a precarious job for me as well as for the viewers in the stands," he wrote. "Luckily, we all got away with it" — and he managed to stay in the air a full seven minutes longer than his contract called for.

The next day, Walden was determined to top his performance. Loading the plane with a better grade of gas, he managed to clear the trees. But he still couldn't climb to the altitude he'd hoped, and found himself navigating around the steeples, houses, flagpoles and towers that lay outside the field. "One steeple in my path seemed exceptionally high," he wrote. "All attempts to steer [around it] made me lose height."

Thinking quickly, Walden dove for the steeple's base, "and with the gained speed and a sudden upward zoom I cleared its pole by mere inches." He then proceeded to use the same method to navigate each obstacle on the way back to the track. The crowd went wild, and Walden basked in his success — plus the $2,000 it earned him.

By the following week, offers to repeat his performance began pouring in from state fairs across the country. "Having only one single plane at my disposal, I could not accept them all . . . however, the total number of accepted contracts exceeded twenty six thousand dollars."

Over the next year, Walden kept up a grueling schedule, traveling from one fair to the next. It was an exciting life, but also a dangerous one: At one fair, he was coming in for a landing when another plane took off directly into his path. Caught in the propeller wash, his plane flipped and the left wing hit the ground. Walden was thrown 50 feet ahead of the plane, which somersaulted across the ground and landed on top of him. "Walden Falls Before 25,000 at Aviation Meet," the New York Evening Mail proclaimed.

Not everyone was thrilled by such exploits. By then, Walden was newly married to his longtime sweetheart, Eva, who considered flying a "harebrained exercise," as the couple's son, Richard, put it. But for a time, Walden persevered. "My father was not the kind of guy that you would say 'no' to," explained Richard Walden. "He was a very determined person."

Then, in 1912, Walden and one of his star pupils, Frank Fitzsimmons, traveled to Maine to demonstrate one of the dentist's planes at the state fair. Fitzsimmons asked to do the flying, and Walden agreed. But as Fitzsimmons took off, the engine stalled.

"His left wing dipped . . . and the plane started into a spin," wrote Walden. "I don't know how I lived through it . . . A fraction of a moment seemed endless."

The plane fell into an alley beyond the field. Incredibly, Fitzsimmons suffered nothing more than two broken legs. But Walden was so upset that he began rethinking his commitment to aviation. "I never shirked at my own risk, of which I was always aware, but it was hard to think of others crippled or killed with tools of my own creation."

By the time his son Richard was born the following year, Walden had given up flying.

From then on, he concentrated on laboratory work, where he also earned a modest amount of fame. In 1915, he developed and patented the first radio-controlled missile, a model of which is in the Smithsonian Institution. And when the United States entered World War I, he formed another airplane manufacturing company in partnership with the owners of a New Jersey lumber mill, and made aircraft wings, stabilizers and fins for the government.

In 1919, Walden and his wife were divorced. He eventually remarried and moved to Great Neck, where the couple raised two more sons. In 1929, he formed a third company, Walden Aircraft, in Long Island City. But by then, aviation was becoming big business, and it was hard for such a small company to compete. Three years later, he closed the plant and went back to tinkering in the workshop adjacent to his dental lab.

The result: More than 80 patents for a variety of devices, among them motion-picture and still cameras that made pictures appear three-dimensional; a mechanical lighting unit for medical photography; an artificial heart, which was used for research purposes at Mount Sinai Hospital; an ink-refiller for ball-point pens; a vegetable slicer for home use; a machine that packed coffee into filter pouches; and an animated electric sign that flashed news bulletins on what used to be the Times Tower in New York City's Times Square — a precursor to the famous Times Square Zipper.

In later years, Walden joined the Long Island Early Fliers, a club of pioneer aviators, where he met Elinor Smith, who herself had set a number of altitude and speed records while flying from Curtiss Field as a teenager in the late 1920s. She recalls being awed by his presence. "We were of such different eras," she recalls. "To meet a man who had actually done these kinds of things was just not to be believed."

Walden also took his sons to air meets and to Roosevelt Field to watch the planes taking off and landing. "But he was dead set against me flying," recalled Richard Walden. "He thought it was too dangerous."

Walden died of cancer in 1964 at age 81 — probably remarkable in itself, considering the perils every aviator faced in those early years of flight. "Of the 16 original pilots who flew out of Mineola, he was the only one who died at home in bed," said Richard Walden.

But Walden's fame didn't end there. Five days after his death, his family was notified that he'd been elected to the National Aviation Hall of Fame in Dayton, Ohio.

Walden never knew about the honor. But if he had, he undoubtedly would have been delighted. For even though he had given up aviation, it was obvious that his dreams of flight never died.

"If I were a younger man," he said in an interview not long before he died, "I would build a spaceship and go to the moon or the stars." ●

Bert Acosta lived hard, flew hard and thrived on adventure — a reckless streak that began early.

'Bad Boy Of The Air'

BY LAURA MUHA

he Navy's newest racing biplane rolled across Curtiss Field and gradually picked up speed. As the plane took off, the pilot kept its nose pointing up. The CR-1 spun around in a loop as it left the Earth.

In the cockpit was 26-year-old Bert Acosta, who, despite his youth, had a reputation as one of the country's most skillful test pilots. He was also known as one of aviation's biggest daredevils.

The date was Nov. 22, 1921, and the young flier knew he was expected to put on a good show. He wasn't about to disappoint.

After a dazzling series of rolls and stalls, he shot up to 7,000 feet and power-dived back to Earth, pulling up again just as his wheels skimmed the ground. He made eight thundering passes of the field at an average speed of 197.8 mph — 8 mph faster than the plane's supposed capability, and a new American record.

For a grand finale, he zoomed a mere 30 feet above the heads of the by-then-terrified dignitar-

Acosta longed to fly in combat during World War I, but when the United States entered the conflict in 1917, he was made a flight instructor.

ies. He did it flying upside down.

As if that weren't enough, another drama was playing out on the ground. A woman in the crowd — the wife of a Long Island millionaire — announced to assembled reporters that she and Acosta were to be married. It turned out to be a publicity stunt — but Acosta, whose reputation with the ladies preceded him, still had to go out drinking with the woman's husband to smooth things over.

From its sensational start to its soap-opera finish, the demonstration was pure Acosta: a breathtaking combination of sheer skill and in-your-face recklessness, executed flawlessly by a pilot so confident of his own abilities that he once boasted he could fly a barn door if it had a propeller and wings.

But Acosta also had a self-destructive streak that earned him the title "Bad Boy of the Air." He'd zoom his plane under bridges, run its wheels lightly along the domes of skyscrapers and do acrobatics just scant feet above bystanders' heads.

Once, when a passenger asked what time it was, Acosta buzzed the clock tower of the Metropolitan Life building in Manhattan. And while living with friends on Long Island, he was known to fly over their house and bounce the wheels of his plane on the roof to let them know when it was time to put biscuits in the oven for dinner.

Back on Earth, Acosta was no better behaved. He was tall, swarthy and cleft-chinned, with a dark mustache that capped a rakish grin. Women found him irresistible, and he felt the same way about them. "Today we'd say that he lived

It's hard to say whether Acosta got into more trouble in the air or on the ground. He poses here with a Curtiss Cox Racer around 1920.

life in the fast lane," says Bob Van der Linden, an early aviation curator at the Smithsonian Institution's National Air and Space Museum in Washington, D.C. "He liked to drink and he liked to womanize. He was being chased all over the place by women, ex-lovers, their husbands."

Or, as a June 10, 1935, profile in Time magazine put it: "[H]e took to the fleshpots on earth as an offset to his work in the air. His life, consequently, became a rowdy romance in which brawls, jails and domestic entanglements were due to play a large part."

Bertrand Blanchard Acosta was born in San Diego in 1895, possibly on New Year's Day, the younger of two surviving sons of Spanish-American mining engi-

neer Alphonse Ferdinand Acosta and his wife, Martha Blanche Snook.

The reckless streak that would lead to his downfall years later was evident even in childhood, as recalled by classmate Waldo Dean Waterman — who himself became a well-known flier — in his posthumously published autobiography, "Waldo: Pioneer Aviator — A Personal History of American Aviation" (Arsdalen, Bosch & Co., 1988):

"Bert had entered the fourth grade in midterm and was assigned a seat near me, in the rear near the window. One day the teacher looked up and saw Bert's jaws moving as if he were chewing gum, a forbidden sin. As was the custom when anyone was caught doing such a dreadful thing, the teacher picked up her ruler and walked down the aisle, prepared to give the offending student a good swat. She said, 'Bert, spit it out!' and Bert sure did spit it out with a great big splatt! It wasn't chewing gum, but tobacco that he was chewing and for that he was immediately marched down to the principal's office. That's the last I ever saw of him around Middletown Grammar School."

By this time, several years had passed since the Wright brothers' famed flight at Kitty Hawk, N.C., and across the country, would-be aviators were experimenting with their own airships. The young Acosta was fascinated by reports of the flying machines, and, with the help of three friends and a picture in a magazine, built his own airplane from balloon silk, bamboo and a two-cylinder engine.

In 1909, he successfully flew the plane off a hill in Imperial Beach, Calif., launching his life's work along with his homemade airship. He was 14 years old.

Two years later, aviation pioneer Glenn Curtiss opened a flying camp on nearby North Island, to experiment with "flying boats," as hydroplanes were then known. Acosta talked himself into a 50-cent-a-day job helping out around the camp.

According to some accounts, Acosta was doing more than just working on the planes; he was flying them early in the morning, before anyone else arrived for work.

Other reports have him threatening to quit unless Curtiss allowed him to fly, and claim that when the

"He was one of the handsomest men you've ever seen," recalled early Freeport flier Elinor Smith of Acosta. Others held the same opinion.

aviator let him take a trial spin, Acosta shoved the throttle wide open and roared skyward. "That's a hell of a way to fly!" Curtiss reportedly commented.

While working for Curtiss, Acosta attended Throop Polytechnic Institute — now the California Institute of Technology — in Pasadena. He was there for three years, studying mechanical engineering, although there are conflicting reports as to whether he graduated.

Acosta also worked as an instructor at Curtiss' flying school on the island, and in 1913 and 1914, barnstormed along the West Coast.

Acosta's taste for adventure was apparent when World War I broke out in Europe in 1914. Since the United States had not yet entered the conflict, he attempted to enlist in the Royal Canadian Air Service. Instead, military authorities — possibly at Curtiss' urging — offered him the job of chief flight instructor for the service. For the next two years, he commuted between Toronto, where he trained Canadian military pilots, and Hammondsport, N.Y., where he tested Curtiss aircraft.

After the United States entered the war in 1917, Acosta unsuccessfully petitioned for a commission that would have sent him to the front. Instead, he was named chief flight instructor at the Army Air Service base on Hazelhurst Field, near Mineola, where he also helped to design the famed Liberty aircraft engine. He also flew for a squadron that searched for German U-boats off Montauk Point, dropped recruitment leaflets over New York City and served as a military test pilot. For his efforts, he was made a captain in the Air Service Reserves.

At war's end, Acosta went back to work for Curtiss. He also flew for several other firms, including the J.L. Co., a New York City outfit that was promoting a German plane called the JL-6. On June 6, 1920, Acosta set an American nonstop distance record in the plane, flying nearly 1,200 miles from Omaha to Lancaster, Pa.

That same year, he traveled to Detroit to try an experimental plane with a new, eight-cylinder engine — a plane that had neither been flown before, nor tested to determine whether its design was structurally sound.

Undeterred, Acosta warmed up the engine and zoomed off. When he returned 20 minutes later, the ground crew realized with horror that one of the plane's wheels was missing — apparently having fallen off during takeoff.

"We expected catastrophe and tried every means of signaling we had to show him what was up," recalled the late aircraft designer William Bushnell Stout in his book, "So Away I Went!" (Ayer Publishing Co., 1979). "He came in, however, set the plane down on one wheel and held it there until the wings lost their lift. When the empty axle touched, the plane gently went over on its back and Bert climbed out unhurt."

On July 29, 1920, Acosta was back in the cockpit of a JL-6 as he and two other pilots embarked on a transcontinental tour — which also unofficially could be considered the first nonscheduled transcontinental airmail flight, since they carried more than 100 letters with them in their trio of aircraft. The first scheduled transcontinental flight by U.S. Air Mail Service pilots would take place the following year.

After reaching San Francisco on Aug. 8, Acosta turned around and started for home, stopping in Reno, Nev., where — although he was married and had two young daughters — he hooked up with a Long Island divorcee named Dorothy Walker. The two had such a good time that, he said later, he didn't sleep for four days.

On the fifth day, however, the tryst came back to haunt him; as Acosta prepared to take off, Walker dashed toward his plane. By yanking the wings up sharply, he managed to avoid hitting her, but in the process, wrecked the landing gear. The story is that he assessed the damage by flying low over the desert and studying the shadow of the plane on the ground, then landed safely and repaired the problem.

After leaving Reno, Acosta and his two companions — including famed Army ace Eddie Rickenbacker — continued east. On the last night of their journey, fog forced them to land in a pasture near State College, Pa. Acosta volunteered to spend the night with the plane, while the rest found a hotel.

Rickenbacker and the others were waiting for Acosta to pick them up at the local airfield the next morning when they heard a plane zoom by overhead. It was Acosta, heading for New York without them. He reportedly had a date, and didn't want to be late — even if it meant his buddies had to return to New York by train.

Despite such exploits, it was hard to get angry at a

man who was as charming as he was reckless. "He was one of the handsomest men you've ever seen, with a real Kirk Douglas chin with that dimple," recalled former Freeport resident Elinor Smith, who got to know him when she was a child hanging out at Curtiss Field with her father.

When Smith's interest in flying became apparent to Acosta, he took her under his wing; although she was just a teenager, he spent hours coaching her on how to handle different situations in the air. In 1930, when she was just 19, she was voted the best female pilot in the country by her peers — an honor she said had much to do with Acosta. "He was a genius at the controls, and he taught me so much," she said. "I will never be able to pay my debt to him."

On Thanksgiving of 1920, Acosta was back on Long Island to take part in the first Pulitzer Cup competition. As 40,000 people watched, he and 37 other pilots raced around a 116-mile triangle that began and ended at Mitchel Field. Acosta completed the course in 51 minutes, 57 seconds — fast enough to take third place.

The following year, the Pulitzer race was held in Omaha. Acosta flew the course so fast that two of the wires bracing the wings of his plane snapped, and the wings started vibrating wildly — but he kept the throttle wide open and won the race, setting a world's closed-course speed record of 176.5 mph in the process.

Then, on June 28, 1922, while he was testing a new single-seat Navy biplane over Mitchel Field, his luck ran out. There are differing accounts of what happened, but in a 1953 interview, Acosta said that smoke started billowing into the cockpit. "When I reached down to see what the matter was I became caught under the cowling. The stick was jammed over to one side [and I] couldn't move it. Before I finally got loose the ship spun into the ground."

Acosta spent the next six weeks in the hospital, floating in and out of consciousness. During his stay, Walker, the divorcee who'd almost been his undoing in Reno, resurfaced, commandeering the virtually incoherent flier and taking him to her Beechurst, Queens, home to finish recuperating. When he was strong enough, Acosta supposedly escaped by sneaking out in the middle of the night.

In the months that followed, Acosta became increasingly reckless. It was during this era that he made his famous clock-buzzing flight; he also

swooped his plane under the Brooklyn, Williamsburg and Manhattan Bridges, becoming the first person ever to do so. (A few years later, he was trumped by the teenage Elinor Smith, who not only flew under those bridges, but the Queensboro as well.)

By this time, Acosta had divorced his first wife and married his second, Helen Belmont Pearsoll, who came from a well-connected Virginia family. The couple lived in Hempstead and had two sons, Bert Jr. and Allyn.

As a father, Acosta was less than reliable but his boys worshiped him anyway, said Allyn's daughter, Christina Acosta Fry, of Savannah, Ga. "My dad loved him fiercely, collected all his pictures," she said. "I've got all these articles that he cut out . . . so I know he cared about him a lot and was very proud of him."

With good reason. Despite the turmoil in his personal life, Acosta continued to set records in the cockpit.

In April, 1927, he and Clarence Chamberlin decided to try and break the world's endurance record of 45 hours, 11 minutes and 51 seconds — not just for the fun of it, but in preparation for what they hoped would be their next milestone: becoming the first pilots to fly nonstop between New York and Paris.

Such a trip had been the goal of fliers on both sides of the Atlantic since 1919, when New York hotelier Raymond Orteig announced a $25,000 prize for the first person to make the flight. Acosta and Chamberlin hoped that by setting a new endurance record of at least 50 hours — the amount of time believed necessary for a transatlantic flight — they'd prove such a flight was possible.

The two took off from Roosevelt Field at 9:30 a.m. on April 12, and the following morning, when they'd been aloft for 23 hours, Acosta dropped a note from the cockpit:

Everything running fine, holding our own. Last night from midnight on was not so very good. However we experienced no difficulty . . . and expect to stick it out all right . . . Just finished light breakfast of soup and water. Pretty good. — Bert Acosta

When the duo finally ran out of gas and landed shortly after noon on April 14, they'd been in the air for a record 51 hours, 11 minutes and 20 seconds, and had broken the previous record by six hours.

An attempt at the transatlantic flight was next in both men's mind. But there was a problem: The

Navigator George Noville, left, and Acosta were part of a transatlantic flying team including Richard Byrd and Bernt Balchen in 1927.

plane could hold only two people, and owner Charles Levine had already hired a navigator — meaning that either Acosta or Chamberlin could make the flight, but not both. Levine attempted to play the two friends against each other, and the navigator, fearing he'd be squeezed out in the process, got an injunction preventing the plane from leaving without him. The 6-foot, 200-pound Acosta eventually settled the matter in an April 27 letter to Levine:

"I cannot help but realize that the sixty pounds difference in weight between Clarence and myself gives him an advantage that can materially advance the possibilities of success, and for that reason I wish to withdraw in his favor . . . I have tried to avoid making this decision — hoping against hope that I would be on the flight — but I do not think that personal considerations should in any way stand in the light of the chief and most important objective — the success of the undertaking."

With that settled, Acosta joined another team consisting of Richard Byrd, Bernt Balchen and navigator George Noville, who were planning to take a crack at the Orteig prize in a tri-motor Fokker named America. But the plane had been damaged during a predeparture crash before Acosta signed on, and by the time it was repaired, it was too late.

On May 20, before the Byrd team — or Chamberlin — could complete predeparture tests, 25-year-old Charles Lindbergh took off from Roosevelt Field, landing in Paris, and the history books, 33 hours, 29 minutes and 30 seconds later as the first person to fly nonstop across the Atlantic.

The Byrd team decided to make the flight anyway, and on June 29, with Acosta at the controls, the Fokker rolled down a 60-foot ramp specially built to help it gain momentum. The ponderous, gas-laden plane lumbered across Roosevelt Field and groaned skyward, barely clearing the row of hangars at the end of the field — that it got into the air at all was a testament to Acosta's skill as a pilot.

"That takeoff was a mighty hard job," he admitted later. "We were a long time getting into the air."

For the next 43 hours and 21 minutes, the foursome endured the deafening roar of the engine and clouds that limited visibility to almost zero.

"I had to stick to the wheel the first six or eight hours — I don't know just how long — till we got past Nova Scotia and the gas cans that blocked the passage to the navigator's cockpit were chucked over-

board," Acosta recalled. "Then Bernt came up and relieved me and we alternated every once in a while the rest of the way over."

When they reached France, the weather was so bad that they were unable to land in Paris. Low on fuel, they headed back toward the Normandy coast, and deliberately crash-landed in the surf about 200 yards from shore.

Waves poured in through the ship's open windows. "All of us were submerged," reported Acosta, who broke his collarbone in the crash. "By the time Byrd got Balchen out I had swum around to the tail. I got out through the side window."

Momentarily disoriented, he started swimming toward open water, then realized what he was doing and turned around. The men arrived on shore to a heroes' welcome; they had officially become the first team to cross the ocean in a multiengine plane.

"MRS. ACOSTA NEVER DOUBTED: Says She 'Knew' the Landing Would Be All Right — is All Smiles at the Telephone," The New York Times headlined the next day, going on to quote her reaction: "Mrs. Acosta was munching a sandwich and said: 'I knew that Bert would bring that plane down so no one would be hurt.'"

In fact, it was Balchen at the controls, not Acosta — something apparently that was a sore point with the latter, for he later went to great lengths to explain: "It was going around in the sleet and darkness that seemed to make me blind. I wasn't absolutely blind, but I couldn't see anything much. That was why Balchen had to take the controls when we came down. I couldn't bring her down. The blindness from lack of sleep and the continual peering ahead through sleet and fog was the only reason I didn't make the landing myself."

There is one other story told about Acosta's time in France: Before heading home, he and the other fliers encountered Edward, the Prince of Wales, at a casino, and were invited to sit at his table.

In the book "Oceans, Poles and Airmen" (Random House, 1971), author Richard Montague describes what happened next:

"With the Prince was a beautiful Hungarian dancer, a chilly blonde whom Acosta eyed with lively interest. Next to Balchen was a very British general with a drooping mustache.

"Wine flowed freely, and Acosta's glass was refilled several times. Couples were waltzing around the floor to seductive music. Suddenly Acosta pushed back his chair and slapped His Royal Highness on the shoulder. 'Say, pal, can I dance with your girl?'

"There was a moment of dead silence. The British general stiffened and looked at Acosta as if he were a worm, but then the Prince laughed. 'Go right ahead, old chap.' "

That night, Acosta didn't return to the hotel room he and Balchen shared, and the next morning, the latter encountered the Prince in the courtyard.

"Where is your friend? He went off with my lady," the Prince said glumly.

Writes Montague: "Acosta was later located in another hostelry with a no-longer-chilly blonde."

Back in the United States, Acosta and his companions were feted in a Broadway ticker-tape parade and at numerous receptions. Helen Acosta brought Bert Jr. and Allyn, then 4 and 2, but they "were dazed by the excitement, and were chiefly interested to hear about their father's broken collar-

Acosta flashes that rakish grin of his from atop a Fokker Universal, the first Fokker designed in the United States.

bone," The New York Times reported.

Given Acosta's newfound international fame, his life should have been golden — but as usual, things took a melodramatic turn. This time, the problem was a series of letters from divorcee Dorothy Walker, which somehow wound up in the hands of Acosta's wife. In 1928, Helen Acosta threw her husband out

The man who would become known as "Bad Boy of the Air" began flying at age 14 — and had his license revoked two decades later.

and filed a $150,000 suit against the divorcee for "alienation of affection," claiming the divorcee had "wrongfully, viciously and wickedly gained the affections of Bert Acosta" by offering him money and encouraging him to move in with her.

Responded the judge: "If it could be arranged to keep this aviator in the air at all times, it would be safer for the homes in this community."

Over the next few years, Helen Acosta also had Acosta jailed several times for nonsupport. At some point, she also filed for divorce — citing a letter from a Sacramento woman who claimed she was pregnant with Acosta's child. "I have been existing in a living hell since you went away," the woman wrote. "You are the only one I ever loved or ever will love . . . O, Bert, come back and see what I am going through and do the right thing." (Acosta's granddaughter, Christina Fry, believes the woman's claims may have been nothing more than a publicity stunt.)

Helen Acosta eventually dropped her case against Walker, apparently forgiving her estranged husband, as well. "He's just a wayward boy and I love him yet," she told the judge.

But Acosta's life remained in turmoil. In 1928, he had started his own aircraft manufacturing firm, Bert Acosta Aeronautical Co., with offices in Manhattan, planning to make amphibious planes. Within a year, he'd lost everything in the stock market crash.

Around the same time, he was jailed for buzzing Naugatuck, Conn. When he later did the same to Roosevelt Field, he was fined $2,000. In 1929, the Department of Commerce revoked his license, although accounts differ as to why; some say it was because he failed to pay his fine, others that he'd

Elinor Smith, second from right, learned to fly under Acosta's wing. The veteran pilot, right, spent hours coaching Smith on how to handle different situations in the air. In 1930, she was voted top U.S. woman pilot.

gone on a drunken flying spree with an expired license. The following year, an unchastened Acosta was again arrested — this time for flying without a license.

In a 1953 interview with the New York Sunday Mirror Magazine, Acosta would describe what happened next: "I went on a five-year binge. I lived on next to nothing, sleeping, mostly, in the Bowery. I had no decent clothes or food. I was drunk all the time. I didn't care a damn whether I snapped out of it or not."

He could, however, snap out of it when required. In 1931, when Elinor Smith was honored at a Freeport dinner, she insisted on inviting the man who'd taught her so much — to the dismay of virtually everyone else, who expected Acosta would show up drunk and embarrass her. (At a similar occasion honoring a Spanish-American journalist, he'd once given the following toast: "We're here tonight to honor this sonofabitch and I don't even know what his name is. So let's all have a drink!")

But Smith was confident Acosta wouldn't do that to her — and he didn't. "Bert came, nicely turned out, sober as a judge, made a nice little speech, came over, kissed me on the forehead, and left," she recalled.

In 1935, Acosta's luck appeared to be changing once more, when the government agreed to let him fly again. "The Department of Commerce, convinced of his reformation, finally lifted its ban, granted him a 'learner's permit,'" Time magazine reported on June 10, 1935. It also noted the inherent irony: "After five hours solo, the best living pilot was scheduled this week to take his flight test for a transport license."

Acosta passed, but his hard times weren't over. His medals and decorations began showing up in pawnshops — although Acosta always claimed they'd been stolen — and his drunken sprees and arrests continued.

Acosta poses with his second wife, Helen. She forgave her husband after throwing him out of their Hempstead home, saying, "I love him yet."

He eventually ended up living in a New York City flophouse — which is where the daughters of his first marriage, Bertina and Gloria, found him in 1936. Although he hadn't seen them since they were babies, the girls lovingly nursed him back to health — and as soon as they did, he was off on another adventure, this time as a mercenary fighting on behalf of the anti-Franco forces in the Spanish Civil War.

Although he managed to shoot down several enemy planes by firing a rifle from his cockpit, the episode was largely a disaster; the planes were ancient, the Loyalists so disorganized that they didn't even issue him a uniform — Acosta flew in the suit he'd arrived in — and they failed to pay him the $1,500 he'd been promised.

After a month, he returned to the United States, where he eventually collected $700 from the Spanish consulate in New York, and talked about making another big flight: Brussels to Tokyo, perhaps, or Paris to New York.

But in 1937, he buzzed a bridge in Connecticut and had his license revoked again — this time for good. He would never fly again. The following year, his estranged wife, Helen, found him working as a dance master in a Harlem cabaret, and had him arrested for nonsupport. When he was released six months later, one reporter described the scene this way:

"Crowds have cheered him, here and abroad. Women have tossed flowers and kisses to him. Leading officials have shaken his hand. But not a soul greeted him when he walked out of the Nassau County jail yesterday."

Acosta's daughters reportedly continued trying to help

him, but little is known of his life between 1938 and 1946, when he went to live in a Franciscan monastery near Peekskill, hoping the monks would help rehabilitate him. He didn't stay long, and once back in New York City, began disappearing for months at a time.

Then, in December, 1951, Acosta collapsed in a New York City saloon. A friend took him to the hospital where doctors discovered he had tuberculosis.

His old flying partner, Richard Byrd, arranged funding to send him to a sanitarium in Colorado, where Acosta apparently spent the last years of his life reflecting on where he'd gone wrong.

"I often think that if I could have just gotten into a plane and kept it in the air without descending to earth, I'd have been so much better off," he told an interviewer.

When Acosta died in the sanitarium on Sept. 1, 1954, at the age of 59, his death was national news.

"With him at his bedside during his last hours was his daughter," Newsday reported the next day. Bertina told the newspaper, "Everyone has been just wonderful to him. He died among friends, believe me."

Acosta was buried in a North Hollywood, Calif., cemetery, along with a dozen other pioneering aviators — including Long Island brother and sister John and Matilde Moisant.

With his death, an era came to a close, as he himself acknowledged in the 1953 Mirror interview:

"The days of stunt flyers are over. I who have done perhaps more sensational flying than any person alive, know this. I was part of an era. Those days are gone, necessary and important as they were at the time. We had fun and the lives lost were not in vain. We were the leavening agent which helped aviation to mature." ●

The Airplanes: Weird, Wild And Waterborne

TAKING OFF
A biplane piloted by Marshall Reed takes off at the Hempstead Plains Aerodrome on May 26, 1912. The plane appears to be a Burgess-Wright aircraft.

I t's a bird, it's a plane — that's right, it's a plane. As imaginations soared, so did designs — resulting in planes made of dreams as well as silk and bamboo. Some looked like flying erector sets, and toys and centipedes. Others had folding wings and mesh-covered motors. Amazingly enough, most of them got off the ground — and the sea, too.

A BURNELLI FIRST
Vincent Burnelli's RB-1, built in Amityville, in flight in 1921 from Roosevelt Field. The RB-1 was the first of Burnelli's lifting-fuselage designs.

FLIGHT OF FANCY
Frank Boland, inventor of a tailless aircraft, flying one of his creations, below, at Mineola in 1912.

COPTER SUCCESS

David Kaplan flies his quadrotor,
above, in Amityville around 1956.
This was the first four-rotor helicopter
to demonstrate forward flight.

BALBO AT SEA

Below, one of 24 Savoia Marchetti S-55
Flying Boats in Jamaica Bay, Brooklyn.
On July 19, 1933, this fleet of planes, led
by Italo Balbo, arrived from Italy.

EXPERIMENT IN MINIATURES

Harvey C. Mummert's 1921 Cootie was an experiment in size reduction. It had an 18-foot wingspan and length of 12 feet.

CIRCULAR REASONING

It didn't work for the 1911 Geary Circular Triplane, below, in Garden City, a post-Wright brothers experimental craft.

HIGH-WING DESIGN

Percy H. Spencer of the Republic Aviation Corp. in Farmingdale pilots the RC-1, a four-seat, all-metal amphibian whose engine was mounted behind the cabin.

WING AND A PRAYER

Or in the case below, on multiple wings. Experimenter Howard Huntington's 1912 contraption sits near his house in Hollis, Queens. This plane did not fly.

AMPHIBIAN AT REST
This quick Fairchild F-91 sits in front of hangar G at Roosevelt Field around 1939.

EARLY PARAPLANE
A McCormick-Dietz paraplane, below, on the ground in Garden City in 1911. There's a parachute in the center tube. It never flew.

THE CLIPPERS AND PORT WASHINGTON *Above, a Sikorsky S-42, which flew from Port Washington in June, 1937, as the Bermuda Clipper. In June, 1939, the Dixie Clipper, below, Pan Am's Boeing B-314, took off from Port Washington on the first regularly scheduled transatlantic passenger service. The 30-hour flight stopped in Portugal twice before landing in Marseilles, France. Port Washington's seaplane history dates to 1913 with the landing of a Curtiss F-Boat; in 1929, American Aeronautical built a factory there.*

Transatlantic Champion

This Curtiss-made NC-4, above, took part in the first transatlantic crossing in May, 1919, a carefully planned naval operation that began in Jamaica Bay, near Far Rockaway, Queens. After stops in Chatham and Cape Cod, Mass., the NC-4 crossed from Trepassey Bay, Newfoundland, to the island of Faial in the Azores. Flight time was 15 hours, 18 minutes. The NC-4 then flew to Lisbon for a total of 2,400 miles.

Lost at Sea

Real estate agent Frances Grayson, pilot Oskar Omdal, navigator Brice Goldsborough and engine expert Fred Koehler took off in this type of Sikorsky amphibian on Dec. 23, 1927, in Grayson's fourth attempt to be the first woman to cross the Atlantic. The trip was to take the crew to Newfoundland and then England, but ended when the plane, The Dawn, crashed off Cape Cod, Mass., killing all aboard.

A Dream Destroyed

Only eight years after the Wright brothers' remarkable feat, teenager Charles Fity built an airplane with foldable wings that, after landing, could be driven like a car. The pictures above, with wings folded, and below, wings unfurled, were taken in 1911 at Nassau Boulevard Field in Garden City. However, the remarkable craft was destroyed by the youthful aviator's father shortly after its third flight. Frank Fity had witnessed his son make a particularly hard landing, which sent a broken piece of propeller flying toward a crowd of bystanders. In his pique, Frank took an ax to the machine. Charles never again had anything to do with aviation.

BULLET ON TARGET

Edson F. Gallaudet, a former physics teacher at Yale University, formed his own aviation company in 1908. One of his first successful aircraft was the Gallaudet Bullet, built in 1912. The aircraft was powered by a 100-hp. Gnôme rotary engine in the nose of the plane and covered in mesh. A drive shaft connected the engine to a pusher propeller in the tail. The plane purportedly could reach 100 mph. Gallaudet occupied a hangar at the Hempstead Plains Aerodrome in 1912. Injuries sustained in an accident in the Bullet on July 24, 1912, cut short Gallaudet's flying career and his development of the plane.

MOISANT MONOPLANE

Mary Simms, a Moisant student who later married Baldwin aircraft designer Albert Heinrich, stands in front of a Bleriot Monoplane in Mineola on Dec. 12, 1912.

Elinor Smith flew to world-class status as a pilot before she grew out of her teens.

Freeport's Famous Young Flier

BY LAURA MUHA

Two thousand feet above Long Island, a teenage girl wrapped both hands around the throttle stick of an open-cockpit biplane and held on with all her strength.

Below her, the lights of Mineola sparkled like diamonds on a jeweler's drape; above her, stars glittered in the moonless sky. But 17-year-old Elinor Smith had no time for scenery-gazing as she struggled desperately to control her plane.

WHAM! A violent jolt of turbulence tossed the craft as if it were a pebble in a wind tunnel. Jamming the throttle open, Smith regained altitude just as — WHAM! — more turbulence rocked the little craft.

Smith's piloting skills landed her a job as executive pilot for Irvin Chute Co. in 1929.

It was just before midnight on Jan. 30, 1929. Six months earlier, the Freeport girl had become the youngest person in the nation to earn a pilot's license. Now she was attempting to break the women's solo endurance record.

When she'd taken off from Mitchel Field at 2:17 that afternoon in a Bird biplane, she had planned to stay in the air at least 18 hours, topping the current 12-hour record by a wide margin. But it was becoming increasingly obvious that she wouldn't last that long. Should she give up now and land in defeat? Or try to stay aloft three more hours — to beat the record by the requisite 60 minutes?

The temperature had been dropping rapidly since sundown, and was now in the single digits. Bitter cold seeped through Smith's custom-made leather flight suit; her fingers, encased in fur-lined gloves, were numb. The chamois mask she wore to prevent frostbite itched unbearably, despite the cold cream her mother had rubbed into her skin before takeoff. And every time Smith exhaled, moisture from her breath fogged her goggles, making it difficult to see.

Clumsily, she loosened her seat belt, hoping to ease the cramps that wracked her legs after hours of sitting. WHAM! A moment later, turbulence hurled her half out of the cockpit.

Heart pounding, Smith tightened the belt again — only to discover that the stabilizer bar was stuck in one position. Without it, she wouldn't be able to keep the plane level as fuel burned off and changed the airship's center of gravity. In order to keep the plane's nose up in flying position, she'd have to keep both arms wrapped around the stick.

For the next hour, the young pilot flew up and down Sunrise Highway, desperately trying to figure out what to do. She could try to land, of course, but doing so before daybreak presented another problem. Despite Smith's considerable experience as a pilot — she had been taking flying lessons since she was 7 or 8 — she had never landed a plane at night, and wasn't sure she'd be able to.

In the days before the invention of sophisticated instrumentation, a pilot's ability to land an aircraft depended largely on his or her depth perception, which

Smith knew could be seriously impaired in the dark. Couple that with an icy, dimly lit field and an airplane half-full of high-test gasoline, and she was facing a literally explosive situation.

"If I hit something," she would say later, "I knew what the outcome would be: Kaboom!"

Although Smith was wearing a parachute, she couldn't justify bailing out and letting her plane plummet into someone's house. Should she fly out over the Atlantic Ocean and jump? The thought of plunging into the icy water was more than she could bear.

Finally, bracing her knees against the stick to keep the plane level, Smith reached for her flare gun and, half standing in the cockpit, fired it once, to let the ground crew know she was coming in. The field lights blinked in response — a signal that the crew had gotten her message.

The only problem that remained was getting down. As Smith circled the field, trying to work up her courage to land, she noticed another aircraft below her. By then, the moon had come out, enabling her to see clearly as the pilot lined up his plane behind two silvery patches of ice. "His movements were so deliberate that I could almost feel him yank the stick as he set down smartly between the two natural markers," she wrote in her 1981 autobiography, "Aviatrix."

The pilot — she later learned it was famed Army flier Jimmy Doolittle, returning from a test flight to Philadelphia — had realized she was in trouble and was showing her what to do!

Afraid to so much as blink, she cut the throttle and followed him in, setting her plane easily on the frozen field. "I just sat there for a minute and thanked God I was down," recalled Smith, who was so tired that she had to be lifted from the cockpit. "It was the worst flight of my life!"

Not to mention one of the most significant. When Smith landed on Mitchel Field at 3:30 a.m. on Jan. 31, 1929, she had been in the air for 13 hours, 16 minutes and 45 seconds.

The 5-foot-3, freckle-faced teenager had just set the first of her many world's records.

Although her name is not nearly as recognizable as that of her friend and fellow flier Amelia Earhart, Smith was considered one of the great pilots of her era. Newsreels of her feats played in movie houses around the country, and front-page headlines proclaimed her a "youthful air queen," "intrepid birdwoman" and — much to her dismay — "the Flying Flapper."

At 15, she became the youngest person of that era to make a solo flight; at 19, she was voted best female pilot in the country by her fellow fliers, beating out veterans such as Earhart to take the title. (By then, she once calculated, she had already flown 158 types of aircraft.) And in 1934, she became the only female aviator ever featured on a Wheaties box.

At the Smithsonian Institution's National Air and Space Museum in Washington, D.C., where Smith's name hangs in the Golden Age of Flight gallery, curator Dorothy Cochrane says Smith deserves far more public recognition than she gets. "She's not a household word, but she probably should be," Cochrane says. "She did some really significant flying."

In her autobiography, Smith says she knew she was destined to be a pilot almost from the minute she saw her first airplane. At the time, she was 6, and she and her younger brother had gone for a Sunday drive near Hicksville with their parents. While motoring along Merrick Road — then a single lane — they saw a sign: "Airplane Rides — $5 and $10."

Parked nearby in a potato field was a contraption that looked as if it had been made from struts, with a bullet-shaped object that turned out to be the cockpit jutting from the front and a propeller affixed to its rear — a design common to aircraft of that era.

"To my brother Joe and I, it was 'Star Wars'!" Smith recalled, laughing.

Smith's father, vaudeville comedian and dancer Tom Smith, pulled over and began talking to the pilot. More than eight decades later, his daughter could still recall every detail of what happened next: how Tom Smith tied her blond braids together so they wouldn't blow around; how he lifted her and Joe into the cockpit and buckled the seat belt over them, the thrill she felt as the plane lurched across the field and into the sky. And then there was the view, more breathtaking than she could have imagined.

"I could see out over the Atlantic Ocean, I could see the fields, I could even see the Sound," she recalled. "And the clouds on that particular day had just broken open so there were these shafts of light coming down and lighting up this whole landscape in various greens and yellows."

From that moment on, she wanted to fly.

Smith's ambition was inadvertently nurtured by her father, who was passionate about airplanes. After wangling introductions to some of the pilots at Curtiss Field, he began spending much of his spare time there, often taking Smith and her brother with him.

In those days, the field was a decidedly unglamorous place: a wide dusty plain bordered by three ramshackle metal hangars with leaky roofs. "You had to be pretty careful where you parked your airplane, or you'd come out the next day and be drowning in the cockpit," Smith recalled. In the dry season, propellers kicked up choking clouds of dust on the dirt runways, and in March and late September, it wasn't unusual to see planes mired up to their wheel hubs in mud. The few patches of grass that remained were spattered with wild buttercups and dandelions, and the scent of the varnish used to stiffen fabric fuselages at the Curtiss Engineering Corp. plant at the far end of the field permeated everything.

The pilots who hung out at the field were a hard-drinking, tough-talking bunch, but they were tickled by the 7-year-old Smith's enthusiasm for flying. She begged them for rides, and usually they complied, letting her take the controls when they saw how much she loved it. By the time she was 10, she was flying regularly, with a pillow behind her back to bring her closer to the controls, and blocks attached to the rudder bar so she could reach it with her feet. On the ground, the little girl peppered her conversation with such terms as "empennage" (the technical term for an airplane's tail assembly) and "ailerons" (the movable section of the wing).

Soon, the pilots' initial bemusement toward Smith turned to respect, as they discovered that she wasn't just enthusiastic about flying — she was talented, driven and courageous.

At 13, Smith was flying over the North Shore with famed Curtiss test pilot Bert Acosta when the radiator burst, releasing a cloud of scalding steam. Acosta, in the front of the two-cockpit airplane, couldn't see anything, so the teenager loosened her seat belt and hung out over the side, directing him to an open field where he could land.

Impressed, Acosta took Smith under his wing and began drilling her on every aspect of airships. ("In those days, we always called them ships; if you called it a plane, we knew you were a civilian," Smith recalled.) He explained the purpose of each part, and made her repeat it back to him. "I'm sure you're going to solo in the next couple of years, and I want you to know everything about this airplane before you get into it, so you don't get killed the first time out," Acosta told her.

In fact, the subject of soloing was a sore one with Smith. It was something she desperately wanted to do, but her father refused to even consider it — at least not, he told her, until she was 18. And to make sure she didn't get any ideas about disobeying him, he privately instructed pilots at the field not to teach her how to take off or land.

In retrospect, Smith said years later, her father was undoubtedly right. "The air is like the sea, and it's just as cruel. It can change on you like that; you have to have adult judgment to know what to do in an emergency."

But at the time, all she could think of was how far away 18 seemed — "those three years stretched ahead of me like 30!" So, in desperation, she did the only thing left for her to do: She went to work on her mother.

Although Agnes Smith had mixed feelings about her daughter's love of flying, she did understand what it meant to have one's ambitions thwarted by parents who didn't take them seriously: Her own mother had denied her the singing lessons she'd craved to cultivate her beautiful voice.

Not wanting to do the same thing to her own child, Agnes Smith waited until her husband was on the road, then told her daughter to report to a small field in Wantagh where pilot Russ Holderman, considered the dean of the local flight instructors, kept his plane.

For the next 10 days, Smith bounded out of bed at dawn, pulled on argyle socks, her brother's knickers and an old leather jacket — "My mother wasn't crazy about that getup!" — and headed for Wantagh, where she spent a half hour with Holderman, practicing takeoffs and landings. Then she'd rush home, change clothes and bike to school, trying to slip quietly into her seat so no one would realize she was late. "I'll always bless my English teacher — she never once marked me absent!" Smith said.

Finally, there came the moment when, after a practice spin, Holderman hopped out of the cockpit. "Take her around," he told Smith. "She's all yours."

Momentarily, the 15-year-old panicked. Why had she thought this was such a good idea? What if she crashed? Then her training took over and she opened the throttle, taxied across the field, picked up speed, and was airborne, becoming the youngest woman in the world to fly solo.

After that, Smith spent every spare moment of that time in the cockpit, practicing takeoffs and landings on racetracks, beaches and ball parks. "Right side up, upside down, crosswind, tailwind or no wind, I learned how to handle everything from a fire on board

By the late 1920s, there were only about three dozen licensed women pilots in the nation.
Here, in 1929, Smith had just set the women's endurance record of more than 26 hours.

to ice build-up on the wings," she wrote in "Aviatrix," adding that her father's pride in her accomplishment quickly overrode his objections at her disobedience.

Yet Smith's problems weren't over. She still needed a pilot's license — and Orville Wright, then chairman of the National Aeronautic Association, wouldn't sign it because he thought she was too young.

Eventually, by pulling some strings, Holderman managed to arrange a meeting between the father of flight and the young pilot. "I felt ridiculous, because he was old enough to be my grandfather," Smith recalled. "But I went to Washington and as it turned out, he thought my parents were exploiting me . . . He had heard they were in the theatrical business, and thought they were building me up to play Loews on 34th Street."

Smith eventually managed to persuade Wright that wasn't the case. "If anything, I was exploiting my parents; they were kicking and screaming because they didn't want a daughter at 15 flying around."

Once convinced, Wright was more receptive. "I became as good friends as you could be with him, because he was fairly crusty," Smith recalled. He was also fair, and not long after that, on Aug. 14, 1928 — just three days before Smith's 17th birthday — he issued her license.

It was around the same time, while idly circling Curtiss Field on a practice flight, that Smith realized she wanted to be more than just another flier. She wanted to become a professional pilot.

Back then, that was a radical career choice for anyone, not to mention a woman. Not even 25 years had passed since the Wright brothers' historic flight, and aviation was barely out of its infancy. Airplanes were primitive — they had no radios or brakes and few instruments — and crashes were frequent occurrences. Pilots were viewed as a cross between daredevils and heroes, risking their lives for a moment of glory — hardly the sort of behavior a woman of that

Former rivals Smith and Bobbie Trout, right, sit on the radios they used during a two-person endurance flight in California.

era was expected to engage in.

Undeterred, Smith convinced her parents to let her postpone college, which she'd been scheduled to begin in September, 1928, and set about making her dream a reality.

She got an unexpected head start two months later, when another pilot, an obscure barnstormer who'd flown in from the Midwest, decided a good way to get publicity would be to fly under the Hell's Gate Bridge between Astoria and Wards Island — a stunt anyone familiar with the area would have shunned because of tricky wind currents and turbulence near the water's surface (not to mention the fact that flying under bridges was forbidden in New York City). Sure enough, the barnstormer crashed into one of the stanchions and, although uninjured, wound up with a suspended license.

Unabashed, the man began hanging out at Curtiss Field, bragging about what a wonderful pilot he was, and claiming that only engine failure had prevented him from clearing the bridge.

Finally, one of the aerial photographers who worked at the field got irritated. "When are you

going to knock it off? Why, even Ellie here could do it!" He turned to Smith. "Couldn't you?"

"Sure," said Smith with a shrug, although she had no intention of trying.

The next thing she knew, the barnstormer was spreading rumors that she'd agreed to duplicate his flight, then chickened out.

"I was furious!" recalled Smith, who saw only one recourse: to prove him wrong by flying under the Queensboro, Williamsburg, Manhattan and Brooklyn Bridges, in that order.

"She's a Daredevil!" headlined the New York Daily News, reporting on Smith's planned exploit.

Smith spent the next few weeks checking bridge clearances and tide tables, and practicing low-level flying around the masts of boats in Manhasset Bay. Then, on Oct. 21, 1928, she took off from Curtiss Field and headed for the East River.

The next day's Daily News told the rest of the story:

"Elinor Smith, Freeport's 17-year-old aviatrix, nonchalantly ducked under four East River bridges yesterday afternoon in a Waco biplane and reported the stunt was easy . . . 'I had to dodge a couple of ships near the bridges, but there was plenty of room,' the high school aviatrix reported." The story was accompanied by a photograph of Smith back at the airfield, casually powdering her nose as if to say, "It was nothing."

To this day, Smith is apparently the only person ever to have piloted a regular plane under all the bridges, something she considers a mixed blessing. "The flight only lasted five minutes, yet when people referred to me in the later years, it was invariably [as] the girl who flew under the four East River bridges!" she said in mock dismay.

The feat made her an instant celebrity — by evening, newsreels of her flight were playing in Broadway movie houses. And it had another, unintended effect as well: Reporters covering the story, knowing she was actor Tom Smith's daughter, referred to her in print as Elinor Smith, not realizing that "Smith" was a stage name. In fact, the family's real name was Ward.

"They [reporters] would call, 'Miss Smith, Miss Smith,' and I'd look around and say, 'WHO?'" recalled the flier, who later legally changed her name.

Although Smith received worldwide attention for her bridge flight, she couldn't afford to rest on her laurels for long.

By the late 1920s, a handful of companies were starting to hire women to demonstrate their planes — "The message was that if a woman could fly it, anyone could," says the Smithsonian's Cochrane — but there were also about three dozen licensed female pilots in the United States, giving Smith plenty of competition.

In March, 1929, Louise Thaden topped Smith's solo endurance record by nine hours. Later that year, Phoebe Omlie became the first woman to fly to an altitude of 25,000 feet. Then there was Earhart, who had set a number of speed records and even had her own publicity manager.

Without such an advantage, Smith knew the only way to land the contracts she needed to fly professionally would be to drum up her own publicity.

So a month after Thaden broke her women's endurance record, Smith earned it back by staying aloft for 26

hours, 23 minutes and 16 seconds — this time in the comfort of a closed-cabin aircraft. Later that year, she teamed with Bobbie Trout on a two-person endurance flight in California; they set a joint record of 42 hours, and became the first women to refuel a plane in midair.

There were other firsts, too: At 18, Smith became the youngest person, male or female, to receive a transport pilot's license, enabling her to fly passengers commercially. The same year Navy Adm. William Moffett invited her to test one of his training planes in Hampton Bays, making her the first woman — and possibly the only one of her era — to pilot a military aircraft. Moffett was so impressed by Smith's demonstration that he gave her his gold aviator's wings, which she made into a ring: More than 70 years later, she was still wearing it every day.

In 1931, when she was 19, Smith also became the first woman to fly to an altitude of more than 30,000 feet, an achievement that almost ended in disaster when the engine of her plane died at 25,000 feet. Trying to restart it, Smith accidentally cut off her oxygen supply and passed out; the plane plunged 23,000 feet. "When I came to, I was in a power dive right into the Hempstead Reservoir."

She managed to steer to a landing on a rough patch of ground near Mitchel Field, only to realize there were two trees looming ahead of her. Rather than crash into them and shear off the wings — "I wanted

Smith, left, and Trout set a joint record of 42 hours and became the first women to refuel a plane in midair in 1929.

to go back up the next week!" — she cut the ignition, slammed on the brakes and deliberately flipped the ship over, crouching in her seat to protect herself.

"Aviatrix, 18, Saves Self by Keeping Head," the New York World-Telegram headlined the next day (she was actually 19 at the time). The paper added that the first people on the scene found Smith walking around her overturned plane, muttering, "It makes me mad. It makes me mad."

The only damage to the plane was a bent propeller, and three of the ribs on the top wing — "It didn't amount to $100," Smith recalled proudly — and so a week later, she went up again, this time setting a new women's altitude record of 34,500 feet.

As she'd hoped, her piloting skills were soon in demand. In 1929, the Irvin Chute Co. hired her as its first woman executive pilot, to demonstrate parachute drops on a nationwide tour; a year after that, she became the first woman test pilot for Fairchild Aviation Corp. She did endorsements for goggles and motor oil. And NBC radio hired her as a commentator covering international flights and air races.

But of all the honors Smith received, the one she's most proud of came in 1930, when the American Society for the Promotion of Aviation sponsored a competition for the best male and female pilots in the United States. Only licensed fliers were permitted to vote. When the ballots were counted, Smith — who'd assumed Earhart would take the title — was stunned to learn she had won.

"It was such an honor to know that my peers considered me the best," she said, adding that she was even more thrilled when her hero, Jimmy Doolittle, was named the best male pilot.

A year later, however, something happened that would indirectly lead to the end of Smith's flying career. Then barely 20, she had gone to Albany to lobby for legislation preventing electric companies from stringing power lines around airports. While there, she met with state Aviation Commissioner Patrick Sullivan, an attorney and political appointee, who, Smith was disgusted to learn, "didn't know beans about aviation. Nothing. Zilch!"

She didn't hesitate to let him know how she felt. "If you're the commissioner, why don't you know anything?" she told him at their first meeting.

Far from being put off, Sullivan, then 23, was intrigued by the feisty blond pilot, so much so that he asked her to dinner.

Two years later, they were married.

For several years and two children after that, Smith kept flying. During that time, she set a number of records, including a straight-course speed record of 229 mph while flying an experimental plane in Miami, and an intercity speed record of 30 minutes between Philadelphia and Long Island.

Sullivan was a good sport about his wife's activities, and about being referred to as "Mr. Smith" by the people they met, but he wasn't crazy about airplanes. "He flew with me a couple of times, but he said it just wasn't for him and we left it at that," Smith recalled. He never asked her to stop flying, but, Smith said decades later, "I can see now that he wanted to."

Then one afternoon while

At the Cradle of Aviation Museum, Elinor Smith Sullivan stands by a plane similar to the one in which she broke the endurance record in 1929.

pregnant with her third child, Smith was aloft in a balky aircraft. "It just struck me: Maybe this is not so smart. I've got two [children], and they need a mother more than I need to fly."

Shortly afterward, at the ripe old age of 29, Smith announced her retirement.

A few times after that, she borrowed a plane from a well-to-do friend, just to go for a spin. But she quickly realized the thrill wasn't there. "If you're doing something professionally, there's always a goal and a focus that you have to maintain," she explained. "To just go up and fly around — it was beautiful, but it just wasn't the same."

For the next two decades, Smith kept busy raising her son and three daughters on Manhattan's Upper West Side. Still, aviation was never far from her mind. "At the dinner table, it was always like this," recalled Smith's daughter, Patricia Sullivan of Manhattan, banking her hand in the air like an airplane to demonstrate her mother's favorite topic of conversation.

In 1956, Patrick Sullivan died after a long illness, and his widow went back to work, writing and editing articles about aviation. Then, in 1960, the U.S. Air Force Association invited her to give a talk at Mitchel Field, which led to an invitation to try flying a T-33 jet trainer. "They didn't have to ask me twice. Discovering the delights and differences between jet and propeller flying opened up a whole new world."

Before long, Smith was back in the pilot's seat, flying C-119s as far away as Puerto Rico for a group of World War II pilots who gave paratroop demonstrations. At 55, a bout with cancer forced her to retire again — but not for long. At 60, she was flying once again, this time with the Naval Reserve in an attempt to save Brooklyn's Floyd Bennett Field, which was being threatened by development. The effort was successful, and during the official celebration that followed, Smith became the first pilot to set a civilian aircraft on the field.

At 89, Smith was living in Santa Cruz, Calif. Although her hearing was no longer good enough for her to qualify for a pilot's license, she still flew with her son, a licensed pilot, and on numerous occasions had "flown" simulators that the military uses to train its pilots — including a Navy F-14 simulator that provided one of her most memorable recent experiences. During takeoff, Smith decided to show off her skill with one of the flashy climbing turns that she could always count on to wow crowds at airshows in the late 1920s. The problem, she admitted, was that she didn't

realize how much more responsive the F-14 was than the small propeller planes she'd once flown. "I gave it just this much" she waved her hand to demonstrate the small amount of power she'd used in the simulator "and suddenly rolled over on my back in the air."

Without missing a beat, Smith rolled the simulated plane right-side up again, and kept climbing. The commander who was "flying" with her was awestruck.

"I've never seen anything like that!" he told Smith.

"I was dying to say, 'Neither have I' — but I didn't!" Smith recalled, laughing.

In March, 2000, she had another first, when she was invited to fly NASA's Challenger simulator, which, she said, "had a console probably the size of the wall."

Actually, she added, "it's a misnomer to say that you fly it. You think you have a throttle, but it's more like a toggle switch, and there's almost no lateral control."

Nor is there any opportunity to correct mistakes. "You've got to make a perfect landing with that thing . . . [or] you crash and burn," Smith said. "If ever I don't express enough appreciation for [astronaut] Eileen Collins — she's 22 feet tall in my book!"

Asked whether she made a perfect landing, Smith laughed. "I managed two — but on a couple of others, they were kind enough to cut the tape!" she said, relaxing in an armchair in what she jokingly calls the "I-love-me room" of her home, because of the memorabilia on display: A 1991 certificate of honor from the National Aeronautics Association "for contributions to the advancement of the art, sport and science of aviation and space flight"; a silver tea set given to her by the village of Freeport; a framed copy of her Wheaties box.

"She didn't want to have any of it out, but I said, 'You've got to — it's only right!' " said her housemate, Lois McFall.

Much as she enjoyed flying the simulators, however, Smith said that neither they, nor the corresponding aircraft, offer anything like the freedom she once felt in the skies above Long Island.

"It's not that we were such daredevils back then, but there was a rapport between pilot and aircraft that I don't think exists today," she said. "You can almost punch in the numbers and fly. You've got flaps, you've got brakes, you've got all the navigational equipment you need, you've got radios."

She paused, reflecting on her early days in the cockpit.

"It was a wonderful, wonderful time," she said wistfully. "I just loved every part of it!" ●

The high-flying Rizzos rest for a pose, circa 1942:
Paul Jr., left, Barbara, Olive, Paul and Beatrice.

A Daredevil And A Dreamer

BY DAVID BEHRENS

From the sky, Long Island's meadows seemed like an almost boundless airfield to Paul Rizzo's generation of aviators.

It was a dashing, crashing era.

On the ground, Americans were getting high on bootleg whiskey and the hot new music of the Jazz Age.

In the air, Rizzo and his cohorts soared through the clouds, brimming with the pleasure of flight. They made certain to carefully mark the next best place for a forced landing, for mishaps were so common in those early days. But how the danger gave an edge to the excitement! For many, in the era between the world wars, flying was almost addictive.

Rizzo was hooked early. Born in 1904 — less than a year after the Wright brothers' famous flight — he took his first plane ride as a teenager. Hanging around Curtiss Field on weekends, he'd offer to do odd jobs for the fliers and his chores often were rewarded with a hop in the sky, a dream come true.

Bert Acosta, one of the maddest of a madcap generation of pilots, gave Rizzo one of his first rides in a plane. Another was Charles (Casey) Jones, who helped to start a fraternity of experienced pilots called QB, the Quiet Birdmen. A decade later, Rizzo would become a member.

Rizzo did not have enough money to buy his own plane until he was 22. He taught himself to fly, reading a how-to book.

At age 94, a year before his death, he was still flying. When he died on the morning of Christmas Eve, 1999, he was Long Island's oldest active pilot and one of the oldest in the country.

His resume reflected the adventurous era: self-taught aviator, entrepreneur and instructor, operator of Brooklyn's first airfield, racing daredevil, stunt pilot, airplane owner and flier-for-hire, chauffeur of joy-riding passengers, wing-walkers and parachute-jumpers. And, during World War II, an officer in the Army Air Corps, ferrying fighters and bombers from factory to air base and then, across the Atlantic and into the war.

Until the very end, he seemed to recall every plane, every flight, every close call — and his three children grew up on his stories.

●

On a warm afternoon in the summer of 1998, Paul Rizzo sat in front of a large TV screen in the living room of his modest East Meadow home. Hanging from the ceiling was a mobile composed of tiny handmade models of the planes of his life — from the famed Jenny of the 1920s and '30s to the B-24 Liberator bomber he ferried to Europe and North Africa during World War II and the lake-hopping Loening seaplane he flew as a charter pilot in the postwar years.

Rizzo was previewing a videocassette, "Daredevils and Dreamers," a one-hour documentary on the pioneering pilots of the 1920s and '30s scheduled for public television stations that week. It was as if he had come across a long-lost high school yearbook. He knew *everyone.*

The film re-created a time when Long Island was the cradle of aviation and Roosevelt and Curtiss Fields were the fields of choice for America's most adored fliers. In those days, ordinary human beings would look up in awe at the sight of a man or a woman in a single-engine biplane, waving from the sky like some goggle-eyed god of another world. And they'd pay barnstormers such as Rizzo as much as two dollars for a seven-minute ride in the blue.

Flying was not just a matter of getting somewhere then — and seeing the black-and-white images of Curtiss Jennys and Taper Wing Wacos and Ryan Broughams, Rizzo was as thrilled as an old grad at a 50th reunion.

Across the TV screen in front of Rizzo, a biplane made a lazy circle over Roosevelt Field. It was a vintage Curtiss JN-4D2 Jenny, driven by a 90-horsepower OX-5 engine.

"There's a Jenny! My first plane!" Rizzo exclaimed, watching the tiny plane trail an arc of white vapor above the landing field. He pressed the pause button on the VCR to relish memories of the long-gone Jenny.

In 1917, in the midst of World War I, 13-year-old Paul Rizzo fell in love with the Jenny — the plane that had been built by the thousands as an Army Air Corps trainer during the war.

One morning, by chance, a Jenny made a forced landing a few blocks from PS 114 in Canarsie, where Rizzo was a seventh-grader. Young Paul had built a squadron of model planes, copies of the combat craft that entranced boys his age. But suddenly, right in his own neighborhood, he had his first close-up look at the real thing.

Canarsie was not an affluent neighborhood. His parents, Joe and Josephine Rizzo, had emigrated from Italy before the turn of the century and settled in Brooklyn. Paul was one of seven children and the youngest of four boys. His father worked as a barber and a day laborer and, to earn some extra dollars, opened a snack stand in front of their house at 9202 Skidmore Ave., selling hot dogs for 5 cents apiece.

His father was making less than $20 a week at the time, so, after graduation from grade school, at 14, Paul had to go to work. He found jobs as a mechanic's helper in Brooklyn garages, showing a natural aptitude for engines from the start.

But planes were always on his mind, and on his days off he schemed to get into the air every chance

Rizzo takes a flight back in time as he watches an image of himself on a 1998 public television special about pioneering pilots of the 1920s and '30s.

he had. Once, in his late teens, he convinced the publisher of the weekly Canarsie Courier to publicize the newspaper by dropping leaflets from a plane.

"He agreed to the price of $25 and Casey Jones took me up in a Curtiss Oriole. I dropped all the circulars and it caused quite a lot of excitement. The publisher was pleased and so was I," Rizzo reflected later.

It was a break-even scheme, but well worth it. Rizzo had an unforgettable half-hour in the sky and happily turned over the publisher's $25 to pilot Jones for the trip over his Canarsie neighborhood.

By 1925, he was buying and rebuilding Model T Fords. One afternoon, when he was 21, he sold a 1922 Ford to a young woman who just graduated from nursing school. Olive Barker paid $125 for the used car. She was delighted with the smooth-running engine and Rizzo was encouraged to ask her out on a date. Three years later, Olive and Paul were married.

While working at the J.J. Hart Ford garage, Rizzo learned that a Jenny was for sale at Curtiss Field. In need of repairs, it had been repossessed because of its owner's failure to pay hangar fees. It was one of thousands of Jennys sold as surplus items after the war.

Now 22, Rizzo was able to scrape together $400 to buy the plane, a simple craft equipped only with oil pressure and water temperature gauges and a tachometer to measure the propeller's revolutions per minute.

Less than a week later, Rizzo suffered his first serious accident. A Model T had jumped the curb in front of the Hart station, fracturing his left leg.

"When the doctor put me in a cast from ankle to hip," he remembered, "I asked him to cut the cast at the knee so I could bend my leg. 'I wouldn't advise you to drive a car,' the doctor said. I told him, 'I'm not gonna drive a car. I'm gonna fly a plane!' He said, 'Young man, you're out of your mind.'"

Rizzo grinned. "Can you imagine people in those days, getting into a plane with a pilot on two crutches and a cast on his leg!"

So at 22, Rizzo was the proud owner of a not-so-new Jenny — and he was not even a pilot.

●

The old pilot stared at a 1920s photo on the TV screen — a slim young man with black hair and a rakishly thin mustache in the style of early Hollywood.

"Oh, there I am," he said.

His own debonair image in an open cockpit reminded him of his first venture as a flier — with a cast on his leg. While he had been a frequent passenger in his teen years, he had never taken over the controls of a plane. So, when he bought his first Jenny, he devoted two full weeks to study a book titled "Fly an Airplane," borrowed from a local library.

"Then I just jumped in and soloed, without a lesson or an hour of flying time."

There was one brief hitch in his first flight. At an altitude of 300 feet or so, the Jenny began to lose power and Rizzo was forced to glide to an emergency landing at the edge of Curtiss Field.

The problem was clearly sabotage, Rizzo said. The previous owner — or someone else — had forced a wooden plug into the engine's cooling system to block the circulation of water. But Rizzo spotted the trouble and was able to complete his first solo.

"I flew all day long, taking off and landing, following what the book said," he recalled. After some 25 hours of flight time, he decided it was time to become a stunt pilot.

Soon after, he asked one of the pilots at Curtiss Field how to spin a plane and bring it out. "He warned me, 'If you try to pull back the stick while you're in the spin, you'll go right into the ground.'" Once again he followed directions without a mishap — and two weeks later he was instructing other people in the art of flying, at $25 an hour.

"I would fly from morning to late evening," he recalled in a memoir he dictated to his wife years later. "The view in nearly all directions fascinated me. By this time, I was used to the controls in the air and the movement became automatic, which permitted me to look around and enjoy the sensation of flight."

In the public television film, Rizzo was relating his first errand in the sky. After his solo flight, he had decided to keep his Jenny and his risky new business venture a secret from his family. But one day, Charlie Moore, a teenage friend, showed up at the his house and told Rizzo's parents he wouldn't be able to take his regular lesson that weekend.

"Paul's teaching me how to fly," he said.

Rizzo's parents were aghast. But his father adjusted quickly to the dawning age of aviation. Soon after, he asked his son to make Canarsie's first air-to-door delivery — a five-pound package of franks — to the Olsen family, one of his best customers.

Flying his Jenny about 50 feet over the Olsen house and slowing to 40 mph, Rizzo made a perfect drop. The story was recounted briefly in a 1927 issue of the Canarsie Courier, under the headline, "Hot Dogs From Above."

The story began: "Mrs. Carl Olsen of 1793 E. 92nd St. was startled by a frankfurter bomb which hurtled out of the sky and landed just outside her kitchen door at her feet."

A few minutes before, the news item went on, "Upon hearing the loud hum of an aeroplane over her roof, she looked out and saw the plane circle twice around the house." Mrs. Olsen had been puzzled at first, until she remembered the Rizzos had a daring son who was an aviator.

In his living room, Rizzo eagerly put the tale in historical perspective. After flying over the Olsen house, he decided to visit a friend, Barney Brinks, who lived two miles away on Barren Island, a small community at the foot of Flatbush Avenue.

By the mid-1800s, the island had become an industrial wasteland: the site of a fertilizer plant which recycled the carcasses of horses, a fish oil factory and later, a city garbage dump.

But by the 1920s, only 1,500 residents lived on the island and one garbage incinerator remained. Flat, sandy and remote, it was an ideal place for an airport, Rizzo decided. He landed on a narrow road near the Brinks house and quickly attracted a crowd, eager as he once was for a close-up view of the classic Jenny.

As Rizzo soon discovered, crowds meant money.

It turned out that his friend Barney's father was caretaker of property on the island and arranged a meeting with the owners. Rizzo rented the land for $15 a month and in 1927, opened Brooklyn's first commercial airfield.

A year later, the airstrip's first hangar was completed, big enough for seven planes and built with the help of Carl Olsen, husband of the recipient of Rizzo's flying frankfurters.

By then, the young flier owned four planes — two Jennys, a Standard J-1 Hisso and a Spartan biplane — and his new airport was an instant success. Hundreds of people came to Barren Island to take flying lessons or a $5 ride in the sky. Before the decade ended, additional hangars were built for a dozen or so other planes, many of them owned by his former students.

Rizzo sold his older planes, none licensed by the U.S. Department of Commerce, and replaced them with newer, safer craft. Among them were a Curtiss Robin, an American Eagle, an OX5 Swallow, an OX5

Challenger and a pair of Waco 10, which featured an automatic starter and brakes — unlike the earliest generations of aircraft.

"The public was starting to get smart about planes," he said.

Barren Island became a famous playground, with Sunday afternoon air shows featuring the most famous daredevils of the day.

Rizzo placed an ad in the Brooklyn Eagle that asked: "HAVE YOU EVER BEEN UP IN THE AIR?" The ad promised "passenger flights every afternoon and Sundays at reasonable rates."

The Sunday show featured death-defying dives, rolls and loops as well as wing-walking and parachute jumping from the astonishing height of 2,000 feet. A Monday item in the New York Daily News observed: "It seems that all the cars in Brooklyn, New York and New Jersey were concentrated in one spot, and that was the Barren Island Airport."

Commercial aviation was still something wondrous at the time, a quality reflected in a story in the Brooklyn Chat:

"One of the most interesting attractions down on Barren Island is the commercial airfield conducted by Paul Rizzo, a 25-year-old aviator, and his assistant, who daily carry many men, women and children aloft for a trip through the ozone over Jamaica Bay and Flatbush," the weekly paper gushed. "No less than six Waco planes, all in apple pie order, are lined up on the Barren Island airfield and one by one taxi across the level field and go into the air with passengers."

But the beginning of the end of Rizzo's Barren Island heyday came when city officials noted his success and began a study of the island for a major airport.

The site was brought to the attention of Mayor Jimmy Walker by Clarence Chamberlin, one of the earliest transatlantic fliers, and construction of Floyd Bennett Field, New York City's first municipal airport, was begun in 1929.

The field was built on land adjoining Rizzo's first landing strip and his planes were often hired by newspapers to photograph the 387-acre airfield. Floyd Bennett opened with a historic air show on May 23, 1931, with 597 planes of the Army Air Corps' First Air Division flying over in the largest pa-

Rizzo pilots a Waco 10 over Jamaica Bay with two wing-walkers along for the ride.

The barnstormer poses with one of his aircraft. Rizzo could recall every plane, flight and close call.

rade of planes of the era. One craft, it was reported by The New York Times, was piloted by Charles Lindbergh, sitting in at the request of a friend.

Floyd Bennett remained the hub of commercial aviation for New York and Long Island until the spring of 1941, when the field was leased to the Navy as a naval air station.

Rizzo had moved his planes to the new facility and continued his barnstorming operations. But the times were changing. Stricter government rules and regulations were enforced, and after the stock market crash of 1929 the demand for airplane rides and lessons began to slacken.

His years at the Barren Island Airport were among the happiest of Rizzo's life. Still, in the 1930s, he was able to fly over the family house on Skidmore Avenue and watch Olive shopping for groceries. Or he might spot her with Paul Jr., their infant son born in 1930, out for a stroller ride in the Canarsie neighborhood.

Sometimes, at midday, Olive might lower a window shade to signal that lunch was ready and her husband would dip his wings and land in a field near the house. While the Rizzos were at their midday meal, a neighbor would look after the plane. There, Rizzo had flown kites and model planes, powered by rubber bands, during his boyhood.

●

On the TV screen, the images of aviation pioneers were flying by.

German ace Ernst Udet demonstrated how to pick up a handkerchief with a hook on his wingtip, dipping over a runway at a mere 30 mph.

"They don't teach slow flying anymore," Rizzo said with a groan. "These fellows today, if their engines quit, they'd overshoot the Sahara Desert."

He loved to talk about the art of flying slowly — how to side-slip and fish-tail to slow a plane while losing altitude for a landing. By getting the air to flow against one side of the fuselage and then the other, a pilot could safely land even with a stalled engine.

There was no traffic control in his day, no traffic patterns, no control towers, no radio guidance, often no runway at all, just grassy fields.

"You took off and you went in any old direction you wanted to. And when you came back, you landed when there was no one in front or in back of you. It was easy. There was so much room. Sometimes, seven planes might land at one time. You'd beat a guy to the field and the others might land on the grass next to the runway. No one had insurance but most of the time, nothing happened."

Curtiss and Roosevelt Fields, part of the spacious Hempstead Plains, soon were called "America's most forgiving runways," where pilots could take off and land in almost any direction with more than enough room for mistakes.

Rizzo still remembered the vast, somewhat bumpy runways, covered with pebbles.

"But taking off was nothing at all. You gave it the gas and felt the pressure on the stick. Once you reached flying speed, with the slightest movement of the stick, the nose came up. We did it all by feeling. There were no instruments in those days. It was strictly by the seat of your pants."

Rizzo counted at least 25 forced landings. There were so many things that could go wrong. There were leaks in the gas lines and leaks in the water lines. There was water in the gas lines and faulty gauges and carburetor fires and broken cables and shaky propellers.

Once, while he was flying a Jenny, the left wheel fell off. He hadn't noticed it until another pilot pointed out the problem as he flew by.

But even with a stalled engine or one wheel, there was no panic and always a place to land. "Long Island was all farms and grassy fields. You'd just put the nose down and go straight. You could land almost anywhere with your eyes closed."

His most serious mishap came on Oct. 26, 1929, when he was competing in the Trenton Air Races at Mercer Airport in New Jersey, celebrating the city's 250th anniversary. The day-long competition drew a roster of famous pilots such as Amelia Earhart, Jimmy Doolittle, Bert Acosta and Clarence Chamberlin.

The New York World reported that a crowd of more than 30,000 looked on as Rizzo's new Barling NB-3 monoplane was clipped by the wing tip of a Curtiss Moth as the planes curved around a pylon during a 30-mile race.

The impact threw Rizzo against the dashboard of his plane and the Barling, which Rizzo had borrowed from a former pupil, crashed to the ground, a total wreck. Rizzo, unconscious for two hours, escaped with only four broken ribs, cuts and bruises and a few missing teeth. He was out of the hospital a few days later and flying again within two weeks. The

winner of the 30-mile race had averaged 127 mph.

Watching "Daredevils and Dreamers," Rizzo grinned at a segment on the Prohibition era. On occasion, he said, he too flew in bootleg whiskey bound for Long Island and New York City speakeasies.

He'd meet bootleggers in their small boats some 15 or 20 miles off Montauk. "You'd carry in 50 cases and make $5 a case . . . No one was scared of going to jail. Coming back, you'd see cops over in one place, so you'd land over in another place. But nobody worried. Lots of cops were in on the deal. Once, in fact, a local police chief helped me unload the seaplane. The bootleggers would stay at Ansel Young's hotel in Greenport, for instance. He was also mayor of the place and the one who appointed the cops. So you figure it out."

On another bootlegging flight, he made a forced landing in the Atlantic and he and two other men sat on one of the wings all night, his son, Paul Jr., who now lives in Virginia, related.

"The plane was listing badly and one of the floats was taking on water. If they hadn't balanced the plane, it probably would have capsized. But then a Coast Guard cutter showed up in the morning, answering a radio distress signal. The cutter tried to tow the plane to shore but it sank on the way."

Rizzo was happy to be rescued but he had no regrets that the whiskey was not. "He seemed quite content that the plane sank before the Coast Guard examined it. Years later, when he talked about the incident, he'd only wink about what he was doing out there," his son said.

When Prohibition ended, Rizzo continued to barnstorm through the 1930s, taking sightseers for flights over Times Square until 11 p.m. for $10 a trip, working summer resorts on both sides of the Hudson, landing his Loening on remote lakes that other pilots considered too small for a seaplane.

In the summer of 1934, he was caught up in another drama on a flight to St. John's, Newfoundland, ferrying two men to see an ailing relative. Plagued by fog and the lack of accurate flying maps, Rizzo navigated with road maps of Maine and the Canadian provinces.

Flying a Ryan Brougham, he had to make several emergency landings in Nova Scotia and Newfoundland. Landing near a mining town, his plane was deeply mired in mud and about 100 townspeople helped move it to another field. Before the return trip, he sent a radiogram that he was taking off, bound for Nova Scotia. But heavy fog forced him to return to Newfoundland, where he made another emergency landing on a beach, damaging his propeller.

Meanwhile, U.S. newspapers reported that his plane was apparently lost in the Atlantic. After repairs were made, using equipment from a nearby railroad yard, he finally reached Boston, 25 days after the two-week trip began. But for many days, Olive Rizzo assumed her husband was lost at sea.

At the time, the country's economic depression had deepened and after Olive gave birth again in 1937, to twin daughters, Beatrice and Barbara, their father was more worried than ever about his ability to support a family as a pilot.

Rizzo had already started night school classes and, also going to summer sessions, he earned a teaching certificate at a college in Oswego. It enabled him to work on and off as a substitute teacher in New York City schools, for $9 a day, teaching youngsters both aviation and auto mechanics.

But barnstorming on weekends, evenings and summer days remained the joy of his life.

In good sunny weather, he might make as many as 60 or 70 takeoffs and landings in a day. He always kept track of the exact number. Once, in a seaplane, he made $560 in one day, taking six passengers at a time at $8 a flight.

On another occasion, he landed in a field on a busy country road near Freehold, N.J. When passing cars just drove on by, he tipped the plane on its nose and waited for drivers to stop and gawk at the crash. They did and he took many for a plane ride at $3 a spin.

●

Paul Rizzo Jr. joined the Army as an infantry lieutenant during the Korean War and retired in 1973 as a lieutenant colonel. He often kidded his father about their respective ranks. The elder Rizzo had retired from the Air Force Reserve in 1962, with the rank of major.

As a young officer, Paul Jr. risked his life in the Korean and Vietnam Wars but he was always terrified of heights. Flying in an open cockpit was never his idea of child's play. But he was often reminded by his parents that he had taken his first flight in his mother's arms — in the front of a Jenny trainer with his father flying the plane from the rear cockpit.

"I was 1½ years old at the time," he said. "Fortunately, I have no memory of the flight."

About the same time, he was unaware that his father had come up with a madcap scheme to save Charles Lindbergh's kidnapped baby. Many years passed before he grasped the full story.

"In 1932, for some reason, my dad had an idea to save the Lindbergh child by offering my mother and me as hostages — temporarily — in exchange for the

He was always busy, giving flying lessons and making charter flights. Below, Rizzo Flying Service brochures

baby. I was only 17 months old at the time. My dad's idea was to make a seaplane rendezvous with the kidnapper in which the baby would be returned. We were never sure what my father had in mind. Perhaps it was something between a heartfelt offer and a bit of a publicity stunt."

Rizzo had become involved when he was hired to fly New York City detectives, assisting in the case, to the Lindbergh home in Hopewell, N.J.

"If you think of flamboyant, that's the adjective to describe my dad. It was a good thing the kidnappers never took him up on the offer."

Reporting the Rizzo plan, an Associated Press story noted that the Brooklyn aviator had made the proposal "with the full approval of my wife, with whom I have lived happily for four years."

Willing to meet the kidnappers on land or sea, Rizzo promised, "I will deliver to them my wife and baby if they will give me the Lindbergh child. I will return the child to its parents, collect the ransom money and fly back with it to them. They can then release my wife and baby by whatever means they desire," the AP story concluded.

In later years, when his children mentioned the story, Rizzo would just roll his eyes. "He never said if he would have really gone through with the baby exchange. And I think my sisters and I were afraid to ask," Paul Jr. said. But he recalls reading a newspaper clipping about his father's offer in a family scrapbook when he was in his early teens. He turned to his father and said: "You meant ME!"

In those years, Rizzo was seldom home, busy barnstorming, carrying charter passengers, dropping circulars over the rooftops of Brooklyn, doing anything to supplement his income. His children were not really aware that their father was one of a generation of pioneers, but they certainly knew he was different.

They lived in the two-family house on Skidmore Avenue, built by their grandfather out of timbers from an abandoned movie house nearby. Their grandparents lived on the first floor, and upstairs, their mother often stepped out onto an open porch to scan the sky to see if their father was on his way home.

"Canarsie Park was nearby and there were empty meadows," Paul Jr. recounted. "My father once landed an Autogiro in a field near the house. It had big windmill-like blades above the wings and a propeller in front. People came around and a policeman watched the plane while my father had lunch. I was somewhere between being proud and embarrassed."

He was only 7 or 8 at the time, he said, and most of the people in the neighborhood didn't even have a car. "And here was my dad landing in an Autogiro."

Someone asked him, "Is that your dad's plane?"

"Well mmmmm yeah," Paul Jr. answered.

But on other occasions he would tell people, "Yes, my dad is an aviator!" He was proud, after all, that his father was doing something so few people were doing.

●

Before the stock market crashed in 1929, Rizzo's air shows were moneymakers and so was his sightseeing business. He'd buy a new plane for $750, charge $3 a flight for a jaunt around Jamaica Bay or Manhattan and the plane would be paid off within a year or two.

Always busy — giving flying lessons, making charter flights, buying and reselling used planes — Rizzo was able to put money aside for the first time in his life. And luckily he did not invest money in the stock market during the Roaring Twenties. But in 1930, a friend convinced him that the time was right to buy stocks at bargain prices.

"I think he bought Montgomery Ward stock," his son recalled. "Then it went down another 30 percent and he finally lost all his money, maybe $10,000 or $11,000, which was quite a lot at the time. From that day on, no one ever dared mention stocks to my father."

The 1930s were tough times for millions of American families. But the airplane continued to be a happy novelty during the first half of the decade — before it became a weapon of total war — and Rizzo worked harder than ever to support his growing family.

"My father was not around as much as we would have liked," his son said. "I remember a cinder track near our house and I always wanted him to run with me. But he'd come home so late or so tired, he never had the time or energy. To some extent, he was an absentee father but I understood later that he had to be absent so much because the times were so hard."

But his father was always full of surprises. Once, when Paul Jr. was 8, his father built an electric automobile for him, using airplane parts and the rear landing wheels of old planes.

"With heavy duty batteries, it looked like a 1920s racing car with a realistic dashboard, and you could

When the open-cockpit era ended, Rizzo took to the lakes of upstate New York in a closed-cabin Loening Commuter Amphibian in the 1930s.

fit two kids in the front seat," said Paul Jr., who never forgot the extraordinary toy and, like his dad, charged kids in the neighborhood a penny a ride.

When the open cockpit era ended, Paul Jr. recalled his first flight in the Loening Commuter Amphibian his father owned from 1939 to 1941, hangared at the Brooklyn Seaplane Base at Mill Basin, off Jamaica Bay.

"It had a closed cabin, fortunately. My father used it for barnstorming the lakes in upstate New York during the summers when I was 9 or 10. I remember he always seemed to be working on the Loening. He'd take me down to Mill Basin and I'd be roaming around, totally bored. When after he fixed something or other, he'd take me up for a ride."

In an open plane, he admitted, he would have been been terrified. "But I was fascinated, looking down at Times Square, flying around the Empire State Building just after it was built in the early '30s."

Every July, Rizzo would fly his wife and the children to his mother-in-law's house in Catskill, N.Y., where the family stayed for the summer. Then he'd barnstorm during his vacation months, dropping into lakes to give people rides.

"But I don't think we ever felt special," Paul Jr. said. "I think we just took things for granted. We'd

tell kids, 'Oh we're flying up to the Catskills to see our grandma.' We'd land in a lake and someone would row out to bring us to a dock. Maybe I did feel special inside. But I didn't really appreciate how special."

•

In 1939, with war looming, Rizzo decided to sign up with the Army Air Corps Reserve. As an experienced pilot, getting a commission should not have been a problem. But after all those flying hours, the veteran pilot *failed* his first military flying test.

"As a barnstormer, he often landed in tiny fields, getting people to rush over and see a real plane. But to land in these small fields, he'd slip-slide in, waffling sideways to slow his plane," his son said.

On military tests, Rizzo admitted, he'd always run into trouble when he used his old barnstorming technique, landing in the least amount of field. The testing officer would yell at him, "What are you trying to do, kill me!" So Rizzo was denied a commission, but he was permitted to remain in the reserves.

After Pearl Harbor, he learned that the Army Air Corps was granting commissions to older pilots to serve in noncombat jobs, such as ferrying planes to the war zones and across the country. With the war in its darkest phase, he was commissioned a first lieutenant.

As an officer, he earned $310 monthly plus flight pay, the family remained in Canarsie and Olive signed up as a plane-spotter, ready to sight enemy planes from her back porch.

At first, Rizzo flew fighters and bombers across the country, from the factories to their air bases. Based in Delaware, he returned to the Skidmore Avenue house only on occasion. From time to time, the children would hear a roar of an engine above the house and they would all run outside on the back porch, yelling, "Daddy, Daddy." They'd see a P-47 or a P-51 circling over them, probably lower than any Air Corps regulation allowed. "My father would circle two or three times and then wiggle his wings," Paul Jr. recalled.

Bea and Barbara Rizzo were old enough to know that their father was away because of the war. And they would all stand on the porch, waiting to see if their father would fly north or south.

"If he headed north, we knew he was landing in Connecticut and he'd be home in a few hours. If you were in uniform, you just had to walk to the nearest road and someone would give you a ride home. My father would say, 'You don't even have to lift your thumb.'" But if his plane headed south, the children knew that their father was returning to Delaware and there would be no reunion.

●

Later in the war, Rizzo made 14 round trips across the Atlantic. Before working the ocean route, he transported new planes such as P-47 Thunderbolts from Republic, B-26 Marauders from Martin and B-24 Liberators from Consolidated to their bases.

As always, he had his share of close calls. Mario Sireci of East Hampton, a close friend, told about one of them — when Rizzo was piloting a B-26 out of Baltimore and his landing gear failed to descend.

"So Paul took the console apart while they were in flight and he found the loose bolt jammed in there. An obvious case of sabotage. But he was able to get the landing gear to work and he saved the plane."

Rizzo served until 1946, when he was discharged as a captain. But the days of barnstorming had ended, and at the age of 42, Rizzo began a new career in the public school system, teaching full time at East New York Vocation High School until the 1960s.

But he wanted to keep flying. And in the first two decades after the war, he continued to work as a pilot during summers and weekends flying charters for wealthy sport fishermen. He also worked part time as a pilot for the New York Daily News, ferrying photographers in the paper's Grumman Mallard during his vacations.

Rizzo had his first taste of air journalism in the 1930s when his plane carried photographers to the scene of two major news stories.

One was the sinking of the S.S. Morro Castle, the cruise ship that burned and was beached off Asbury Park, N.J., in 1934. The other was the crash of the German dirigible Hindenburg, which exploded while landing at Lakehurst, N.J., in 1937. Rizzo also made a dozen trips to show sightseers the scene of the disasters.

When his charter flight days ended, Rizzo concentrated on buying, rebuilding and reselling dozens of old Rolls-Royces and other vintage cars. Collecting cars had begun as a hobby after the family moved to East Meadow in 1951. Over two decades, he bought and restored more than 60 Rollses and a dozen other antique autos, including Packards, LaSalles and Pierce Arrows. Eight of the best Rollses were used in a limousine service the Rizzos started, with Olive handling the reservations for 16 years, until the early 1980s.

But Rizzo never lost his taste for flying. At 94, he still flew a small plane at least twice a month with his friend Mario Sireci, sharing the controls. He had decided his soloing days were over and flew only with veteran pilots in planes with dual controls.

"We met at a Quiet Birdmen meeting and we became very good friends," said Sireci, a former naval aviator now in his 70s. "In the mid-1980s, Paul still wanted to fly and I had an airplane, so we'd go up on weekends. I was there in case he had a problem but the guy was an excellent pilot."

Rizzo often told his co-pilot his favorite stories, including one about his first official flying test. "Paul had taught himself to fly long before the government required licenses and flying tests. So when he was asked for his log book, he asked: 'What's a log book?' But he always kept his gas receipts so he could estimate his flying hours, and he went to Washington to get his license from the Civil Aeronautics Authority, which was part of the Department of Commerce then."

The government had assigned an inspector to give Rizzo a flying test in 1929, Sireci went on. "But the

Paul Rizzo was an aviator until the end. He continued to fly until he was 94 years old, opting to not "just sit around and watch the grass grow."

guy refused to get in the plane with Paul. 'You take off and land it and I'll watch you from here,' the guy said. That's the way he got his license, years after he was flying all over the place."

Rizzo did receive the license — after running an airport for two years, teaching dozens of fliers and putting in more than 750 hours of flying time.

•

The Rizzo twins, Bea and Barbara, were 4 years old when their father went off to war. Like their older brother, they had no idea that their father was a pioneer. Not until they were much older.

"We knew he ran an airport and that he flew all the time," said Bea Kochen, who now lives in Florida with her husband. "He was always talking about flying. But we were like most kids. It didn't really impress us at the time. We were so used to flying. Everyone was impressed but us."

The twins spent every summer at their grandmoth-er's home in the Catskills until they were 14 or so, Bea said. "One year, my father was flying all of us back home, as usual, but this time something went wrong and we made a forced landing in the Hudson. The seaplane just glided down but it was very fright-ening. After my father landed, some nuns from a con-vent along the river rowed out and took us ashore. But even then, we must have been used to flying be-cause my sister doesn't remember anything about that day."

During the war, they worried about him a great deal. "There were all sorts of terrible war stories and I still remember the blackouts and practicing for air raids in school," Bea said. "Then when we got older, he worried about us."

Rizzo was especially concerned about his daugh-ters going out on dates when they were teenagers.

"He'd always say that some day, we'd see that he was right," Bea said. "In the 1950s, when we were going to Hempstead High, we had to sneak out of the house to have a cigarette. He was very strict about cigarettes and about makeup, too. Once, my sister and I put on eyeliner and makeup for a date. Later, my mother told us that my father was so upset he was in tears."

Bea and Barbara both married when they were 21. Later, their father was delighted to take his grandchildren for airplane rides. "It was a thrill for him and them but not for us," Bea said. "We had flown so much by then, it was old hat."

Her father was mentally sharp until the very end, she said. "Then after his last surgery in 1999, he thought he was in a resort hotel. It was a blessing, really, because he never knew he was in a nursing home. He was insulted if anyone called him a senior citizen. He'd say he didn't want to be around a bunch of guys who talked all day about their aches and pains."

When he was younger, he was demanding, but he was such a cheerful man, Bea said. "If we ever complained about anything, he'd tell us to get up and go out and get busy and forget our pains. He would never cater to sickness. But then, when my mother was dying of cancer, he took wonderful care of her."

He never seemed angry or glum, she remembered. "In the morning, at the breakfast table, he'd be singing and patting everyone on the back and saying what a great day it was . . . The teaching job was for security. Flying was his true love."

Once, Rizzo built a model airplane for his son, when Paul Jr. was 4 years old.

"It was made of very fragile balsa wood with tissue paper to cover the wings and fuselage," his son remembered. "Apparently, I sat on it accidentally."

Father and son kidded about the accident for years. But later, the incident set the stage for a sentimental twist of fate. When Rizzo was very old, his son made a number of model planes for him — some of the early planes such as the Jenny and some of the ones he flew during the war. Rizzo decorated his living room ceiling with them.

The model of the Jenny is buried with him at Long Island's Calverton National Cemetery. In the grave beside him is Olive Rizzo. Before he died, Rizzo spent a great deal of time at the graveside, talking to his wife of 68 years. After Olive's death in 1996 — at age 93 — Rizzo still refused to leave Long Island.

"He said he didn't want to just sit around and watch the grass grow," Paul Jr. said. "So we agreed to help him stick it out in East Meadow as long as he could."

Most of all, he wanted to be buried beside his wife, the woman he had called Honey for almost 70 years. "If we didn't bury my father there," Paul Jr. said with a smile, "we knew he would haunt us for the rest of our lives."

On their father's tombstone, his children wrote a brief inscription:

Pioneer Aviator
Pilot at Age 94
New York's Oldest Aviator

Nearby, they inscribed these words on their mother's gravestone, after Paul Rizzo's death:

His Honey
Devoted wife
Partner for 70 wonderful years
Together again

The Failures: Tragic Consequences

EARLY FAILURE
This early Curtiss aircraft was wrecked while Glenn Curtiss was instructing would-be flier Alexander Williams. The photo was taken July 18, 1909, on the Hempstead Plains.

I f there was triumph, there also was tragedy as humankind took to the sky. Crashes were frequent on Long Island's airfields. Some fliers walked away from wrecked and burning biplanes, trainers and home-built aircraft, but more often, fatalities and serious injury resulted. In a few instances, the airborne danger scarred the earth as planes plunged into yards and roads and sprayed wreckage across suburban neighborhoods.

FATAL 'ANSWER'
Joe James and Viola Gentry stand astride The Answer, a 110-hp. Paramount Cabinaire biplane. The aircraft crashed in Westbury, below, while pilot Jack Ashcraft was attempting to set an endurance record in June, 1929. Ashcraft and Gentry had hoped to surpass 150 hours without refueling, but lasted less than 10 before crashing. Ashcraft was killed and Gentry seriously injured.

MOTOR PARKWAY MISHAP

Bill Hilliard and A. Leo Stevens were en route to Montauk Point on April 17, 1911, when they flew low over Motor Parkway on the Hempstead-Garden City border to have their pictures taken. Without warning, the plane took a sudden dive and crashed, above. Both men walked away in good condition.

TOUGH BREAK

The U.S. Army had only two flying fields when America entered World War I in 1917. One was Long Island's Hempstead Plains Airfield. Training accidents were common. Below, a forlorn student sits on the wing of his wrecked Curtiss Jenny at a Long Island potato farm, circa 1918.

NOSE DOWN

This Standard Pursuit Trainer crashed at Hazelhurst Field in Garden City, circa 1918. This plane appears to be a single-seat model E-1 with an air-cooled rotary engine. The Plainfield, N.J., Standard Aircraft Corp. built 128 of these open-cockpit biplanes.

MILITARY
WRECKAGE

A De Havilland military aircraft crashed near Hazelhurst Field, circa 1920. This model, the DH-4, had a gun ring mounted around the rear cockpit. It was used extensively during and after World War I.

TAKEOFF DISASTER   *A 1926 attempt to become the first aviators to fly from New York to Paris ended in tragedy. This giant Sikorsky S-35 biplane began its takeoff from Roosevelt Field on Sept. 21, 1926, and after three minutes lay in a burning heap. Mechanic Jacob Islamoff and radio operator Charles Clavier, both stunned in the crash, were unable to escape the mangled plane and burned to death. French ace René Fonck and Lt. Lawrence W. Curtin, seated in the cockpit, survived. The crash was blamed on overloading, as the plane's right landing gear broke and the plane cartwheeled. Capt. Fonck was unable to stop the machine before it fell down a 20-foot slope at the end of the runway.*

HOME-BUILT NIGHTMARE

An aircraft described as "home-built" crashes and burns on Long Island, circa 1930. Many early aviators built planes in their yards; often those planes never made it off the ground.

RESCUE EFFORT

Workers with overalls clearly marked "Roosevelt Field Service Hangar D" at the scene of a Fleet 2 airplane crash near the airport, circa 1930. The Fleet 2 was a two-place open cockpit biplane built by Fleet Aircraft of Buffalo.

NEIGHBORHOOD
NIGHTMARE
*At about 12:30 p.m.
on Aug. 3, 1954, an
Air Force Republic
F-84 Thunderjet
roared out of the sky
and crashed in the
center of Denver
Road in Wantagh.
The pilot was killed
in the crash, which
sprayed jet fuel and
chunks of metal over
a wide area.*

THEY SURVIVED *Air Force 2nd Lt. Andrew Wallace took off from Mitchel Field on a
routine training flight the morning of May 4, 1949, but his F-82 Twin Mustang interceptor
failed to gain sufficient speed to clear a fence. Wallace pulled up the plane's nose, but the
F-82 stalled and nosedived into a partially built home on Fulton Avenue in Hempstead.
A crew member suffered burns. Wallace walked away from the crash — his second in 10
days. "Just one of those things," he said later. "Or two of them."*

AIR FORCE DISASTER *This crash of a C-123 transport, from Mitchel Field, on the Southern State Parkway in October, 1958, indicates why it became dangerous to continue to operate military aircraft in increasingly populated suburban areas. The plane smashed three cars, killing one motorist and injuring four others.*

COMMERCIAL CRASH *An American Airlines DC-3 crash-landed at Gilgo Beach, east of Jones Beach, in January, 1947. The plane ran out of fuel and the pilot got lost in a storm, but miraculously, the 16 passengers and crew survived the accident.*

*Leroy Grumman was Red Mike, left, and Leon
(Jake) Swirbul was The Bullfrog*

Red Mike And The Bullfrog

BY DREW FETHERSTON

T o the men who built airplanes on the production floor, they were known as Red Mike and The Bullfrog.

They seemed unlikely partners: Red Mike was almost crippled by shyness — "a very timid person," remembers one longtime employee. The Bullfrog, meanwhile, had a genius for making friends, and "would have made the greatest politician in the world," according to the same worker. Red Mike wanted to run a small, family-size company; his partner always looked for ways to grow.

Though they didn't share the same vision — and often had loud disagreements in the small office they shared — they managed to create an aviation company that played a crucial role in winning World War II in the Pacific, put men on the moon, and helped shape the face and economy of Long Island for more than 50 years. During much of that half-century and more, their company — Grumman — was the Island's largest employer.

Leroy Grumman was Red Mike, so called because he had red-blond hair. Leon A. (Jake) Swirbul was called The Bullfrog for no reason that any of his colleagues could recall.

Long Island had shaped both of them, and Grumman's industrial saga played out here because it was the place that they knew and liked best.

Grumman, the man, was born Jan. 4, 1895, in Huntington, into an old family that had Connecticut antecedents. His father had been a carriage maker and, later, a postal worker. He graduated second in his class at Huntington High School and went on to attain a degree in mechanical engineering from Cornell University in 1916.

Swirbul was born three years after Grumman, on

Leroy Grumman, former Naval Aviator No. 1216, later one of the owners of Grumman Aircraft Engineering, in the cockpit of a G-32A in 1938

March 18, 1898, in the Yorkville section of Manhattan, but his family moved to Long Island when he was a child. He grew up in Sag Harbor, where he graduated from Pierson High School. He, too, went to Cornell, where war found him in 1917. Swirbul left school to enlist in the Marine Corps.

Grumman was working for the New York Telephone Co. when World War I broke out. He joined the Naval Reserve and applied for pilot training but was turned down, apparently because he had flat feet. The Navy instead sent him to Columbia University to study gasoline engine mechanics.

Later, the Navy sent Grumman to the Massachusetts Institute of Technology, where he discovered he was in a course meant for pilot trainees. He said nothing, and his studies carried him on to the Naval Air Station at Miami, where he received flying lessons. He took advanced flight training in Pensacola, Fla., was commissioned an ensign, received a certificate identifying him as Naval Aviator No. 1216, and became a flight instructor.

Later, the Navy again sent Grumman to MIT — to study the new discipline of aeronautical engineering.

By this time, any observer could imagine the men each of these boys would become. Raymond P. Applegate, who taught Grumman to fly, recalled several years ago that the young pilot "was very, very reticent. Most of the guys, after they [learned to] fly, they became tougher than hell. Grumman didn't."

Swirbul was a good athlete — he played basketball well enough to earn money at it as a young man — and a cheerful, outgoing companion. Yet there was a secrecy about him that almost matched Grumman's shyness. Swirbul did not and would not speak much about himself.

At the height of World War II, when he was executive vice president and general manager at Grumman — a company that then employed 25,000 and was playing a crucial role in the Pacific war — his official company biography covered the first 30 years of his life in a single paragraph.

In 1951, when his achievements were already acquiring the gloss of legend, an admiring Forbes magazine article noted that Swirbul's dossier at the Institute of Aeronautical Sciences held a single yellowing newspaper clipping, while those of lesser aviation executives bulged.

Grumman and Swirbul met in 1924 at Loening Aeronautical Engineering Co. in New York City, one

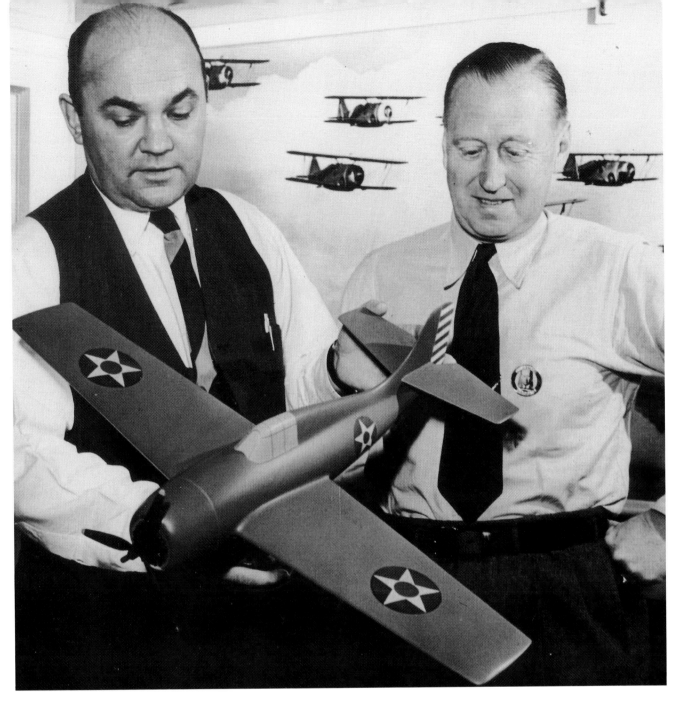

Jake Swirbul, with Leroy Grumman, holds a model of an F-4F Wildcat in the pair's office in 1941.

of the many small aircraft firms that sprang up after World War I.

The belief at the time was that the airplane would soon play much the same role in American society as the automobile.

"Land and get out in a small field, ball park, golf course, beach, country road," ran an advertisement for The Ace, a $2,500 biplane offered in 1919 by the Aircraft Engineering Co., a small Long Island manufacturer. "After flying, simply pick up the tail and put it away." The company slogan was, "The Country Road Your Airdrome."

When the dream of a biplane in every backyard failed to materialize, the Aircraft Engineering Co. — and many other such ventures — folded and disappeared.

But Loening, which had been established by two brothers, Grover and A.P. Loening, was more successful: It survived.

In 1919, when the firm landed a contract to build 50 monoplanes for the government, the Navy sent Grumman to oversee construction. He so impressed the Loenings that they hired him. Swirbul, who had worked in aircraft shops after the war, became a civilian inspector for the Air Corps. This work brought him to Loening in 1924.

In the 1920s, aviation was a glamorous industry that catered to celebrities. Mechanic Charles Solarski recalled Grover Loening tapping him on the shoul-

*Grumman Aircraft's early inner circle, from left, Leroy Grumman,
Bill Schwendler and Jake Swirbul*

der while he was working in a cockpit, asking him to
move so that a client could try it out. The client was
Charles Lindbergh.

Lindbergh's historic transatlantic flight and a soaring stock market fueled a boom in aviation. A wave
of mergers and acquisitions swept the industry, and
in 1929 the Loenings sold out to Keystone Aircraft,
which announced it would close Loening's Manhattan factory and move all operations to Bristol, Pa.

The Loenings cautioned the new owners about the
closing, noting that many of their workers didn't
want to move. "If you haven't got the men," Grover
Loening said, "you haven't got anything."

Grumman, Swirbul and Bill Schwendler, a Loening engineer, flew down to look at Bristol. None liked
what he saw.

Swirbul wanted to work for himself. Grumman,
Schwendler recalled, "liked Long Island. He liked
boats." Schwendler and others connected to Grumman were interviewed in 1971 for a company history.

Just who proposed that they quit and set up a new
company is lost in the mists of time. But the agreement was quick and firm; Grumman mortgaged his
house and Swirbul's mother borrowed $6,000 to set
up Grumman Aircraft Engineering Corp.

Schwendler joined them, along with two other men
who would form part of the company's inner circle of
management for the next 50 years: Ed Poor, who had
handled Loening's business affairs, and E. Clinton
Towl, a 24-year-old who had just quit Wall Street.

On Dec. 15, 1929, Towl traveled to Baldwin to look
over the headquarters that Swirbul had found. It
was a small building that faced south to the Long Island Rail Road tracks near Grand Avenue. Once the
Cox-Klemin Aircraft Co. factory, it was by this time
an abandoned auto showroom-garage.

"It was pretty run-down," Towl said. "The windows
were broken, skylights were broken, there was about
four feet of oak leaves on the floor . . . And I thought,
'Dear God, what have I put my money into now?' "

Grumman Aircraft officially came into being on
Jan. 2, 1930, with $64,325 in capital. Grumman, who
put in $16,875, and Swirbul, who contributed $8,125,
were the biggest shareholders.

It was precisely the wrong time to go into business,
of course. The stock market had crashed weeks before
and the nation — and much of the rest of the world —
was sliding helplessly into the Great Depression. "In
those days," said Norman Egloff, an executive who
joined Grumman in 1933, "they used to say that the
average life of an aircraft company was five years."

All the company had at first — except for the considerable engineering abilities of Grumman and Schwendler, and the business savvy of Swirbul — was a
contract to repair damaged Loening amphibians.

This work nearly wrecked the company within days
of its founding. On a bitterly cold day, Grumman and
Towl drove to the freight yards on Manhattan's West
Side to pick up a damaged airplane. They hitched it to
Grumman's car, a Hudson Super Six, and drove it over

the Queensboro Bridge and out to Baldwin.

They arrived after dark — police had stopped them on the bridge for an explanation — and the plane wouldn't fit inside the small building. A long pontoon was left protruding into the dark street. A few hours later, a motorist hit the pontoon, damaging it and his own car. The motorist threatened to sue, which promoted a soul-searching meeting between Swirbul and Grumman.

"The question in their minds was, 'With this sort of a risk, I wonder if we should go ahead or not in this business?'" Towl recalled. The partners quashed the suit by agreeing to fix the car, but it brought the company near to insolvency. "They had to sit down and count," Towl said.

Repair work on planes was only "a means of keeping the front door open," Towl said. The real hope was to get contracts to produce aircraft for the Navy. Even that work was risky, because government contracts then were fixed-price and didn't pay cost overruns. A single bad bid could ruin a young firm.

The company had been nudged in this direction by a Navy admiral of Grumman's acquaintance who hinted that anyone who came up with a good retractable set of landing wheels for Navy amphibians might make a fortune.

While Leroy Grumman worked on the retractable wheels, the company, which had hired some former Loening mechanics, paid the bills by using their metal-working skills to produce aluminum truck bodies. In time, Grumman received a contract to build pontoons for the Navy — then another contract, to build two prototype fighter planes.

The XFF-I was a stubby two-seater biplane, with a fat fuselage designed to accommodate its retractable landing gear, a first in military aviation.

Despite its bulk, it was very fast for its time. It flew 198 mph in level flight; a competing Boeing fighter could only achieve 178 mph.

Grumman got $75,000 for the two prototypes — enough to yield a profit — and a contract for 37 additional planes. A further order for more planes followed, and Grumman was off the ground.

There were hard times in those early years, to be sure. The company once ran out of money and had to send its workers home, payless, for a week. Grum-

The original brain trust packed the engineering talent of Grumman, left, and Schwendler, center, as well as the business acumen of Swirbul, right.

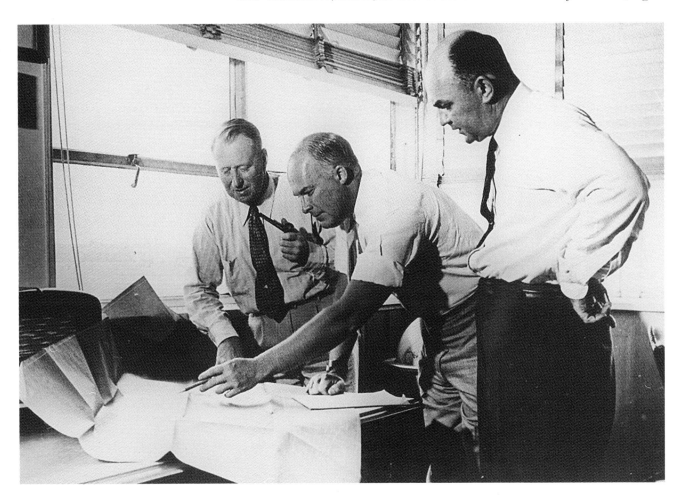

man could only afford to insure its planes for the hour in which they underwent their flight tests.

Money was so tight that Grumman and Swirbul would pick up scrap metal from roadsides for use in the shop. But the peculiar mix of Grumman's and Swirbul's talents quickly began to shape an unusual and successful company that "sang with harmony," one of its engineers said.

The harmony didn't always emanate from the company's founders, a kind of Odd Couple of aeronautics. They shared an office, of necessity at first in their cramped Baldwin building, but by choice later as the company expanded and moved to bigger quarters — to Valley Stream in 1931, Farmingdale in 1932 and finally Bethpage in 1937.

They faced each other across matching desks, under an ever-growing fleet of model Grumman airplanes. The two men often didn't agree, and passersby in the corridor sometimes heard loud and harsh words exchanged. But there was one inflexible rule: Neither Grumman nor Swirbul would leave the office until an argument had been resolved. The decision that emerged by the end of each day was always unanimous.

"It was a gentlemen's agreement between themselves," Towl said. "When they started the company they had enough sense, I guess, to realize that two men were not going to get along as smooth as silk on every question that came up."

Curiously, for partners who worked so closely — or maybe not so curiously, considering their personalities — Grumman and Swirbul didn't have much contact with each other outside work. Both lived in Brookville and were enthusiastic golfers and sometimes played a round together, but the relationship was almost strictly business.

Grumman Aircraft was not a democracy, but it was an organization founded on equality and respect. Swirbul and Grumman and their fellow top executives thought nothing of peeling off their jackets, rolling up their sleeves and going to work on the factory floor.

James Wallace, a mechanic who had come from Loening, recalled the two men sewing fabric on wings: "Grumman would see what was going on and what we were doing and say, 'Come on, Jake, we can do that.' And out in the shop they'd come and they'd be working right with us."

Towl, whose whole career had been behind a desk, occasionally would be called on to help fix an air compressor or buck rivets. "We didn't enjoy the privilege of having any fancy titles," he said. "It was a lot of fun."

Leroy Grumman's shyness was well known, but no one presumed to take advantage of him. Indeed, it had the odd effect of increasing workers' respect. Most recognized that Grumman's shyness concealed what one man called "a whim of iron."

"There was nothing Milquetoast about him. He was shy, but nevertheless he could stand up and make speeches," said Joseph Stamm, an original employee. While everyone in the plant felt comfortable calling Swirbul Jake, no one ever called Grumman anything but Mr. Grumman.

And there was no doubting Grumman's skill as an airplane designer. He was, said one engineer, "a master of the educated hunch" who could foresee technical problems and their solutions. He also knew the Navy intimately, and seemed able to anticipate the service's demands.

Grumman, said Charles Solarski, who joined the new venture, "was like the Michelangelo, and Jake was the guy who cut the marble for him. And Jake was the sort of a guy who had influence there [in Washington]. He knew how to give the schmaltz to the people."

Swirbul did far more than quarry marble for Grumman to sculpt. He created a management style that was uncommonly successful in creating a profitable and smooth-running corporation.

Some of Swirbul's innovations later became standard practice in American industry. When he noticed workers clock-watching on their regular Saturday-morning shifts, he asked them if they'd like to try to finish their week's work on Fridays and take the whole weekend off. Production soared, and the five-day week was adopted.

Another time, Swirbul resisted efforts to punish workers found smoking in the bathrooms. Instead, he sent a maintenance man in to mop the bathrooms constantly, driving out the smokers. He then created spaces where they could take a break, smoke and have a cup of coffee. The coffee break thus became part of the Grumman workday.

As competitors soon discovered, Swirbul's style was easy to admire but very hard to emulate. His door, he liked to say, was always open.

"He always had his desk where he could see through the door," his wife, Estelle, told an interviewer in 1971. "He always said it was the hardest thing

Workers build an F-6F Hellcat, the only fighter aircraft developed by the United States during World War II. On a good day, Grumman could turn out 27 Hellcats.

in the world for a man to go in and see the boss — that they would get right to the door and then turn around. So when Jake saw a man walking up and down, he would say, 'Want to see me?' "

With Swirbul as its organizing genius, Grumman in the 1930s was just the sort of company that Leroy Grumman wanted: small, familial and incidentally profitable. On the eve of World War II it was hardly an industrial giant: In 1939, Grumman still managed to protect all of its property with the services of a single security guard.

The German invasion of Poland later that year brought war to Europe and the first wave of change to the company: France and Britain ordered F-4F Wildcats, the 330-mph fighter planes that Grumman had first flown in 1937.

Few companies responded as well as Grumman to the challenge that followed Pearl Harbor. Employment rocketed from 700 in 1939 to 25,500 in 1943. Grumman's sales for 1940 were $4 million; its 1943 sales were 100 times that sum.

The production floor performed prodigies: In 1944, the Navy had to ask Grumman to slow its production — to 500 airplanes a month — after Swirbul said he could build 700 a month. In March, 1945, Grumman built a record 664 aircraft.

Yet the company could turn on a dime to react to changed conditions. When the Navy wanted aircraft retrofitted with bulletproof fuel tanks, they sent an aircraft carrier to the waters south of Long Island. The airplanes flew from the carrier to Bethpage, were refitted overnight, and returned to the carrier.

Grumman designers turned out a supercharged twin-engine fighter, the XP-50. The Army Air Corps liked the plane. Bob Hall, a test pilot, recalled that "Mr. Swirbul said, 'All right, you give us an order for 1,000 and I'll build them. I can't fool around with smaller quantities because the Navy wants everything we can build.' So the Air Force hemmed and hawed and decided they couldn't take 1,000 . . . The performance [of the XP-50] was excellent; it was far better than the P-38."

The airplanes that did get built performed their own prodigies in the skies. The secretary of the Navy, James Forrestal, once said, "In my opinion, Grumman saved Guadalcanal." Grumman Hellcats

— the only fighter aircraft developed by the United States during the war — once shot down 369 Japanese aircraft in a single day.

On a good day, Grumman could turn out 27 Hellcats. Grumman Aircraft accomplished all this without changing the fundamentals of its management. Grumman's technical brilliance brought forth innovative and very marketable airplanes, while Swirbul kept morale up with his inspired (and sincere) paternalism.

As he had since the beginning, Swirbul organized recreational activities for employees — everything from Ping-Pong to bocce.

When the war swelled the ranks, there were more than 40 in-plant softball teams, with Swirbul and Grumman playing alongside the newest and most junior employees.

Designing new planes was challenging, but build-ing them in wartime with a huge force of new and un-trained workers was even more difficult. Swirbul set up training programs for new employees, in some cases outside the company plant; Sewanhaka High School in Floral Park, for example, taught machin-ing and sheet-metal work to many, including women.

Swirbul set up a system of wartime incentive bo-nuses: Employees received half of any savings from increased production. This frequently worked out to 30 percent of a worker's annual wages; by the end of the war, the program had paid out $38 million.

Other Swirbul programs during the war included the "little green car" that would pick up any worker whose automobile broke down, and when turkeys became scarce, Swirbul arranged to buy eggs and have them hatched and raised so that the company could continue its tradition of handing out Christmas turkeys.

Grumman, left, and Swirbul stand in front of a Wildcat. After war erupted in Europe, France and Britain put in orders for the fighter.

Any worker with a medical problem that couldn't be treated on Long Island was sent at company cost to the Mayo Clinic in Rochester, Minn., as was any member of his or her family. Though some tried, Grumman workers never came close to bringing in a union to represent them.

"Other businessmen thought I was crazy to care about things like a big sports program and air shows and music," Swirbul told an interviewer for Fortune magazine in 1948. "They said such mollycoddling didn't pay off. I only tell them it does pay off."

Grumman's labor turnover during the war was half that of the other aircraft makers, and the company's profit margin was better as well.

Grumman succeeded by keeping things simple, even at the height of its wartime production. The company never overreached itself; it ranked seventh among airplane makers during World War II. It ran lean: In 1948, it had an engineering staff of 500, compared with more than 2,000 at the Glenn L. Martin Co., a competitor.

During the war, Grumman's operating profit held around 10 percent, while other aircraft makers watched theirs slip as low as 4 percent. In 1946, Grumman showed a profit when all other airplane makers posted losses.

No secretary guarded Swirbul and Grumman from callers. When Grumman went to visit the Navy brass in Washington, he didn't take a briefcase, preferring instead to take notes on an envelope. On those business trips, his idea of an evening's recreation was to collar a co-worker and go bowling.

While other airplane makers struggled with complex inventory systems, Grumman relied on empty oil drums filled with parts. Each had a red line painted around the inside a few inches from the bottom. Above the line were the words, "When it gets down to here, tell Joe."

Swirbul's management system wasn't hierarchical; questions did not have to go to the top of the executive pyramid to get answered. If someone saw something that had to be done, he or she did it.

As the end of the war approached, Grumman and Swirbul faced a new problem: With Navy war contracts about to be canceled, they had to shrink the company without killing it. They asked supervisors and foremen to draw up lists of essential workers. When peace arrived, they fired the entire work force, then rehired 5,000 within 10 days.

Grumman poses with a Wildcat. His technical expertise produced innovative aircraft.

Leroy Grumman told George Titterton, a company executive, to make every effort to keep anyone who had been with the company 10 years or more.

"Everybody would have expected Jake to do this, but it was Roy," Titterton said. "Deep down, he was really loyal to his people."

The smaller company was much to Grumman's liking, and he set about designing several small civilian airplanes. Only one of these succeeded: the Agcat, a crop-dusting biplane that one aeronautical engineer called "a pure 1926 aircraft." The Grumman company made a few, then licensed the design to another manufacturer who produced 2,646 of them.

Swirbul thought Grumman could only survive by growing and finding new markets for new products. When the Korean War broke out in 1950, Grumman received a contract for hundreds of S2F Tracker anti-submarine planes.

A lot of people thought this was too much to handle. Swirbul, however, told his colleagues to take everything they could get. "And he was right," said Tit-

Above, Rose, left, and Sarah Ficaro, real-life Rosie the Riveters, helped the WWII effort at Plant 3.

At left, workers build a G-21 Goose amphibious plane, in the foreground, and F-4Fs in the background. During the war, Grumman's labor turnover was half that of other aircraft makers.

Workers pose with a TBF Avenger torpedo bomber. The Avenger first saw action in the Pacific at the Battle of Midway in 1942.

terton. "Korea didn't last that long, but we had 700 on the books of the company and delivered them over a period of, like, 10 years."

Grumman's no-frills management was responsible for other successes. Henry Schiebel, a Grumman executive, recalled the meeting that led to the risky decision to build the Gulfstream, a civilian executive airplane, in the late 1950s: "Jake turned to Grumman and said, 'Roy, Henry wants an answer on this thing.' So Grumman said, 'I'd like to build this.' Jake turned around and said, 'Anybody got any objections?' "

When there were none, Schiebel was told to go ahead and build the Gulfstream. The entire meeting took less than four minutes. Grumman sold more than 200 Gulfstreams, and turned a profit after the first two dozen.

Within a few years, though, illness and death broke up this successful partnership. Swirbul contracted colon cancer. "When Jake was ill, the union [organizers] put out a little pamphlet," Swirbul's wife recalled. "They didn't say anything about Jake dying, but they did ask the question, 'What's going to happen to you when Jake's not there?' "

Swirbul died in June, 1960, just as the company began a space program that would put the Grumman-made Apollo Lunar Excursion Module on the moon before the end of the decade. Grumman's plants closed to let workers go to his funeral at the Brookville Reformed Church, and thousands of them attended.

Grumman didn't live to see his company acquired by Northrop in 1994. A smaller crowd turned out for his funeral in Manhasset in 1987; time had thinned the ranks of those who remembered his presence and role in the company. He had retired from any active role in the company in 1966, at the age of 71, three years before the moon landing.

Those who came to Grumman's funeral spoke of his shyness, of how he would roam the plant looking at his shoes to avoid making people nervous by looking at them. Someone remarked to Grumman's son, David, that his father would have been pleased by the simple service that marked his passing.

"He would probably just as soon dispense with the whole funeral," David Grumman replied. ●

Grumman Aircraft's men and women worked so hard the Navy had to ask the company to slow production to 500 aircraft per month. In March, 1945, the company built a record 664 planes.

Cecil (Teddy) Kenyon grew up yearning to fly.
She finally became one of Grumman's test pilots.

She Tamed Grumman's Hellcats

BY LAUREN TERRAZZANO

The green and white Arrow Sport soared high above Long Island, the ground slowly disappearing beneath it. Teddy Kenyon, her hair tucked smartly under a brown aviator's cap and the arms of her coat snapping in the wind, turned back to her sister, Barbara.

"Would you like to play in the clouds?"

The horizon beckoned that spring morning of 1937, an expanse of periwinkle sky dotted with translucent pillows of white. Their elbows hung off the sides of the tiny plane as they sat one behind the other in the two-seater, 20 minutes away from a luncheon at a North Shore estate. At top speed, the little plane could go 60 mph. There were no weather reports back then, no charts. Kenyon used road maps to navigate.

As always, Kenyon was the picture of quiet confidence. As they dipped in and out of the clouds, Barbara felt as if the two were back in Kent, Conn., tobogganing down the snowy hills of their childhood on a frosty February morning. Teddy would always sit at the helm of the sled.

And now she was at the controls. She always was. It was emblematic of the life she would come to lead — flying machines that soared like birds.

During World War II, Kenyon was one of three female test pilots at Grumman Aircraft Engineering

Kenyon logged 1,000 hours of flight time at Grumman during the war. Here, she's in a Hellcat.

Corp. in Bethpage who would test warplanes known as Hellcats and Avengers, putting them through rolls, dives and other maneuvers before they were shipped to the Navy for combat.

"Climbing in that plane was like being shot out of a gun. A fantastic roar and a rush of air. It mesmerized me," she would later tell an interviewer. Kenyon spent nearly three years doing what was commonly known as a man's job back then. And despite some early resistance from the men she flew with, she eventually became something of a celebrity among plant workers as well as pilots.

"She had this way of looking at you when she talked to you and making you feel as if you were the only one in the room," said Corwin Meyer, a former test pilot.

Kenyon even appeared in a Camel cigarette ad with the slogan, "I tame Hellcats," though she never smoked, and in a Cutex nail polish ad, though she never wore nail polish.

By most accounts, flying was a freeing force for Kenyon at a time when most women stayed home, cooked and tended house.

"Flying liberated her, clearly," said her sister Barbara, 90, a soft-spoken silver-haired woman living in a brown wood-frame house on a hill in Westwood, Mass. Kenyon's aviation exploits endure most powerfully now in the memory of her sister, who was interviewed in the spring of 2000. Her home includes a spare room filled with pictures, newspaper clippings and a hand-painted trunk full of Kenyon's red leather flight logs, each with the name Cecil Kenyon etched in gold lettering on the front.

The lines of time were etched gently across Barbara Magaletta's face, but her blue eyes came to life at the mere mention of Kenyon's adventures in the cockpit. Teddy was her best friend, a big sister, whose love affair with flying began at age 10. All it took was for a

Grumman's female production test pilots, from left, Barbara Jayne, Elizabeth Hooker and Cecil (Teddy) Kenyon, in 1942. At first, many male pilots didn't believe women could do a "man's job," and the avoided trio.

plane to roar overhead and Teddy would run outside their Connecticut farmhouse to gaze at the sky.

The woman who would play in the clouds was born Cecil Woolsey MacGlashan on Sept. 11, 1905, in New York City, the second child of a lawyer, Archibald MacGlashan, and a socialite, Cecil Woolsey Hamilton. After her birth, the couple moved to a 15-room white house on Oliphant Avenue in Dobbs Ferry, eight miles north of Manhattan. For much of her life, her family called her Molly, a nickname that lasted until she was a teenager. But her older brother, Arch-

ie, saw his tomboyish sister one day wearing brown coveralls — her preferred choice to dresses — and re-marked to their mother how much she looked like a teddy bear. The nickname was born.

When she was 8, her father had a heart attack and the family moved to a farmhouse on Skiff Mountain in Kent. She went to a one-room elementary school until the eighth grade, and then was privately tutored. In 1919, Teddy went to live in Bermuda with her stepgrandmother to attend the Bermudan School for Girls. A year later, she received a telegram that her father had died. She was unable to attend the funeral because there were no commercial flights, and a steamer would have taken several days. It was with great regret that she found herself unable to return to Connecticut. It may have been another reason she would spend much of her life in the cockpit of a plane.

"No doubt, she thought, 'If I could have flown home, I would have been there,'" her nephew, Don MacGlashan said.

When Teddy Kenyon was 16, the sky got a little closer. A barnstormer flew to a Kent farmer's field to offer rides to anyone willing to take the risk. This was Kenyon's first true brush with a plane. Her mother wouldn't let her go up, but she walked up to the aircraft one day, mesmerized by the mere sight of it.

"My God, it's made of cloth."

Two years later, her mother wasn't home when Kenyon took her brother's new motorcycle for a spin. Kenyon was very interested in anything mechanical, and very good at understanding how things worked. As she sped down the road, her mother drove by with a friend. Alarmed to see her daughter whipping along, Mrs. MacGlashan made her friend turn the car around to follow Teddy. Every time she would catch up, her daughter would speed up. When they got home, Teddy was forbidden from riding the motorcycle, which hadn't been inspected for safety. It wasn't something proper young ladies did.

That same year, she moved to Boston to do what proper young ladies did — attend the very correct Miss Erksine's Finishing School. In Boston, she met a dashing young man named Ted Kenyon. He was well mannered and well educated, a senior studying electrical engineering at the Massachusetts Institute of Technology. But he was also a pilot who barnstormed on weekends to make money.

"Here was this nice-looking guy full of beans and having a good time," she later told her nephew, who recorded those sentiments in a family history.

After she finished school, Teddy's mother took her traveling to Europe. Throughout the trip, she and Ted corresponded. For 18 months they communicated this way. When Teddy got off the boat with her mother in New York, Ted was waiting on the pier. The couple married a few months later in 1926.

By this time, Ted was a pilot with an airline that flew passengers from New York to Boston. The married couple were well matched; Ted had found a vivacious woman who doted on him, would keep house

and cook meals for him in their Cleveland Circle apartment in Boston, but who also shared his love of adventure.

They were barely married a year when Teddy began to barnstorm with Ted on weekends at the East Boston Airport, now known as Logan International, which was then a 1,300-foot cinder strip in the eastern corner of the city. Overlooking Boston Harbor, the airstrip was surrounded by brick tenements filled with Italian immigrants struggling with the onset of the Depression.

But the newlyweds evaded hard economic times. Ted was making a good living as a pilot and was able to buy his Arrow Sport. Every Saturday, she would sign people up for the rides and Ted would fly them. And they ended up making more money there on weekends than he made all week during his regular job.

"Loved it," she scribbled on a timeline she wrote for a flying club history of their barnstorming days.

In 1929, Ted taught Kenyon to fly, to her mother's dismay. "It's too bad two such nice young people will have to die so young," Mrs. MacGlashan said at the time.

An engineer by trade, Ted was methodical and thorough about every facet of flying. He insisted she learn it all.

"When she learned to fly, she not only learned the coordination, but the physics and mechanics of the plane and how everything worked," Teddy Kenyon's nephew recalled. "She would say, 'You maybe fly 10 hours in the plane and then you work 10 hours to fix it.'"

After just four hours of instruction, she soloed on Aug. 1, 1929. With only 10 hours and 20 minutes of experience in the air, she got her federal pilot's license at Roosevelt Field two months later. The license took two figure eights, three precision landings and a 20-question written test.

"She's one girl who knows what flying is all about. She knows the feel of a ship. When she lands she settles just right and sets the plane down just where she intended," her husband said in an article written about her in a Boston newspaper at the time.

But while Ted was extremely proud and confident of his wife's abilities, he did worry. He made her promise she wouldn't even consider going up at the hint of bad weather and got very nervous when she attempted stunts. Later on, he expressed his caution in the naming of a plane they purchased, GWWP: God Willing, Weather Permitting.

In the '30s, Teddy began entering air-stunt contests. Her first was sponsored by the American Legion. She had this to say in the handwritten timeline, which she called "Teddy K's years of flying":

"American Legion convening in Boston — for flying ability and appearance of self and airplane, and manner. Won It." She flew home with $300 in $20 gold pieces, and the title "Miss America of the Air."

In October, 1933, two months after Amelia Earhart made her first record-breaking transatlantic flight, the Kenyons flew to Roosevelt Field, where Teddy competed in the National Sportswomen's Flying Championship, a three-day contest in which both men and women demonstrated their proficiency in air stunts ranging from turns to dives.

She borrowed a Waco plane from Fred Magaletta, an aviation friend who would later marry her sister, Barbara.

"I don't think she was ever afraid of anything," recalls Don MacGlashan, who now lives in Maryland. Two days into the contest, she was near the top of the point scale.

But even for Kenyon, anxiety was running high. On the third day, she would have to demonstrate her proficiency in a type of turn she had never done before. Magaletta flew down from Boston to show her how to do the maneuver, known as an Immelmann turn, a maneuver to gain altitude and change direction by doing a partial loop.

High above Roosevelt Field, the two practiced for a few hours until she got it just right.

The next day, she pulled it off perfectly. She scored more overall points in the contest — 1,017 — than all women, and men, too.

"Entered charity air pageant at Roosevelt. $5,000 is prize and silver trophy — won it." She gave Magaletta $1,000 for the use of his plane and spent the rest on a Waco of her own.

In 1936, she and Ted moved to Long Island, to a wood-frame house on Cherry Lane in Huntington. Ted, now an inventor of aviation instrumentation, had gotten a job at Sperry Gyroscope Co. and later Grumman as an aviation research engineer specializing in automatic pilot instrumentation. Also, he grew up in Smithtown and wanted

Kenyon won a 1933 flying contest at Roosevelt Field, and walked away with a trophy and $5,000.

to return to an area closer to his family.

In 1937, the couple bought a Fairchild 24, and installed Ted's autopilot invention, with both of them testing it for months on end in the skies.

By most accounts, it was a happy life. He dabbled in photography. She constructed her own dining set. They had their friends, and their plane. And they played in the water as well as the air — exploring Long Island Sound in their 40-foot sailboat, the Sea Spray. Teddy mostly stayed at home, testing Ted's flying instruments in her spare time. But even though she still got to fly now and again by testing Ted's inventions, she missed doing it regularly.

Already flying for 13 years, Kenyon was slowly being joined by a legion of women taking to the air. By March, 1940, there were 906 licensed women pilots in the United States. Every chance she got, Kenyon would tell other women that it was as easy as driving a car, and that flying was clearly the "sanest, safest and most comfortable way to travel."

"They've turned out better than I expected," chief test pilot Selden Converse said of Grumman's female fliers. Barbara Jayne is at left.

She wrote those words in a newsletter for the Ninety-Nines, a nationwide women's flying club that she helped found.

But to call Kenyon an early feminist was a bit of a stretch. Her sister said she might have even balked at the word, which was used sparsely at the time. Kenyon was becoming a defender of women's rights in the air.

She loved to cook dinner for her husband after his long days at Grumman. She wore red lipstick, red slippers and a red scarf when she flew. She did wear pants usually, and preferred jodhpurs, not for political reasons but "because they didn't get tangled up in the foot pedals," she once told her nephew.

Conversation usually stopped when she breezed into a room, her confidence and immediate interest in whomever she was talking to put most men at ease and made their knees turn to jelly.

"Teddy had a special presence. She had a walk. Not a flat-footed walk. She bounced on her feet. She would come into a room and quite literally, everyone would turn to this very good-looking woman who had a terrific smile, and they would immediately respond to her," Don MacGlashan recalled.

She simply believed that women were capable of flying as well as men. And she proved it time and time again.

In the March 23, 1940, edition of the aviation newspaper Flying Time, Kenyon wrote a column voicing opposition to the Civil Aeronautical Authority's rule that grounded women during their pregnancies. The order required them to go through the entire training process again after childbirth and forced them to reapply for pilot licenses.

In addition to praising pilot Betty Gillies, the wife of her future boss at Grumman, for vociferously fighting the rule, she wrote: "Tell me, how many graduates of schools and colleges would care to be called back to take their final exams again, after several years absence . . . It doesn't make sense that you should have to go through this long procedure with each and every offspring." The rule was ultimately changed.

Two years later, Teddy got a job with Grumman in Bethpage and flew airplane parts to and from the plant in a Fairchild, in what were known as "milk runs." She also joined the Civil Air Patrol and carried parts and personnel to East Coast bases. She volunteered to track German submarines, but was turned down. "They didn't feel we should do that sort of thing," Kenyon later told a Connecticut newspaper.

Then, one day in the spring of 1942, the head of testing and flight operations at Grumman approached Kenyon and two others, Barbara Jayne and Elizabeth Hooker. Bud Gillies, whose own wife was a pilot and who realized the shortage of male test pilots in the company, had a proposal. Would they like to test warplanes?

The answer was yes.

"As of next Monday, you're going to be on the Grumman payroll, as production test pilots," Bud Gillies told them, according to the company's history.

Although Grumman was the first company in the United States to use women as test pilots, the Navy would never dream of allowing them to fly in combat. Yet, these women would be putting the planes through all their maneuvers to make sure they were working right for Navy fliers.

None of them had ever flown a plane such as the Goose — a powerful twin-engine plane used to train the women — and Kenyon was impressed by Gillies' faith in them.

COLOR PHOTOGRAPH BY ALLAN GOULD FOR THE AMERICAN MAGAZINE

Hellcat teasers

A "GREEN" PLANE is one that has never been off the ground before. A "hot" plane is one so fast it is difficult to handle. At Bethpage, Long Island, three iron-nerved young women work 10 hours a day flying war planes that are both green and hot. They test the new Grumman Hellcats, speedy navy fighters. These women—Teddy Kenyon (wearing red hat), Barbara Jayne (right), and Elizabeth Hooker—make a trio of America's first feminine testers of combat planes. They streak the planes through the sky at about 400 m.p.h., put them into slow rolls, snap rolls, and grueling dives. Each new plane gets a full hour's

punishment. All during a test, the pilot keeps her eyes glued to the instrument panel and jots down notes on the plane's speed, balance, motor performance, landing gear, etc. The girls are casual about the hazards of their jobs and only reluctantly tell of close shaves, such as the time Miss Hooker found her Hellcat's hydraulic system had failed and had to force the landing gear down by bodily might. A Smith College grad, Miss Hooker has been flying since she was 15, was a flight instructor before her present job. She's the only brunette and unmarried girl of the trio. Mrs. Jayne gets a special kick out of testing Hellcats, because her husband flies them for the Navy overseas. Mrs. Kenyon was taught to fly by her husband, who's now a Grumman flight engineer.

American magazine published a 1944 article about Hooker, left, Kenyon, in cockpit, and Jayne.

"He said, 'Girls, get out there and go,' " Kenyon would tell Grumman historians. "And so the three of us just went out there and got in the planes and went."

Grumman actually closed the airfield on the first day and told personnel to go home just in case things didn't work out. The three women donned coveralls, leather jackets, caps and goggles for their test run, which the media were invited to watch.

"I've always thought it took a good deal of courage

for Bud Gillies to send us off like that in ships we'd never flown before," Kenyon would recall.

The strip at Bethpage, flanked on either side by factory buildings, was humming with activity during the war. During their first few months of flights, the trio was featured by major newspapers and magazines. All photogenic with dazzling smiles, they were celebrities to the outside world. News photos tell the story: In one shot, the three women are posed casually and smiling against their planes. Another Life magazine picture shows Kenyon standing gleefully on the wing of her plane in Bethpage, her leg slightly outstretched as if she were about to do a ballerina plié.

But while things went smoothly for the women in the air, they weren't particularly easy on the ground.

When Bud Gillies first told the men about the new fliers, he didn't ask their permission. He simply told them: "Gentlemen, you will now have three women among you."

The men couldn't fathom the idea of women doing their jobs. At first, they avoided the women when they walked into the so-called Ready Room, where pilots went to read and relax before flights. They even threatened to quit. But when Gillies told them to go right ahead, they quickly changed their minds.

Corwin Meyer, an experimental test pilot for Grumman at the time, was one of the few men who didn't have a problem with three women flying planes.

"If you got someone with skill and a brain, it didn't matter what color, sex, religion or height they were," Meyer, 82, who retired to Ocala, Fla., said in 2000. "However, most of the other fellows did not have the same feelings I did. Their macho feelings came out. They felt that women were not suited for this job."

But, he said, "The gals, all three of them, were so talented and had such good personalities, they fit in immediately. They also fit in because Bud Gillies said they were going to fit in, and he was the boss."

Eventually, their male colleagues came to accept them. "They've turned out better than I expected," said Selden Converse, then the chief test pilot. "They're good fliers and they're regular guys."

From that point, things went more smoothly. Each day, they would begin around 9 a.m. with a long checklist of what had to be tested. With Grumman producing about 500 planes a month during the war, there was always plenty of work. The average test run would last about an hour.

In the air, Kenyon would have to go through an intensive drill. On each leg, she carried a flight card, which consisted of four or five pages of information she was expected to fill out, documenting engine characteristics: fuel pressure, oil pressure, movement of flaps, precision of hydraulic system and landing gear. She would have to take the plane into a dive at various altitudes to see whether it performed to Navy specifications.

Just as she said in the Camel cigarette ad she posed for, she really did tame Hellcats and other Grumman craft, logging about 1,000 hours in the air. In the cartoonishly dramatic ad, she was portrayed as returning to base just before a fog rolled in. "Brother," one male pilot was shown telling another, "that Kenyon girl can fly!"

She even tested one Hellcat equipped with an autopilot designed by her husband, making sure it was safe before he flew it to military bases to demonstrate the device. Clearly, the Hellcat was one of Grumman's most powerful planes, the pride of its fleet.

Sleek and silver, it was one of the fastest fighters of its day, able to achieve 400 mph and able to fly at heights of up to 35,000 feet. And she loved and nurtured it like a child, alternately pushing it to its full potential and coddling it when the great machine needed it. And sometimes it did.

One afternoon in 1943, her colleague, Barbara Jayne, was called to the field in what she later referred to as one of her most memorable moments at Grumman. Kenyon was at 6,000 feet testing a Hellcat, when the left aileron of the plane jammed, hindering its ability to turn. Other test flights were rerouted while Kenyon tried to regain control of the plane. Fire engines and rescue vehicles were parked on the field, their occupants waiting anxiously to see if they would have to spring into action. The tower urged her to fly over the Sound and dump the plane.

"They said to her, 'Do you want to jump?' And Teddy said, 'I wouldn't hurt this aircraft for anything,'" Jayne recalled.

"I couldn't bear the thought of losing that lovely new fighter," Kenyon would say later, "so I made a wide turn and lined up with the runway, heading into that nice strong wind. That was one time I prayed for a perfect landing."

She got her wish.

When the war ended, Kenyon's two-year career at Grumman began to wane. Orders for warplanes diminished rapidly. In addition, thousands of men flooded back from overseas, grabbing their slice of suburbia in Levittown and other postwar developments, and trying to reclaim their jobs at the aviation giant.

"VJ day ended that barrel of fun," she wrote in 1979 in the Ninety-Nines' 50th anniversary yearbook, reflecting on her two years as a test pilot.

Luckily, Ted was still testing aviation instruments and needed his most reliable co-pilot to continue helping with his research. The couple bought three warplanes: a Steerman PT-17, a Voltee BT-13 and a Lockheed Lightning P-38 for their automatic pilot research, and used the planes for fun.

In 1952, they left Long Island, frustrated with the pace at which it was being developed and hopeful to find peace and tranquillity in Connecticut. Teddy was 47. They constructed a Frank Lloyd Wright-style house on a hill overlooking the Connecticut River, and constructed a separate building next to their home to house Ted's instrument company, Ken-lab.

Kenyon continued to fly, getting her helicopter license when she was 54 because Ted was developing instrumentation for choppers. "1959 — got helicopter license," she wrote in her timeline. "And would need extra pilot! (Me)"

"My dream," she wrote later, "is to have a helicopter in our own backyard. It's a great and wonderful machine."

The two were married for 52 years, remaining partners in their business and their marriage for all of that time. In 1970, she purchased a Piper Cherokee, and used it in tournaments she would fly for the next few years. She resurrected the name from their earlier craft, God Willing, Weather Permitting, paying homage to her husband's careful approach to flight.

Ted died suddenly in November, 1978, of a heart attack. Teddy died seven years later on Dec. 12, 1985, from complications resulting from a stroke. The simple eulogy she had written for her husband would also apply to her life.

"Let our dreams be our dreams of the future, but when life is over on Earth, let there be no sadness. Only joy for the golden days we had." ●

The Triumphs: Celebrating The Firsts of Flight

HERRING'S DERRING-DO *Freeport resident Augustus Herring, who was among the first Americans to fly a fixed-wing aircraft, stands ready for takeoff in a contraption he built based on a German Lilienthal glider. Herring successfully flew from a bluff on the shores of Lake Michigan in 1896.*

In the beginning, almost every other flight was a first. The first transcontinental flight, which was sponsored by a soda company. The first successful flight by a woman. The first official airmail flight. And the most glorious first of all — the epic journey of the lone eagle, a 25-year-old flier named Charles Lindbergh, who took off from Roosevelt Field in May, 1927, and flew the Spirit of St. Louis across the Atlantic nonstop to Paris.

UP, UP AND AWAY

A poster depicts the "Grand Aerostatic Ascension of Charles F. Durant" in the early 19th Century. The history of lighter-than-air flight on Long Island goes back to June 15, 1833, when Professor Durant ascended in a balloon from Manhattan and touched down at the Union Course racetrack in Woodhaven, Queens.

TRANSATLANTIC AIRSHIP

The British dirigible R-34 sits tethered at Roosevelt Field in July, 1919. The 643-foot-long airship, piloted by Royal Air Force Cmdr. G.H. Scott, with a crew of 30, reached a top speed of 62 mph during a 108-hour trip from Scotland. It was the first transatlantic trip by an airship.

MAN CAN FLY   *A. Leo Stevens, in an airship of his own design, makes the first successful powered flight in the United States. The Sept. 30, 1902, flight lasted 35 minutes and thrilled thousands along the Brooklyn shore. This image was taken at Brighton Beach.*

RECORD-SETTING GIRL   *Four months after Charles Lindbergh's crossing, Ruth Elder attempted to become the first woman pilot to cross the Atlantic, taking off from Roosevelt Field on Oct. 11, 1927. Elder and George Haldeman flew a Stinson plane named American Girl 2,623 miles, establishing an over-water distance record before being forced down by mechanical problems. They were rescued by a freighter 325 miles northeast of the Azores.*

The Flight of the Vin Fiz

Pilot Calbraith Rodgers and the Vin Fiz, above, take off from the Sheepshead Bay racetrack on Sept. 17, 1911, on the first-ever transcontinental flight. The airplane, named for the Vin-Fiz soda company, which sponsored the publicity stunt, met with myriad obstacles on its 75-town, 4,231-mile hopscotch journey across the United States. It was struck by lightning, attacked by a bull in an Indiana pasture and besieged by crowds that darkened its wings with autographs. Rodgers himself was battered, knocked unconscious and punctured with metal shards when his radiator overheated. After 49 days — and no fewer than 12 crashes — Rodgers arrived in Pasadena, Calif. Right, an advertisement celebrates the voyage.

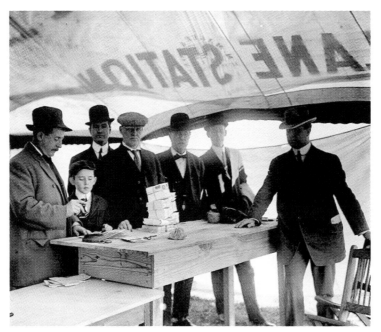

MAIL CALL

The nation's first official delivery of mail by air took place at the 1911 International Aviation Meet on Sept. 23 in Garden City. A mail sack was flown by pilot Earle L. Ovington about six miles and dropped in Mineola. Ovington is shown here reenacting his pickup with Postmaster General Frank H. Hitchcock. At left, the first airmail post office, set up at the air meet.

SPECIAL DELIVERY

On May 15, 1918, workers at Belmont Park loaded letters from a truck onto a plane for the first regularly scheduled airmail flight. The service exchanged mail between New York City and Washington, D.C. Below, the proud crew of the U.S. airmail facility at Belmont Park.

FEMALE PIONEER *Bessica Raiche of Mineola was recognized as the first American woman to pilot an airplane when she took off in a Wright-type craft from the Hempstead Plains on Sept. 26, 1910. Raiche and her husband, Francoise, built the plane in their living room. Eventually, Raiche gave up flying for health reasons and embarked on a career as a medical doctor, becoming one of the nations's first obstetrics and gynecology specialists.*

BUILDING HER OWN
Raiche works in her Mineola back yard, above, where she built a pusher biplane with help from her husband. At right, a medal Raiche received for her efforts.

GIANT IN A JUMPSUIT

Charles Lindbergh became an American legend in 1927 when he made the first nonstop flight from New York to Paris. The 25-year-old accomplished the mythic transatlantic feat alone in a tiny silver monoplane called the Spirit of St. Louis. Overnight celebrity followed him home from Paris as he took a nearly year-long tour around the United States, Latin America and Canada to promote aviation.

BEST OF LUCK

At right, while working on the Spirit of St. Louis and waiting for clear skies, Lindbergh took visitors from rival camps in his hangar at Curtiss Field. Clarence D. Chamberlin, right, and explorer Richard E. Byrd, center, both were preparing airplanes nearby in hopes of beating the others to Paris. As he got ready to take off, Lindbergh was told the other planes were still in hangars. In a book about the flight, Lindbergh recalled thinking, "I'm glad this flight to Paris hasn't become a race. Now I can set my throttle for range instead of speed, hoarding gallons of gasoline for that worried hour when extra fuel means the saving of a flight."

CAPT. CHARLES LINDBERGH.   RICHARD E. BYRD.   CLARENCE CHAMBERLAIN.

AWAY HE GOES

Lindbergh's plane a few minutes out of Roosevelt Field. Describing the moment years later, he wrote: "The great landscaped estates of Long Island pass rapidly below; mansion, hedgerow, and horse-jump giving way to farms and woodlands farther east." Legend has it that shortly after Charles took off on his perilous journey, his mother, Evangeline, told a friend: "For the first time in my life, I realize that Columbus also had a mother."

BIENVENUE!

In a borrowed suit, Lindbergh is cheered in Paris, left, a day after his arrival. After his 33-hour, 30-minute flight, Lindbergh landed at 10:22 p.m. Paris time on May 21, 1927. People pulled fabric and parts from the Spirit of St. Louis for souvenirs. At the U.S. Embassy, the pilot finally got to bed at 4:15 a.m., his first sleep in 63 hours. "I awoke that afternoon," he later wrote, "a little stiff but well rested, into a life which could hardly have been more amazing if I had landed on another planet instead of at Paris."

BACK HOME!

Throngs of well-wishers greeted Lindbergh at Roosevelt Field, below, upon his return from Paris.

PROUD WELCOME

Members of the Nassau County Police Department motorcycle division congratulate Lindbergh after his return to Long Island on June 16, 1927.

TICKER-TAPE PARADE

Lindbergh received a New York City welcome on June 13, 1927, when he rode up Broadway in a ticker-tape parade celebrating his New York-to-Paris solo flight. The tons of confetti dimmed the sky and newspapers heralded that there had never been such an event in the city's history.

Chuck Sewell was more at home in a cockpit than anywhere else. Here, he's piloting an F-14.

Lightning In The Sky

BY JAMES KINDALL

Chuck Sewell had flown, crash-landed, nursed home and manhandled more than 140 types of airplanes during his danger-filled life, but even he had never seen anything like the X-29.

Stuffed with new technology, NASA's first "X" plane in 14 years was an aerodynamic razor blade. Composite materials kept it light. Three computers sent 40 commands per second to its control surfaces. Engineers at the Grumman Corp. had spent thousands of hours preparing for its 1984 debut at California's Edwards Air Force Base. As the company's chief test pilot, Sewell had worked for months in a simulator learning the controls. Everything was set. That was the good news.

Despite their confidence, company engineers knew an independent evaluation commissioned by NASA had concluded that the X-29's design made it too unstable to fly. One chief worry, for instance, was that with the plane's unorthodox shape and blurring speed, a computer error could rip off a wing in one-fifth of a second.

Sewell couldn't wait to grab the stick.

Support technicians — frustrated for weeks by rains and wind — were cheered when Dec. 14 dawned calmly. Deputy director for development Glenn Spacht quickly gathered the staff. Sewell wedged himself into the cockpit and became so excited he flubbed the countdown (the group kidded him later, "Yeah, you're qualified to fly; but you can't count"). Then, he hit the throttle and was up in the sky putting the mystery plane through its paces.

Altitude? On the money. Speed? Perfect. Everything was precise.

"It was like watching a maestro," Spacht said.

It was a perfect ride, the cap to a remarkable career.

Sewell, left, and Kurt Schroeder, another Grumman test pilot, walk away from the experimental X-29.

All in all, the intense, 54-year-old Oklahoman rode the futuristic plane four times in the next year. His third trip probably best reflected his matter-of-fact, daredevil life. On his way in, he flipped the plane in an unauthorized roll while doing five "G's" — five times the force of gravity. Instead of plodding through a safely arranged series of tests to determine the X-29's viability, Sewell knocked off an entire list of maneuvers with one move. Furious military officials grounded him temporarily. Grumman people grinned.

It was just Chuck.

"He pushed the envelope right to the edge," Spacht said.

Of all those involved in Long Island's aviation history, probably none pushed the envelope with such dedicated glee as test pilot Charles A. Sewell. During a 20-year military career, he risked his life in combat missions over Korea and Southeast Asia. Later, during 17 years at Grumman, he tempted fate on a routine basis, punishing untested planes in the sky until they revealed their weaknesses — he'd once considered an airline job, but said he couldn't spend all his time, "flying right side up."

Not that he was foolhardy. He studied his planes like a surgeon to reduce the danger element. His wife, Bonnie, sometimes grew tired of the endless procedures. "Even when we flew in a little airplane he would go down a long preflight checklist. I would say, 'Do we have to do this every time?' He would shake his head and say, 'Just one little omission.'" But he also accepted the fact that accidents were sometimes unavoidable in his high-speed profession — a price paid by men like himself for maintaining America's tactical superiority. How you responded to an adrenaline-edged moment was what mattered.

Here, Sewell was a master.

"The first thought when you're in a hairy situation is, 'This can't really be happening to me.' But it disappears and you revert to your training," he said in an interview. "It's survival instinct."

Of course, the odds finally caught up to him. Just not in a way anyone imagined.

Two years after his X-29 triumph, in 1986, a vintage World War II Grumman-built bomber he was trying to ferry across Long Island Sound for a friend blew an engine after takeoff. The virtuoso who had made it back with so many crippled aircraft tried to return to base one last time. While circling, the craft plunged to earth, killing him instantly. News of his death

"He pushed the envelope right to the edge," said Grumman's deputy director for development, Glenn Spacht, right. Sewell sits in an X-29.

stunned the flying world. But everyone realized that the soft-spoken man with the Texas drawl who liked to tear the wings off jets had died doing what he loved.

Roger Fergueson, a Grumman pilot who had known Sewell since his military days, put it best.

"He was only here to fly."

During his 36 years in the air, Sewell accumulated one of the most impressive resumes in aviation. As a Marine, he logged more than 330 combat missions, earning the Legion of Merit, two Distinguished Flying Crosses, 15 Air Medals and two Purple Hearts. At Grumman, he flew virtually every plane in the company's inventory and became known for his ability to solve deadly flight problems in midair. Twice he won the Kincheloe Pilot of the Year Award given by the Society of Experimental Test Pilots, an organization that included the legendary test pilot Chuck Yeager, as well as historic astronauts Alan B. Shepard

Jr. and Neil A. Armstrong. Sewell also garnered several awards for his technical papers.

In his role as a test pilot, he radiated confidence, a trait that some described as a consuming ego. Others contend his professional fierceness was mitigated by unswerving loyalty and a big heart.

"He worried about his men. To him, they were all his sons," said Bonnie.

His longtime secretary, Lauren Drake, remembered him as a fun-loving boss who always had cake and presents for her birthday and was constantly trying to fix her up with dates. When she threw a Halloween get-together, Sewell and his wife came dressed as Mickey and Minnie Mouse.

"He had a soft interior masked by the macho exterior," she said.

When it came to airplanes, Sewell remained a child all of his life. Even after reaching lofty flying plateaus in his profession, he still built plastic models of the planes he had flown and displayed them in his office. And, just as when he was a toddler growing up in Oklahoma, whenever an aircraft flew over his Setauket home, he rushed into the yard to see what it was. He told his wife before they were wed that he'd married an airplane first. She found out quickly he wasn't kidding.

"I was a young bride in 1952 and he was stationed at the Marine Air Station at Cherry Point, N.C. I'll never forget the first hurricane we had. The Marines wanted to fly all the planes inland to protect them. I said to him, 'I've never been in a hurricane. Don't leave me here!' He looked at me and said, 'Sorry, gotta go.' "

His passion to get into the air was overwhelming.

"You'd cut your best buddy's throat for a flight," he said.

Chuck Sewell may have been extraordinary in the sky, but little about him attracted attention on the ground. He was average in height and weight with a muscular build and a wicked grin. By early middle age, his hair had retreated to a sandy fringe. To keep in flying shape, he ate health food, took vitamins, jogged, worked out and ran up the 100 steps to his Grumman office. The result was an upper body strength that allowed him to endure eight and a half G's in a jet.

"He even kept hand grips in his car," said Drake.

At the office, he was a demon for the work ethic, often carrying home his technical work. But he liked socializing. Parties were common among the close-knit flying staff and Sewell was always there. He teased the women, told jokes, but limited himself to one drink. Domestically, he was a churchgoer with deep patriotic beliefs and a conservative strain. Cynde Goodwin, his daughter, once went out with a young man in high school who had long hair and an earring just to shock her dad.

"You should have seen his face when he opened the door."

But get him in a plane and he was a unique animal.

"He was wired different," Spacht said. "He had abilities that even other test pilots didn't have. Test pilots are a breed above other pilots and Sewell was the best of the best."

His specialty was to take a new plane to 35,000 feet and throttle the engines back. Then, he would

Sewell, the former Marine aviator, took pride in responding to an adrenaline-filled moment, but he also was careful to take care of routine matters such as an aircraft inspection.

At Grumman, Sewell flew almost every plane in the company's inventory. Here, he's in the cockpit of an F-14A Tomcat to test its aerodynamics.

put the craft into a steep dive, adding a bit of spice by making it spin. The essential skill for test pilots — the satisfaction at the heart of terror — is overcoming unexpected circumstances in midair. In other words, finding a solution before you became a pancake. Somehow, hurtling downward like a locomotive, Sewell would fight off the forces tearing at his body, restart the jets, stabilize the situation and head happily back home. He performed the maneuver again and again. Those who flew the planes after him studied his notes and thanked their stars for crazy people who did such things for a living.

"He was the best spin pilot in the world," said Bill Rasmussen, a fellow test pilot who clashed with Sewell before becoming a close friend. "He was a real hero."

During his lifetime, Sewell had more hairbreadth escapes than a bad Hollywood script.

While on a combat mission over Korea, his plane was hit and he bailed out behind enemy lines. Despite a shrapnel wound in his arm, he evaded searchers for three days, feeding himself with dried fish stolen from the roofs of Korean homes. He made it to the ocean hoping to swim to an American-held island 10 miles offshore. His pursuers were so close, bullets hit the water around him as he swam. The U.S. military spotted him and he was plucked from the water by a helicopter. After a short recuperation time, he was back in the air doing it all over again.

His testing specialty got him in trouble in 1974. It came while testing on an F-14 over the Atlantic about 30 miles off Long Island. After Sewell shut down the plane and twisted it into a violent spin, a chemical from an emergency power unit leaked into the left engine. Flames shot out, melting the side of the craft. The sensible reaction would have been to bail. Instead, Sewell revved up the engines and headed back to base flying at an angle that kept the flames blowing away from the fuselage. The plane touched down with no brakes, slowed only when the tail hook caught the runway wire. Waiting firefighters put out the blaze. Engineers estimated the plane would have turned into a comet in another 40 seconds.

Sewell admitted later he should have ejected, but he didn't like the idea of losing a $40 million investment.

Of course, there was also the matter of his pride.

"I hate to leave my airplane out there," he said.

At least on one occasion, his escape from death was a matter of pure luck. One of his chief delights in life was traveling with his children, Richard and Cynde, mostly on adventure sport activities such as scuba diving. "He was forever showing me the world," Cynde said. In the 1970s, he took her with him to the Paris Air Show. They were invited to ride in a giant experimental Russian version of the SST. Sewell wanted to stay at the show, but his teenage daughter threw a tantrum because she hadn't seen Notre Dame. He capitulated and they did a day tour, but got back just as the Russian plane was taking off. It crashed minutes later, killing all aboard.

Charles Sewell was born in Fort Worth, Texas, in 1930, the son of department store worker who died when he was 2. His mother moved to Marietta, Okla., a whistle-stop agricultural town on the state's southern border, where she opened a restaurant with her brother. It was the Great Depression. Money was always tight, said Ken Sewell, Chuck's brother and an aerospace researcher and author living in Dallas. The boys' only spending money came from cutting lawns, doing farm work. The two built model planes and pored over books about aircraft. In the evenings, their mother read to them from a set of encyclopedias.

"She taught us to enjoy reading and it proved to be our way to explore the world," Ken said.

Even then, Chuck was known for his intensity.

"Chuck did have a fierce pride," said his brother. "He began lifting weights while a teenager and walked with a rigid posture. Some said it looked like he had a rod for a spine. Although he had an ego, he always had a soft heart for others."

No one knows quite how airplanes became his obsession. His parents once took him on a ride in an old Ford Tri-Motor when he was a toddler, according to his brother. In an interview, Sewell mentioned being so affected at age 5 when a plane landed near his grandfather's farm in north-central Texas that he couldn't stop yelling. But getting into the air was no easy task.

By age 14, Sewell was working on construction gangs to earn money for flying lessons. Two years later, he got his private license. He enlisted in the Navy at 17 when a military recruiter told him he could make flight school by passing a two-year college equivalency test. After winning his wings in 1950, he opted to be a Marine pilot for the chance to fly Grumman's Panther jets. From there, he went on to become a fighter tactics instructor at the Marine Air Station at Cherry Point, N.C. One of his students was John H. Glenn Jr., the first American to orbit the Earth.

In Korea, his plane was hit on 15 missions in a row and shot down on the 16th one — his run to the ocean. By January, 1952, he was told he had flown too many missions and was to be sent home. To stay, he volunteered to be a forward air controller with the Marines on the ground calling in air strikes. While the unit was

taking a hill, his left arm was shattered by rifle fire.

"He had bullet holes all over his body," said Rasmussen.

The second time Sewell was wounded he ended up in a naval hospital in Oakland, Calif. At a dance on base, he was introduced to a nurse named Bonnie Yeager, who so impressed him that he took his date home, then came back to talk to her. They were married six months later and had two children.

Although he rushed into Vietnam with patriotic enthusiasm, Sewell returned a disillusioned man. The military was never allowed to engage the enemy, he complained. He told how even after spotting missile sites or war material being unloaded in Hanoi Harbor they were waved away.

"We were fighting with one hand behind our backs," he said.

Four men in his fighter squadron died.

"I lost a lot of good friends," he said.

Sewell knew his family worried when he was in Southeast Asia. Once, he wrote his children telling them he had a secret. In the next letter, he sent a photo of himself with his shirt open revealing a Superman costume. But aside from his colorful escape (after returning from Korea, he had nightmares during which he would shout and break out in cold sweats), he never mentioned his war experiences.

"That's as much as he would talk about," said Bonnie, "and if I pressed, he would just say, 'Forget it.'"

Two of the family's happiest years came after Vietnam when he was assigned to an aerobatics unit in England. Sewell was so respected that he became the first American to command a Royal Air Force squadron. Flying buddies there gave him the nickname Chuck, saying, "We can't call you Charlie" (the English equivalent of a "ninny"). "We were the only Americans on base, so we were treated like royalty," Bonnie said. Several times over the years, the family returned to visit friends.

His career took another leap forward when he was accepted to the Navy's celebrated test-pilot school in Patuxent River, Md. He described the intensive classroom work in mathematics, physics and aerodynamics as a "year in jail." Continuing to climb the military ladder would have meant accepting a desk job at the Pentagon. But being kept on the ground wasn't an option for Sewell. In 1968, after 20 years of flying, he chose to retire as a lieutenant colonel and look for a job elsewhere.

*"He was the only man I ever knew who never dreaded going to work,"
said Sewell's wife, Bonnie. The flier ran his test team like a squadron.*

Grumman, one of the Navy's traditional aircraft suppliers, was in the market. The company heard about Sewell's plans and realized he was experienced, but still relatively young at age 39. "He was a catch," said Bob Smyth, the former Grumman chief test pilot who hired him in 1969. They also liked his hard-flying reputation. "He was strictly a jet pilot; a testicle pilot."

Sewell knew the risks involved in the job.

Testing new planes has always been a dangerous business, a fact reflected by the test pilot society's high fatality rate. In 1967, two Grumman test pilots were killed during the takeoff of a controversial bomber, the TFX, the first military jet with moveable wings. Another was killed in 1972 in an early F-14 model while preparing for an air show. Anything could go wrong in the air and sometimes did. As an example, in 1958, a Grumman pilot had the distinc-

tion of being shot down by his own machine gun. The incident occurred when the bullets fired by the plane lost momentum and were sucked into the engine, sending the plane crashing to earth. The pilot escaped with only a broken leg.

But dealing with the unexpected called for what Sewell called the "black art" of do-or-die improvising. Keeping your head was the main thing. "You can't afford to get frightened and survive."

No one ever questioned Chuck Sewell's nerve.

After hearing a rumor that a number of F-14 crashes had resulted from the plane's tendency to spin uncontrollably when the power was uneven, he set out to prove it wrong. Flying at a low speed 7,000 feet above the Mojave Desert, he shut down one engine and held on as the plane pitched downward and began to revolve. At a mere 2,000 feet, he got the en-

Sewell in the cockpit of an F-14 in 1986. The south shore of Long Island, and Montauk Point, are in the background.

gines going again and pulled out.

But even with a cool-headed pilot, the situation could easily get out of control.

In 1981, on a routine test flight, both engines of his F-14 failed for unknown reasons. The plane sank in the Atlantic 25 miles off Southampton. He and his co-pilot parachuted into the ocean and were picked up by a Grumman helicopter. Sewell broke three ribs during the bailout, but he was back in the air two days later. "We never found out what happened," he said. "We only picked up little pieces."

Naturally, he wasn't above a little grandstanding now and then.

Once, while testing the limits of the F-14, Sewell pulled a "Top Gun" maneuver that raised the hair of everyone watching. He swooped in at 200 feet above the ground, skidded almost to a stop in a nearly vertical position, then roared off. A Grumman official observed, "He was riding on his tailpipes."

"He was the only man I ever knew who never dreaded going to work," said Bonnie. "Every morning he got up with a smile on his face."

Being a hard-charging test pilot didn't necessarily translate into a compatible corporate player. Even family members admit he had a quick temper, and didn't like to be contradicted.

"Chuck was a tough guy," Smyth said. "He was a super guy to have work for you, but I'm not sure I would want to work under him. I spent a lot of time picking up broken glass after him with upper management."

While at Grumman, Sewell tested and refined the F-14, A-6 and F-111 fighter bombers while directing a staff of 12 pilots, two helicopter pilots and nine weapons operators. He ran the team like a squadron. Not all were fans. A staff pilot who asked to remain anonymous classified Sewell as a caring person, but one with an inflated self opinion who let others do the "dog work." "His ego was insatiable. He took the best assignments for himself under the guise that he was the only one who could do it. His opinion of himself was that there wasn't a better pilot in the world."

Sewell had heard the comments before.

"Every test pilot says he's the best in the world," he said. "You have to believe that, or you wouldn't be doing the silly thing."

Probably the peak moment in his flying life was climbing into the X-29, one of the most radically designed ships ever to sail into the skies. His daughter remembered him being "absolutely thrilled" to be involved in the program. He talked about its high-tech components and showed people pictures. She was having dinner in a Florida restaurant when news of the successful flight came over television.

"I ran around the restaurant and told everybody, 'That's my dad!'"

Everyone at Grumman from the technicians to the pilots knew experimental planes were extremely rare and only the best got the opportunity to test them. The legendary Chuck Yeager, the chief figure in Tom Wolfe's best-selling "The Right Stuff," placed himself in the history books when he climbed into the Bell X-1 in 1947 and broke the sound barrier.

"You knew it was the most joy you were ever going to have in your life, which was exciting and sad at the same time," Spacht said.

Although the X-29 was a pure research aircraft, the company hoped to make it an appealing supersonic fighter, or at least use its technology on later models. The company had injected $50 million of its own money in the project on top of the $93 million provided by the Defense Department. Sewell picked out the man to handle its initial flights with his usual aplomb. "I decided objectively I was the best one for the job."

The unauthorized roll that got him in trouble came simply out of professional curiosity, Spacht said.

"By the third flight, you could tell Chuck was getting comfortable with the airplane. At one point, he was actually slapping the stick to get it to do something wrong," Spacht said. "To be honest, when you get to be a test pilot, if nothing's going wrong, it gets pretty boring. As sophisticated as the X-29 was, it was starting to get into the boring hours phase. Meanwhile, the airplane really is a fighter . . . the ultimate sports car. So, we got to the end of the flight card for the day and he still had some fuel left. We told him to run it out. That's when he threw in the unplanned roll. What Chuck was curious about was, if you did a tactical fighter maneuver with all those flaps and computers, would it wiggle in harmony? And it did. He did it for his own education. The military was the only ones upset. Chuck's attitude was, 'What's the big deal?'"

In reality, the X-29 was never adopted by the Navy, although some of the research was used in other military planes. One of the advanced Russian fighters looks strangely similar to the Grumman plane, Spacht pointed out. After being flown 242

times, the remarkable X plane was retired in 1988.

Sewell once told his secretary that he planned to keep flying until he was 96, but the rigors of test piloting were beginning to show. Once, while experiencing "lateral G's" that slam a pilot from side to side, he clamped his jaw so tight he sheared off the top of a tooth. Drake and others worried about him when they heard his labored breathing via a helmet microphone during some of the more arduous tests.

"Sometimes when he came down you could see it took a toll on him," Drake said.

He could have flown at Grumman only six more years before mandatory retirement. After that, he said he planned to begin building kit planes at home. Like all Grumman pilots, he loved the company's older models. Drake recalled how enthusiastic he was about the chance to fly the WWII bomber he

Forty-eight-feet long, the X-29 had forward swept wings in back and horizontal stabilizers in front.

died in. A workhorse of the Pacific theater, old Avengers were used after the war by crop dusters and fire departments for battling forest blazes.

"He just loved flying those planes," Drake said.

His plan that day was to ferry the vintage plane, which belonged to a friend, from Connecticut on to Florida with a stopover at the Grumman plant in Calverton. Smoke puffed from the plane's cowling just after it left the field. Witnesses said it seemed to wallow in the sky. As it continued to lose altitude, Sewell sent a garbled message that sounded like he going to return to the runway. Suddenly, spectators heard his voice boom out over the small airport's loudspeaker, "I'm going to crash." Seconds later, the plane rolled and hit the trees.

Rasmussen had been at his Florida condo at the time and was supposed to be Sewell's chase plane. He called his friend Sunday night to say he couldn't make it because of bad weather. The next morning, he had a "bad feeling" after leaving his house. He returned home and called Grumman. They had just received word of the accident. His theory is that Sewell felt obligated to bring the craft back in for his friend. It was a tough Grumman plane; he should have simply belly flopped to the ground. "If he had come straight ahead into the woods he would have been OK. You could fly [an Avenger] into the Empire State Building and survive, but you can't survive if it's inverted."

Drake still breaks down remembering that day.

"You'd think you'd get over it, but you never do."

Sewell was buried in the Arlington National Cemetery. After Sewell's death, Grumman chairman John C. Bierwirth said, "Our aircraft are America's front line of defense because of men like Chuck, who pushed them to the limit."

Around her neck, Cynde wears a gold figurine in the shape of the X-29. She planned to give one to her dad that Christmas. After the crash, she had two made, one for herself and her brother. They wear them every day, she said.

Sewell once told an interviewer he had a recurring dream that after much flapping of his arms, he was able to rise into the air and fly like a bird. Cynde believes her father lived that dream on Earth, or at least got as close as any mortal can get.

"He was totally happy and at peace with himself." •

The pilot and an uncompleted X-29: Sewell couldn't wait for the day he took the X plane up in 1984.

Chuck Sewell died in a plane crash in 1986. At top, firefighters in Brooklyn, Conn., inspect the wreckage of the propeller-driven Avenger torpedo bomber Sewell was flying. He was planning to transport the old plane to Florida for a friend. Above, three years before his death, the pilot posed with another Avenger. At left, he stands in front of an F-14, a plane he tested time and again for the Navy.

Tom Kelly and his Grumman crew helped put Americans on the moon — and get them back to Earth safely.

Father Of The Lunar Module

BY MICHAEL DORMAN

I t all began when Thomas Kelly started meticulously building balsa model airplanes as a 10-year-old Merrick schoolboy.

"They were pretty fancy," he would recall six decades later. "You made a skeleton out of the balsa wood and you covered it with paper. Then you could paint it with all kinds of designs. Some of the planes took a couple of months to build. Most of mine were rubber-band models. You could wind up the propellers and get them to fly. I only had a couple of gasoline-powered models."

The childhood hobby blossomed into a lifelong fascination with the phenomenon of flight. And that fascination would propel Tom Kelly into a pivotal role

Kelly, fourth from left along railing, directed more than 7,000 people on the LEM project. At the top of the railing in this 1968 photo are Apollo 9 astronauts Russell Schweickart, far left, and James McDivitt, second from left.

in one of humankind's great adventures — the landing of American astronauts on the moon.

Kelly would oversee the design and construction of the lunar excursion module (LEM), the spacecraft that would carry the astronauts to and from the moon's surface. It was a project that would engage more than 7,000 employees of the Grumman Aircraft Engineering Corp. in Bethpage and propel Long Island into the center of the race for space. Kelly would

serve as Grumman's top troubleshooter not only on the initial 1969 moon landing but on lunar missions that followed. And his engineering work would earn him the sobriquet "the father of the LEM."

For Kelly, the moon project came as the climax to a career that had seen him do everything from performing manual labor on a Grumman assembly line to designing propulsion systems for warplanes and missiles. Those who worked with him on the lunar

With NASA's encouragement, Grumman volunteered to develop, at its own expense, a space vehicle proposal. Kelly, right, stands with Apollo spacecraft manager Joe Shea.

project said he knew the aviation-aerospace business inside out and that he repeatedly demonstrated calm in the face of pressure. "There were a million engineering problems that had to be answered each day," said one of Kelly's longtime LEM associates. "He made those decisions."

Kelly — a short, slender man with a twinkling eye, a ruddy countenance and a hearty chuckle — lived on Long Island through much of its history as an aviation hub. He was born in Brooklyn on June 14, 1929, but moved to Merrick with his parents before he was 2. His mother, Irene, tended the home. His father, Wilfrid, worked in advertising for a newspaper chain. When Kelly was 6, a brother named Bob was born.

"I had a normal, happy childhood," Kelly said in an interview in the spring of 2000. "I liked school. I liked sports, but wasn't any good at 'em. I did a lot of musical stuff — played trumpet in the school band." He would continue to play the trumpet into his

70s — performing with the community band in Greenport, near the home in Cutchogue where he moved after his retirement from Grumman.

Kelly not only liked school; he did exceedingly well at it. He was the valedictorian of his class at Wellington C. Mepham High School in Bellmore. And he was one of 10 Long Island high school graduates in 1946 who won coveted Grumman engineering scholarships. The scholarship helped put him through Cornell University and provided him with a summer job at Grumman during his college years.

Although the summer job carried the title apprentice engineer, Kelly and the other students actually did grunt work in Grumman's aircraft shops. "They used to rotate us around to different assignments — putting airplanes together," Kelly recalled.

"The chores that nobody wanted to do they saved for us. I remember one miserable job we did on a civilian amphibian called the Mallard. It had an aluminum hull that could float. To make the hull water-

Some of Grumman's key engineering and management personnel gather for a photo in Houston in July, 1969. They were there for the Apollo XI mission to the moon. Kelly stands at center.

tight, they put a strip of sealing tape on the rivet lines where the pieces of aluminum were joined. They put the tape on first, got it all lined up, then drilled the holes and put the rivets in. Getting that tape on was one of our summer kids' jobs. It was a pain in the neck. It was fussy work. You had to get it just right. But it was very interesting seeing how everything really went together."

In 1951, the year of his graduation from Cornell with a mechanical-engineering degree, Kelly married the former Joan Tantum. His wife shared his enthusiasm for birding, a seemingly natural extension of his passion for the process of flight. Five sons and a daughter were eventually born to the couple.

Direct from college, Kelly went to work full time for Grumman as a propulsion engineer on a supersonic missile program. "That got me into the high-speed end of the aircraft business," Kelly said. "So, after that, I worked on some of the advanced Navy fighters — the F-11F and the F-11-1F. The F-11-1F was a Mach 2 supersonic fighter, very advanced."

He rose quickly to the job of engineering group leader on such projects, working on them for almost five years. During that time, Kelly also earned a master's degree in mechanical engineering from Columbia University. He would later win a fellowship to the Massachusetts Institute of Technology and take another master's in industrial management.

Kelly, who held a second lieutenant's commission in the Air Force Reserve, was called to active duty in 1956. He was assigned to the aircraft laboratory at Wright-Patterson Air Force Base in Dayton, Ohio. "That was pretty neat," he said. "For two years, I worked on all the latest Air Force airplanes under development — and they had a lot of them at that time. There were quite a few fighter planes and there was a supersonic bomber called the B-58. I went around to all the manufacturers, participating in reviews of their work."

In 1957, while Kelly was still in the Air Force, the Soviet Union took the lead in the space race by firing the Sputnik satellite into orbit. "That got me interested in space. So, when it came time to get out of the Air Force after two years, I looked around at all the aerospace companies — instead of just going back to Grumman. I went out to Lockheed in Sunnyvale, Calif., because I wanted to work on space, and Lockheed already had a couple of space projects."

He worked as a group leader on several Lockheed rocket-propulsion projects for about a year. "But the people at Grumman kept working on me over the phone to go back there," Kelly said. "They said they were going into space and wanted me to help them get into space. Finally, they talked me into it. I did come back, in 1958."

Immediately after his return, Kelly was assigned to work with a special group of engineers to develop preliminary projects for space. In 1959, Grumman won a government space contract — to develop an Orbiting Astronomical Laboratory (OAL). "It was a big telescope launched up into space," Kelly said. "It was the forerunner of the Hubble Space Telescope. It did basically what the Hubble does, except with a somewhat smaller instrument. It was very successful. It was supposed to last a year and it was still going strong after eight years. When they finally shut it down, they ran out of things to do with it and money to fund it. But, once Grumman won that OAL contract, we were as qualified as anybody to bid on space work."

By 1960, the National Aeronautics and Space Administration had begun preliminary studies on a possible manned landing on the moon. Grumman assigned Kelly to lead a small team of engineers exploring NASA's plans for the lunar mission and whether there might be a role for the company in the project.

"We found out what NASA was doing," Kelly said. "It was all pretty much 'what if' studies at that point. What would it take to land men on the moon? How would you do it?"

Then, in 1961, President John F. Kennedy — in a State of the Union address — laid down a dramatic challenge: "I believe that this nation should commit itself to the goal, before this decade is out, of landing a man on the moon and returning him safely to Earth."

That declaration, Kelly recalled, "upped the ante" considerably. "All of a sudden, it went from 'what if' studies to 'here's something we're going to do.' The question became what Grumman could do to get a piece of the action."

With NASA's encouragement, Grumman volunteered to develop at its own expense a proposal for the space vehicle that would actually land on the moon — a vehicle known then simply as the Bug. There was stiff competition among various companies for contracts on the project.

Three methods were considered by NASA for carrying out the mission — a direct ascent to the moon's surface using an enormous rocket; an Earth-orbiting rendezvous technique; and a plan that would place a command vehicle in lunar orbit, where it would release a two-stage spacecraft for a round trip to the moon and then return to the Earth.

Wernher von Braun, the noted rocket scientist, was among those arguing for an Earth-orbiting rendezvous. But that would have required launching two huge spacecraft separately from Earth. "We thought the rendezvous in lunar orbit was much more efficient than the other ideas," Kelly said.

"I liked the idea of a single launch. It was far more efficient than any of the other schemes. But there was one other thing that was very good about it. It required that you develop a specialized lunar landing vehicle, separate from the command vehicle that was going to re-enter the Earth. And the requirements of those two spacecraft were diametrically opposed. How you would ever fulfill those requirements with a single vehicle I still don't know.

"The command vehicle, to re-enter the Earth, had to be very dense, strong, heavily insulated, so it could go through the fiery re-entry with high forces. The lunar module didn't need any of that. It had to be extremely lightweight because, for every pound of weight that went out to the moon and came back, you had to add three pounds of propellant. So, in seeking something extremely lightweight, we wound up with a sort of spindly, anemic-looking vehicle. With two separate spacecraft, you could deal with the diametrically opposed requirements separately. We helped persuade NASA to go to a lunar-orbit rendezvous."

Grumman, in competition with eight other aerospace companies, bid on the contract to build the LEM. While Kelly and his colleagues were drafting designs for the project, Long Island political leaders were simultaneously working to win the contract for Grumman — since it would be worth billions of dollars and thousands of jobs for the local economy. Nassau Democratic Chairman John F. English, a close ally of Kennedy, visited the White House repeatedly with Nassau County Executive Eugene H. Nickerson to lobby for Grumman's proposal.

On Peconic Bay in 1998, the engineer could still visit the stars with his telescope. Every lunar module — more than a million parts — was handmade by crews such as this, right.

These combined efforts paid off on Nov. 7, 1962, when NASA awarded Grumman the LEM contract. The news sent cheers and shouts sweeping through the Bethpage plant. Initially, the contract provided for $350 million worth of work. But, by the time the project was completed, it brought Grumman $2.3 billion and Long Island subcontractors many millions more. Kelly would direct the work of more than 3,000 Grumman engineers and 4,000 other employees on the LEM.

Many of them said the dramatic nature of the mission ignited an unusual esprit throughout the company. Grumman employees would gather in the parking lots after the end of the workday, using their fingers to draw diagrams in the dust on their cars — speculating how problems on the LEM could be resolved.

"We were able to let our imaginations run wild," Kelly said. "We realized pretty quickly that we didn't have to worry what the LEM looked like. It didn't matter what it looked like. It didn't have any aerodynamic requirements, so nothing had to be streamlined. You could just figure out what you needed functionally to do the job."

That job was to carry two astronauts from the command vehicle to the moon and back to the command vehicle. A third astronaut would remain in the command vehicle for the lunar orbit while his mates made the round-trip to the surface. Kelly's plan called for the LEM to use a descent stage to reach the moon, then for an ascent stage to separate from the other section on the lunar surface for the return trip. Much of the LEM's weight would thus be left on the moon during the flight back to the command vehicle.

NASA eventually changed the vehicle's official name, dropping the word "excursion" from the original lunar excursion module and revising the acronym from LEM to LM. The theory was that the word "excursion" might sound frivolous and call up images of picnic journeys. But, for most, the LEM remained the LEM.

Slowly, the LEM took form in the Bethpage shops. It did indeed bear a resemblance to a bug — and not an especially attractive one. A lumpy midsection surmounted four spindly legs. Parts seemed to stick out of the structure at weird angles.

Roger Carpenter, who worked under Kelly as a

member of Grumman's engineering materials review board, said in an interview that many people did not comprehend how the spacecraft was constructed. "The LEM was not mass-produced," Carpenter said. "It was entirely handmade." That meant human hands installed more than a million parts on each LEM. All told, Grumman built more than a dozen LEMs — all different.

Among Kelly's recurring problems was trying to reduce the combined weight of those million parts. The less the spacecraft weighed, the less propellant it would need. Thus, the LEM sacrificed beauty for engineering efficiency.

"Form followed function," Kelly said. "It came out the way it came out."

One means of cutting the spacecraft's weight was discovered when Kelly's team realized the number of certain propellant tanks could be reduced from four to two. But the placement of the tanks removed an element of symmetry. "It made it look as if the LEM had mumps," Kelly said. "One tank was sticking farther out than the other. But, since we didn't care how it looked, we did it that way."

Other problems arose constantly in the design and manufacture of the spacecraft. "A big problem was just getting the parts to fit," Kelly said. "We also had persistent problems with leaks in the fluid systems — propellant tanks and so forth. We had to do a lot of work on seals and closures before we finally got the leak situation under control. When we were placing clusters of small rocket thrusters, we had to try a number of variations before we finally hit one that seemed to satisfy all the constraints we could think of. There was a lot of opportunity to innovate as we went along."

Roger Carpenter recalled problems arising every day — some involving the LEM's windows. "The LEM, of course, had to be able to withstand very high temperatures," he said. "But, when heated, these windows would crack into thousands of pieces. We worked and worked on it, and determined it was a bonding problem. We worked with the suppliers and corrected it."

In view of the monumental risks confronting the astronauts, the engineers built a huge array of redundant systems into the LEM to ensure against possible operations failures. Where it could be done, they installed backup systems upon backups upon backups. But total redundancy was impossible because of the weight limitations.

Most important, there could be no backup system for the vital rocket engine designed to lift the LEM from the moon for the return to the command vehicle on its way back to Earth. A failure by that engine would be catastrophic. The astronauts would be stranded on the moon.

"There would be nothing we could do except watch them die a long, slow death," Kelly said.

Steven Hornacek, a Grumman telemetry engineer, described participating in sensitive tests on the ascent engine. The engine contained numerous valves. "All of them had to open at exactly the same time and with the same force," Hornacek said. "The tests had to assure that they would do that."

Kelly, for his part, said, "The ascent was something you could worry about, but you couldn't do much about it. The beauty of it was that it was all over in a flash. You pushed that button, and it either worked or it didn't. There wasn't any long, drawn-out period of worrying. It was more than the ascent engine that I worried about, too, because there were a whole string of explosive devices that had to function to separate the ascent stage from the descent stage. All of that had to come off at the same time as the ascent engine fired up. By the nature of explosive devices, you're relying on statistical testing to assure that the devices are reliably functioning."

There were also tests where the LEM was moved into a hangar at the Bethpage plant, surrounded by conditions approximating the moon's gravity, and dropped about 20 feet to simulate a landing on the lunar surface. Later, there were two preparatory unmanned LEM flights months before the first attempt at a manned landing. On the second unmanned mission, called Apollo 10, the LEM flew within 40,000 feet of the moon and sent back striking pictures of the surface.

All together, seven years passed between the time Grumman received its initial LEM contract and the first attempt at landing astronauts on the moon. Kelly and his team advanced from simulated flights to actual limited test flights and then the two preliminary test flights.

There were failures, corrections and refinements at every stage. But then, inevitably, it was time for the LEM's biggest test — the actual manned flight.

In the early morning hours of July 16, 1969, the glow of floodlights illuminated a huge Saturn V rocket standing on a launching pad at the John F. Kennedy Space Center in Cape Canaveral, Fla. The heaviest vehicle ever fired aloft — weighing 6,484,289 pounds — it was poised to send three astronauts racing into the skies on a planned eight-day mission.

Neil A. Armstrong, 39, was the commander of the Apollo 11 crew. Edwin (Buzz) Aldrin, also 39, was assigned to accompany Armstrong in the LEM to the moon. The third astronaut, Michael Collins, 38, would pilot the command vehicle — named Columbia — from which the LEM would be launched toward the lunar surface. Collins would orbit the moon until the LEM brought Armstrong and Aldrin back to the command vehicle for the return to Earth.

At 9:32 a.m., the Saturn V rocket lifted off the launch pad amid waves of reverberating roar. Twelve minutes later, another rocket boosted the spacecraft into the Earth's orbit. After the vehicle had circled the Earth for 2½ hours, an engine fired and sent the spacecraft bursting through space at 24,245 mph. It pulled out of the Earth's gravitational force and sped toward the moon.

The LEM — named Eagle — separated from the moon-orbiting command vehicle and began cruising toward the lunar surface. "Eagle has wings," Armstrong radioed the ground controllers.

Tom Kelly was stationed for the flight at NASA's Manned Spacecraft Center — later named the Lyndon B. Johnson Space Center — in Houston, where the mission was being directed. "I was in a small, windowless room right across a corridor from the big Mission Control Center everybody saw on TV," Kelly recalled.

"This small room was called the Spacecraft Analysis, or SPAN, Room. We had the senior people there from the spacecraft and guidance contractors on the project. We had a few NASA people in with us and flight-control consoles that showed us the instrumentation readouts coming down from the spacecraft. We were also hooked into the voice network, so we could talk back and forth."

Grumman was permitted only three people in the SPAN Room. But another 20 Grumman engineers were stationed in a nearby Houston building and about 80 were monitoring the flight at the Bethpage plant.

"Our job was to deal with problems that arose during the flight," Kelly said. "How we reacted depended on how much time we had. If we only had a couple of minutes, I would have to give them an opinion right in the SPAN Room. If we had a little more time, we could talk to our guys in the other building in Houston or back in Bethpage and to our suppliers all over the country. The spacecraft was always showing what NASA called anomalies. Anything that was a deviation from the strictly normal was an anomaly. Whenever an anomaly was reported — either from instrumentation or something the crew reported — we had to explain them. Most of them were not significant, but some were."

Neither Kelly nor his Grumman colleagues had the answers to all the problems that arose. As the LEM made its final descent to the moon, for example, there came what Kelly called an unexpected event. "The guidance computer issued a program alarm with a software warning that the guidance computer had stored in it," Kelly said.

"It actually had a whole string of these program alarms. The computer would just give you program alarm No. 21 or No. 23 or something like that. That's all it told you. When one of these came up during the descent, nobody had ever seen one before. We'd never in all our simulations triggered one of those alarms. But, fortunately, one of the NASA flight controllers had made it his business to memorize all these alarms and know what they were for — what their importance was. So he was able to tell immediately that it wasn't a serious problem. It's a good thing because he was the only one in the whole operation — ground or flight crew — who knew what it was."

When the LEM drew even closer to the moon, a far more dangerous problem developed. The Eagle was inadvertently being steered by its guidance computer down into a boulder-strewn crater on the moon. A landing in the crater might prove fatal. The LEM might crash into a boulder. The spacecraft might topple over. It might land at an angle greater than 30 degrees from the vertical — making a return takeoff impossible.

Armstrong made a critical decision. He took control of the spacecraft away from the computer and flew the LEM manually past the rocky crater. But Aldrin then issued a warning, telling him: "Quantity light."

A signal light indicated they had only 114 seconds' worth of fuel remaining for the descent engine carry-

Commander Neil Armstrong took this photo of the lunar module at the Sea of Tranquility with a special lunar-surface camera. Astronaut Edwin Aldrin Jr. works with scientific experiments near the module.

ing them toward the lunar surface. But Armstrong still had not seen a likely spot to land.

The voice of Charlie Duke, the capsule communicator at Mission Control, soon crackled over the radio. "Thirty seconds," he said.

Thirty seconds' worth of fuel — perhaps even less, for such estimates were not infallible. At last, Armstrong spotted a potential landing site more promising than the rocky crater. He steered toward it.

"Forty feet," Aldrin radioed Mission Control. "Things look good. Picking up some dust. Drifting to the right a little. Contact light! OK. Engine stop." When the engine shut down, by some estimates, the fuel tank was empty.

A short time after the shutdown, Armstrong radioed: "Houston. Tranquility Base here. The Eagle has landed."

It was 4:17 p.m. EDT on July 20, more than four days after the astronauts had been fired into space.

Cheers, applause and tears filled Mission Control and the Grumman plant as well as a multitude of other spots around the world. Humans had done what had long seemed impossible — making the 225,000-mile journey to the moon.

But Tom Kelly and other experts on the ground had little chance to savor the moment. For, almost immediately after the landing, another potential disaster confronted them.

"We noticed that the pressure and temperature were building up in a small section of propellant line that went from the shutoff valve on the descent engine to a heat exchanger that warmed the cold helium gas," Kelly said.

"Apparently, there was still some helium flowing at shutdown and it had frozen a slug of the liquid fuel in the propellant line. This made a sort of trap because you had the slug of fuel on one end and the shutoff valve was closed at the other end. The engine, of course, was very hot. As it sat there after the landing, the heat flowed back into the adjacent areas."

As a result, it heated up the segment of propellant line containing the trapped fuel slug. "We didn't like that because the fuel itself was an unstable chemical," Kelly said.

"If you heated it up much beyond 300 degrees Fahrenheit, it was liable to explode on you. So that made us very concerned. And, as we watched, the temperature went over 200 degrees and it was climbing pretty fast. So we held a hasty conference with our own propulsion experts and the NASA experts. We decided on a sort of desperate measure called burping the engine. We were going to ask the astronauts to flick the engine on and then immediately off just to relieve the pressure momentarily in the line."

Until then, the astronauts knew nothing about the problem. "The ground was just about to radio them and explain it to them and ask them to burp the engine," Kelly said. "And then the problem went away by itself. The temperature got high enough that the slug of frozen fuel melted. That relieved the pressure. So, all of a sudden, we saw everything go back to normal. Only then were we able to relax and realize: Wow, we really made it to the moon."

Armstrong and Aldrin were scheduled to take a rest period after the LEM set down on the moon. But they were fired up and not sleepy, so they got permission to embark immediately on their next activity — actually walking on the moon.

John Devaney, a Grumman engineer working with Kelly in Houston, was especially concerned about one aspect of the planned walk. "The landing gear on the LEM was designed to crush during the landing on the moon," Devaney said in an interview. "It was

Astronauts Neil Armstrong, left, and Edwin (Buzz) Aldrin visited Grumman on Long Island in September, 1969, to thank the LEM crew for its work.

full of crunched tinfoil, so it would crush on touch-down. But Armstrong and Aldrin put the LEM down so gently that the landing gear didn't crush. That left the LEM higher off the moon's surface than we expected. I was worried that, when Armstrong dropped off the ladder to the surface, the bottom of the ladder would be so high that he couldn't climb back into the LEM."

It was 10:56 p.m. on July 20. Armstrong, bundled into his bulky pressurized suit, began descending the ladder for his heralded space walk. He dropped gingerly from the bottom step to the lunar surface.

"That's one small step for man, one giant leap for mankind," he said in becoming the first human to set foot on the moon. Actually, he had misspoken. He had meant to say: "That's one small step for a man, one giant leap for mankind." But the misstatement — which did not quite make sense — was recorded for posterity.

Armstrong shuffled cautiously about the lunar landscape. "The surface is fine and powdery," he radioed Houston. "It adheres in fine layers, like powdered charcoal, to the soles and sides of my boots."

Before long, Aldrin joined him. They set up a television camera to capture their movements for a fascinated Earth audience, then walked and jumped across the lunar surface. In all, the space walk lasted 2 hours, 14 minutes. During that time, the astronauts deployed equipment for a series of continuing experiments and collected 21 moon rocks. They also planted an American flag as a symbol of national pride — but not a claim of conquest. Then they climbed back into the LEM, encountering no trouble in ascending the ladder despite the uncrushed landing gear.

Later, when the time came for Armstrong and Aldrin to take off on the return trip to the command vehicle, they were well aware that they were staking their lives on the 172-pound LEM ascent engine designed to lift them from the moon. Grumman had tested the engine successfully more than 3,000 times. But the astronauts recognized that, if it somehow failed to work, they would be stranded on the lunar surface.

Inasmuch as there could be only one ascent engine, Kelly and his team had designed a simple device they hoped would present a minimum of risk. "It was pressure-fed, with no pumps," Kelly said. "The propellants ignited on contact, with no ignition system."

As the astronauts awaited the ignition's critical test,

Mission Control reported: "You're clear for takeoff."

"Roger, understand," Aldrin replied. "We're No. 1 on the runway."

Within seconds, the engine fired amid a burst of energy. The LEM's ascent stage separated from the descent stage and began rising from the moon. The ascent engine performed flawlessly.

Kelly, in the SPAN Room, knew instantly that the liftoff was a success. "We were very worried about it because the engine and a lot of other things have to work simultaneously," he recalled. "It either goes or it doesn't. Fortunately, it went."

It took the LEM four hours to rendezvous with the command vehicle. The two aircraft docked, and Armstrong and Aldrin slid through a passageway into the command vehicle.

Apollo 11 splashed down in the South Pacific at dawn on July 24 not far from the Navy aircraft carrier Hornet. Six-foot swells almost immediately capsized the spacecraft. But a recovery team of Navy divers swiftly righted the vehicle by using large flotation bags. After being scrubbed down on a life raft with disinfectants to combat health hazards confronted on the mission, the three astronauts were lifted by helicopter to the deck of the Hornet to begin 18 days of quarantine.

At Mission Control, the traditional splashdown cigars seemed to appear everywhere. A huge television screen that usually displayed flight information was showing Kennedy's speech passage challenging Americans to land a man on the moon and return "him safely to Earth." Then a message flashed across the screen: "Mission accomplished — July, 1969."

Tom Kelly was back in Bethpage by that time, since the LEM mission had effectively ended when the vehicle docked with Columbia. He and about 100 of his colleagues viewed the splashdown on a television screen in Grumman's big Mission Support Room.

"It was a moment of triumph," Kelly recalled. "We were watching the people in Mission Control on television, lighting cigars. We didn't have any cigars, so we cheered and patted each others' backs."

Four months after the initial lunar mission, two other astronauts — Charles (Pete) Conrad and Alan Bean — flew another LEM to a successful landing on the moon. Kelly was again stationed in the SPAN Room in Houston for the Apollo 12 flight. The LEM performed so well that Kelly did not consider it necessary to be in Houston for the third scheduled manned lunar mission. Instead, he was studying for his master's in industrial management at MIT.

On April 13, 1970, three astronauts aboard Apollo 13 — James Lovell, Fred Haise and Jack Swigert — were cruising through space 205,000 miles from Earth. Suddenly, a loud bang was heard.

A liquid oxygen tank aboard the spacecraft's command service module, built by North American Aviation, had exploded. The explosion crippled the mission and seriously endangered the astronauts. The remaining oxygen in the command vehicle was quickly being used up. Without oxygen, the command vehicle could not produce necessary electrical power and water. Its controls would become useless. The astronauts abandoned the command vehicle and entered the attached LEM — hoping to use it as a lifeboat that would enable them to return the entire spacecraft to Earth after scrubbing the attempt to reach the moon.

Tom Kelly was awakened by a telephone call in the middle of the night in Cambridge, Mass., and asked to return to Bethpage to direct Grumman's efforts to help rescue the astronauts. "Grumman sent a light plane to Boston to pick me up," Kelly said.

"I came down to Bethpage and went to our Mission Support Room. Even though it was about 3 in the morning, people were pouring in to work just like it was the start of a normal workday. All the people on the program who had heard about the problem decided they were going to come in without being called in. It was a good thing they did because there was plenty to do."

The possibility that the LEM might need to be used as a rescue vehicle had been raised in a study years earlier. "We knew it was possible to do this, but none of the details had been worked out," Kelly said. "It hadn't been rehearsed with the crews. So it had to be developed on the fly. There was a lot of hectic activity to determine what was the best way to get the astronauts back to Earth, what was the best trajectory and how long it would take."

A major problem confronting Kelly and his colleagues was determining the amounts of consumables — such as water, oxygen and electrical power — the astronauts were using in the LEM and how long they would last. "We wanted to know not specification numbers but the real numbers from the equipment that was up there," Kelly said.

"We had to know how close we were going to cut it. We got on the phone with all the manufacturers all over the country. In some cases, we asked them to run special tests for us. And we determined how much of the equipment we were going to have to shut off in order to stretch the consumables until the astronauts got back to Earth. It turned out to be a lot. We had to shut most of the equipment in the LEM off, which was a problem because we had to figure out how to reorient the LEM after that period of shutdown."

But somehow it all worked. On April 17, the astronauts splashed down in the Pacific near the aircraft carrier Iwo Jima. Within an hour, they were safely on the carrier's deck.

"Apollo 13 was the finest hour for the LEM," Kelly said. "We were the lifeboat that rescued the crew."

For his work as "father of the LEM" and the broad range of his efforts on the space program, Kelly was awarded NASA's Distinguished Service Medal. But that was not his only honor. When Newsday was seeking nominations in 1998 for Favorite Long Islander of the Century, one of Kelly's sons, Peter, suggested his father. "Because he's my father," Peter Kelly wrote.

"And besides his tremendous contribution and vision in engineering and space technology, he is a person of utmost integrity who instilled his family with love and hope."

Tom Kelly retired in 1992 after holding a series of Grumman executive jobs — among them vice president for engineering. Three years later, he and his wife moved to their home in Cutchogue.

One spring day in 2000, Kelly sat in his living room — near a telescope providing glimpses of waterfowl taking flight over Peconic Bay — and reflected on both the 20th-Century events that had marked high points in his career and what they might mean for the future.

"The first lunar landing firmly set NASA on a course of exploration of the solar system — of the planets and even the universe — that it's still on today," he said. "It established that space exploration was a practical thing to do — a very worthwhile thing to do."

As for the personal satisfactions his work had brought him, he said, "The whole Apollo program and the lunar module, that was certainly a great satisfaction. The LEM behaved wonderfully in all the flight missions. Everything the LEM was supposed to do, it did."

Did he have any regrets?

"The only regret is that I wasn't able to go to the moon myself," Kelly said. "I would have loved to go. It was a great adventure." ●

Thirty years after the Apollo 11 moon landing, Kelly stood inside a mockup of the lunar module, which is on display at the Cradle of Aviation Museum in Garden City. At left, he stands before a mural at the Grumman plant in 1992.

Memories of Long Island's Golden Age of Aviation

GOLDEN FLYER
In front of what could be considered the first "hangar" on Long Island, Charles Willard, standing without hat, and Glenn Curtiss, second from right, pose on Aug. 12, 1909.

Times and places and people and planes. Memories are made of these. An aviation tournament in 1910, featuring a race around the Statue of Liberty. An early pilot hand-cranking his aircraft. Airborne bootleggers loading liquor. Cars of the curious lining Curtiss Field on a Sunday in the 1920s. An exclusive country club in Hicksville that was a playground for the aviation set in the 1930s and '40s. Howard Hughes at Roosevelt Field.

SEE YOU
AT THE RACES

The world's aviation community, including the esteemed Wright brothers, came to Long Island for the biggest aviation event of the day. The International Aviation Tournament, whose program is at right, hosted fliers from England, France and the United States who competed for speed and altitude prizes in October, 1910, at Belmont Park. There also was a round-trip race to the Statue of Liberty. Thousands of New Yorkers glimpsed an airplane for the first time at the tournament. Among planes on display was the French Demoiselle, below, flown by future World War I ace Roland Garros.

INTERNATIONAL
AVIATION
TOURNAMENT
BELMONT PARK
OCTOBER 22ND TO 30TH
1.30 P. M. DAILY

FRENCH FLYER
This Antoinette aircraft, left, considered by many to be aerodynamically advanced, flew at the Belmont tournament in 1910. The Antoinette's long, thin fuselage and cruciform tail made it one of the most beautiful flying machines of the pre-World War I era.

RACETRACK IN THE SKY
Belmont racetrack's grandstand enabled tens of thousands to watch races at the October, 1910, international tournament.

LAST-MINUTE ADVICE

Pilot Ralph Johnstone talks to flight pioneer Orville Wright just before starting on a record-breaking, high-altitude flight of 9,714 feet at the 1910 International Aviation Tournament at Belmont Park.

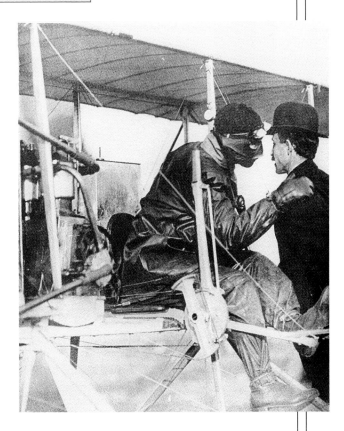

THE WRIGHT STUFF

At the 1910 Belmont Park tournament, Wilbur Wright and his sister, Katharine, watch the Gordon Bennett trophy race — worth $5,000 in prize money — which was won by English flier Claude Grahame-White.

GEORGE BEATTY, PIONEER

George Beatty, above right, was one of early aviation's pioneers. After receiving his license in 1911, he spent the years before World War I teaching and flying exhibitions. In February, 1914, he helped establish a school near London that specialized in the instruction of military pilots. Above, he is paired with railroad heir Lt. Col. Cornelius Vanderbilt of the New York National Guard in a Wright aircraft in 1912 on the Hempstead Plains. Below, Beatty and K.M. Turner demonstrate in-flight radio communication, also in 1912.

AVIATION FIELD AT BAYSHORE, L. I.

PASSED BY CENSOR, WASHINGTON, D. C. ©I.F.S.

U. S. ARMY AEROPLANE IN FULL FLIGHT. SERIES NO. 12 222673

POSTCARDS FROM THE EDGE *The image above, from a postcard, shows a Curtiss Jenny in flight over what appears to be a set of land-based wood frame hangers. Although the postcard says "Aviation Field at Bay Shore, L.I.," this may well be a generic image and not Bay Shore. Below, "Back from its Morning Flight," depicts a Curtiss Flying Boat being pulled up a runway by students of the Naval Aviation School at Bay Shore. Both cards appeared around the time of World War I.*

COPY BY COMMITTEE ON PUBLIC INFORMATION

BACK FROM ITS MORNING FLIGHT, U. S. AERO STATION, BAY SHORE, L. I., N. Y.

FIFTH DIMENSION

Douglas O25-Cs of the Fifth Observation Squadron, based at Mitchel Field, in flight over Long Island, circa 1933.

SMART COMMUTER

Aeronautical engineer Lawrence Sperry commuted from his Hempstead home to his factory in Farmingdale in this Messenger aircraft. It was only a short walk from Sperry's Garden Place house to a small pasture north of Atlantic Avenue in Garden City, where the aviator housed his plane in a barn. Sperry, a true innovator, was lost at sea on Dec. 13, 1923, while flying from England to Holland. Nicknamed "Gyro," among his many inventions were the automatic pilot, the parachute pack and instruments for all-weather flight.

BOOTLEGGING

In the 1920s and '30s, plenty of new uses were found for aircraft, including aerial advertising, freight transport, mapping and even bootlegging. Above, bootleggers prepare to transport illegal alcohol somewhere in eastern Long Island, circa 1930.

ANTARCTIC CHAMPION

Explorer Richard E. Byrd's South Pole plane lands at Roosevelt Field in June, 1928. Byrd made history with a flyover of the North Pole and six missions to the South Pole. His successful polar flights were aided by his World War I experience of flying over water out of sight of land.

BANKING
A Burgess-Wright aircraft flies over the Nassau Boulevard Aerodrome in Garden City during an international air meet in September, 1911.

START 'ER UP
An engine is cranked up before a flight at Mineola, circa 1910.

AERIAL F STOP
Frank Dart, left, a New York Herald Telegram photographer, prepares to take off with an unidentified pilot in a Wright aircraft from Nassau Boulevard Aerodrome in 1912.

CHUTING STAR

Henry (Buddy) Bushmeyer, poised on the wing of a plane 2,000 feet up, gets ready for his regular Sunday afternoon parachute jump which, along with other stunts, brought thousands to Roosevelt Field from 1927-31.

BOMBERS
AWAY!
*Curtiss B-2
Condor bombers
in flight over
Long Island
around 1931.
Civilian models
of the Condor
were used to
transport
passengers and
to take up
Roosevelt Field
parachutists.*

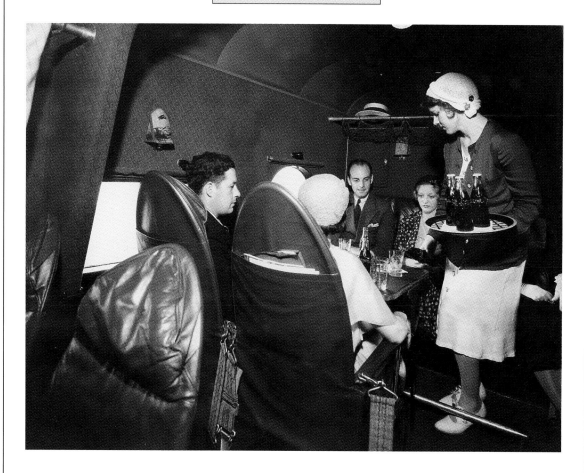

First Class
Because of the high cost of airline tickets in the 1930s, all seats were considered "first class." Above, aboard a Long Island-built Curtiss Condor airliner, passengers enjoy the novelty of dining in the air, circa 1930.

Lear and Hughes
Aviation giants, including William P. Lear, left, and Howard Hughes, center, were drawn to Roosevelt Field in the 1930s and '40s. Lear (1902-1978), who later designed the Learjet, was a pioneer in aircraft communications; between 1930 and 1950, he was granted more than 100 patents for communications equipment.
In 1938, Hughes (1905-1976) still was best known for his air racing.
At right is Sidney Nesbitt, a Lear pilot.

WINGS OF ANGELS
Frank and Lisett de Kapri Steinman operated an air ambulance in the 1940s and '50s from Roosevelt Field. Above, a patient is loaded into the couple's Cessna T-50; Frank Steinman is third from the left. At right, the inside of the T-50 was a mini-emergency room that could treat heart-attack victims or auto-crash casualties. Steinman is at the far left.

FIELD OF DREAMS   *Two views of Curtiss Field, Mineola, in the 1920s. Part of the original Hempstead Plains Aerodrome, in 1917 the field was renamed Hazelhurst Field in honor of Army Lt. Leighton Hazelhurst, who was killed in a flying accident. In 1921, part of the airport became Curtiss Field. Later it was incorporated into Roosevelt Field, which closed in 1951 to make way for a shopping mall of the same name.*

WELCOME HOME, LINDY   *Roosevelt Field was the scene of a tumultuous celebration on June 16, 1927, as thousands joined in a reception for Charles Lindbergh upon his return from Paris after his historic flight aboard The Spirit of St. Louis. Lindbergh embarked upon his epic voyage from Roosevelt Field on May 20, 1927, arriving in Paris 33 hours and 30 minutes later. Lindbergh returned to the United States aboard the USS Memphis on June 11, 1927. By the 1930s, Roosevelt Field, below, was the largest and busiest civil airport in America, and crowds would gather on weekends to watch the colorful aviation activity.*

ISLAND PRIDE

Long Island's World War II soldiers were proud of their roots. At left, a B-25 bomber from the 42nd Bomb Group in New Guinea bears the "nose art" of an unknown Long Island resident. Exactly who the "Long Island Belle" was we probably will never know. Below, soldiers at Roosevelt Field adjourn on Aug. 18, 1943, after a flying demonstration and pep rally from noted pilot Al Williams.

COUNTRY CLUB LIFE
The Long Island Aviation Country Club in Hicksville, right, was an exclusive flying and social club for the wealthiest of aviators in the 1930s and '40s. Aside from social events on their airfield, a variety of excursions also were held, including the one below to Sands Point in 1936. Relaxing on the beach are, from left, Mrs. John Rutherford, Mrs. Robert Love, Betty Gillies, and Mrs. Grover Loening.

THE JET SET
Today, airports are generally viewed as noisy, congested places to be avoided when possible. However in the 1940s and '50s, families often went to airports just to watch the planes take off. Sadly, the observation promenade at LaGuardia Airport, left, circa 1955, no longer exists. Above, the approach to newly opened LaGuardia, circa 1940.

IDLEWILD CONSTRUCTION

This 655-acre "Terminal City" development, started in 1942, eventually would grow into Kennedy Airport. The small cinder-block administration building, center, was the only passenger terminal facility at New York International Airport when it opened in 1948. Commonly known as Idlewild Airport, New York International's name was changed to John F. Kennedy International Airport on Christmas Eve, 1963, to honor the slain president.

HOME OF
THE THUNDERBOLT
Republic Aircraft Corp. and its airfield in Farmingdale played a key role in World War II. Republic built the P-47 Thunderbolt, which entered combat over Europe in May, 1943. By war's end, more than 15,000 were produced, combining for 546,000 sorties. Republic Airport, seen here in 1943, sat along Route 110. It was still in use nearly 60 years later.

George C. Dade came of age at Roosevelt Field.
He finally got off the ground in July, 1929.

Starry Eyes And Flights Of Fancy

BY GEORGE DEWAN

T hanksgiving, 1929, was a cold and windy day at Roosevelt Field, with a threat of snow in the air. Seventeen-year-old George Dade lived with his parents in a converted hangar at the airfield, where he worked after school and on weekends selling tickets for airplane rides and making public address announcements. For the tall, gangly Hempstead High School junior, the airfield was a world of wonders, the sky above a magic kingdom.

The teenager, whose schoolmates called him "Our Lindy," would soon become one of the youngest persons in the country to earn a pilot's license. Before going to bed that Thanksgiving evening, he went through his usual routine of writing down the highlights of the day in his diary.

"Boy, maybe I haven't got a lot to be thankful for," Dade wrote on Nov. 21, four days before his license was issued. "Health, home, happiness and last but not least being able to fly."

If aviation was born at Kitty Hawk, N.C., it was raised and nurtured on the Hempstead Plains. And George C. Dade was one of its handmaidens.

From the time he left Minnesota at age 9 with his family in 1921 and set foot on what was then Curtiss Field to the day he died on May 27, 1998, at age 85, Dade was connected in some way with the world of flying and its pioneers. Yes, he met and mingled with the great ones: Charles Lindbergh, Jimmy Doolittle, Amelia Earhart, Elinor Smith, Igor Sikorsky, Glenn Curtiss, Bert Acosta, to name just a few. But Dade's life was much more than just rubbing elbows with aviation celebrities.

Dade made his own mark, but not as a daredevil flier or an airplane builder. He developed a system that revolutionized the business of crating aircraft for shipping, and in World War II his company packaged more than 33,000 newly built American fighter aircraft for overseas delivery. He also built more than 700 sets of wings for the CG-4A gliders that participated in the Normandy invasion. And later, he was a driving force behind the development of the Cradle of Aviation Museum at Mitchel Field in Garden City.

Every old plane has a story to go with it, and Dade wanted the planes in the museum to not just sit there and look pretty, but to illuminate a piece of history. For instance, there is the first airplane ever owned by Lindbergh, a 1923 Curtiss JN-4 — known as the Jenny — found by Dade badly damaged and deteriorated in an Iowa farmer's barn in 1973. Dade purchased the remains and had them shipped to his home in Glen Head. There, he and more than two dozen other members of the Long Island Early Fliers Club restored the historic plane in his basement.

It's hard to say how life would have turned out for Dade if his parents, Jesse and Eleanor Dade, had not come East, but had stayed in Blackduck, Minn., where young George was born on July 26, 1912. A homesteader, his father was postmaster of the little town at the time.

By 2000, Blackduck was a city with a population of 750, about 65 miles from the Canadian border, with two sawmills and a large drapery manufacturer as the major employers. Incorporated as a village in 1901, it was named for nearby Blackduck Lake. It soon became a rip-roaring, Paul Bunyan frontier town, catering to swarms of lumberjacks, some from as far away as Scandinavia, who moved into northern Minnesota to level huge forests of white and Norway pine for the burgeoning lumber industry. There were soon 1,200 people, 16 hotels, three brothels, 20 saloons and three churches. In 1903, the first play came to town, T.S. Arthur's temperance melodrama, "Ten Nights in a Bar-Room: And What I Saw There." By the time Dade was born, Blackduck had gone dry.

Jesse Dade was also a partner in a lumber mill, and became expert in woodworking. One day he read a newspaper article — either in the local weekly, the Blackduck American, or in a Minneapolis paper — that a man named Glenn Curtiss had opened an experimental aircraft factory in a place called Long Island, outside of New York City. And he was hiring skilled men who could work with Sitka spruce from the Northwest, which has the highest strength-to-weight ratio of any softwood in North America, ideal for building early 20th Century airplanes.

"This seemed like a challenge, and shortly after, dad severed his connection with the lumber mill and the family was on a train headed east to Long Island," Dade wrote in a 1987 memorandum. He took a job with the Curtiss Engineering Corp. on Stewart Avenue in Garden City, and was immediately assigned to the woodworking mill.

Curtiss had purchased the western section of Roosevelt Field, where the shopping center is today, and renamed it Curtiss Field. He had converted a number of World War I buildings at the airfield into housing for his employees. In the fall of 1921, the Dades moved into part of what had been the base hospital. For the first time in his life, George Dade was living smack in the middle of a hotbed of aviation. At one point there were 30 hangars in the area.

"As a 9-year-old exposed to all this aviation activity, my eyes were always bulging and my heart was always throbbing," he once told a reporter.

As the family trudged around the field looking for their new home, Dade saw his first airplane close-up.

"We were walking along this grassy field where Macy's department store stands today, and here

*Dade, left, poses with pilots of the Roosevelt Flying Corp. The plane, a
Fairchild FC-2, was built in Farmingdale at the Fairchild plant around 1927.*

came this flying machine," he said in a book he
wrote with journalist George Vecsey, "Getting Off
the Ground: The Pioneers of Aviation Speak for
Themselves." "It seemed to be bearing down upon
us, tail high, propeller spinning, roaring like a thousand buzz saws. I was sure it was going to slash
right through my whole family, but it rose trium-
phantly from the ground like an awkward bird and
passed over our heads, belching huge clouds of
black smoke. Later on I found out it was Bert Acosta, the bad boy of aviation, an Errol Flynn type,
fond of liquor and women."

The smell of an airfield running at full throttle
was one that Dade never got out of his nostrils.
Never wanted to, in fact. One thing he remembered
until the day he died was the pungent smell of ba-

nana oil lacquer, or dope, applied to tighten and
strengthen airplane fabric.

For a boy about to become a teenager, there was excitement everywhere, and not just in seeing planes
constantly taking off and landing, and sometimes
cracking up. At neighboring Roosevelt Field in 1924,
Encore Pictures made a seven-reel feature film, "The
Sky Raider," full of aviation acrobatics, disaster and
heroism. Over at Hangar 17, the famous aircraft designer Igor Sikorsky tinkered around with new
ideas. On Saturdays, Dade would carry his father's
lunch pail to the Curtiss shop, where planes were
being made for some of the big names in flying,
names such as Al Williams, the stunt flier, and
Jimmy Doolittle.

"In our way, we were joining the brigade of pio-

*Charles Lindbergh, left, was a hero of Dade's in the '20s. Almost 50
years later, Dade, right, restored Lindy's first plane, a Curtiss Jenny.*

neers — the inventors, mechanics, kids off the farm,
veterans from World War One, people willing to risk
their lives to be pilots," he said in "Getting Off the
Ground." "They were flocking to an airfield Glenn
Curtiss had developed on the Hempstead Plains. He
came down to New York City, looking for a flat place,
and when he came to Long Island he must have felt
like Brigham Young when he crossed the last mountain and said, 'This is the place.'"

It was the place for Curtiss, and it was the place
for 9-year-old George Dade. This was Dade's new
home, and it made him forget Blackduck, Minn.
When Bert Acosta came roaring down the field with
his plane belching smoke, Dade fell in love with avi-

ation. He was only a kid, but he wanted to be more
than a spectator. There was plenty of unpaid work
for a starry-eyed youngster to do. His next-door
neighbor in the converted hospital was Jack Whitbeck, division manager for the U.S. Air Mail Service, which began in 1918. (The first official airmail
flight in the United States took place in Garden
City in 1911 when pilot Earle Ovington took off
from nearby Nassau Boulevard Aerodrome and
dropped a bag of 640 letters and 1,280 postcards
over Mineola, 6 miles away.)

At that time, airmail came into Curtiss Field once
a day, about 5 or 6 in the afternoon, so in the winter-
time the airfield was in darkness. Also, there were

no paved fields, and no airfield lights. When Dade and his young friends heard the airmail plane roaring over the field, they raced out and jumped on Whitbeck's old Model T truck, where he kept pots of kerosene. After Whitbeck pointed the truck into the wind, the kids lit the pots and set them out in a line to guide the plane down.

As part of his operation, Curtiss had a school where, for $800, men could learn to assemble planes and fly them. There often would be a couple dozen such students. "There would be wings in one building, tails in another, engines in a third," Dade said in "Getting Off the Ground." "I can remember one building where there must have been one thousand OX-5 engines. These fellows were always looking for someone to help them steady a wing or go locate an eighth strut. If a man had a ripped wing, he'd let me sew it up or paint some dope on it.

"It was a love. You couldn't have a finer, more exciting childhood than I had."

Jesse Dade's job was threatened in the postwar years when Curtiss started laying off workers. So he quit, and he and his brother, Charles, started their own business in Hangar 60, the oldest hangar on the field. Dad Dade, as his son later referred to him, got the idea of building prefabricated garages and small bungalows. In 1924, he moved his family from the converted hospital to a demonstration bungalow he had built inside the hangar.

George Dade haunted the hangars at Curtiss Field. In 1926, when he was 14, he got his first paying job, one that couldn't be done by a grown man. Although he eventually grew to be 6 feet, 4 inches tall, Dade was then still small, and he was hired to crawl into the narrowing inside tail section of plywood amphibious airplanes to apply varnish to keep out the moisture. In that enclosed space, the fumes almost knocked him out a couple of times, but someone was always nearby to rescue him.

The following year, big excitement came to Roosevelt Field. For seven years, no one had been able to win the $25,000 prize put up by New York hotelier Raymond Orteig for the first person to fly nonstop between New York and Paris. In the spring of 1926, three teams had attempted the trip; two had crashed on takeoff and one was lost at sea. On May 20, an obscure airmail pilot named Charles Lindbergh had his Ryan monoplane, the Spirit of St. Louis, rolled out of Hangar 16 at Curtiss Field and

moved to the end of the runway at Roosevelt Field. At 7:54 a.m., Lindbergh's epic flight began.

Dade missed it. He was on his way to school. When Lindbergh landed in Paris and made himself a worldwide sensation, Dade regretted ever going to school that morning. But when Lindbergh returned to Roosevelt Field, Dade helped lay out a big circle of cars to welcome him. From that moment on, Lindbergh was Dade's hero, inspiring him toward a career in aviation.

Before long, Dade moved on to better jobs at Curtiss Field, a place that he loved more than the classrooms at Hempstead High. He soon had the job of operating the public address system. And he also sold tickets for short airplane rides. Here was his typical spiel:

"Only one more seat at $5 now, over Long Beach and return in a large Ford Tri-Motor, folks, it is the sensation of a lifetime." Or:

"There she goes, boys, get your tickets now — the next trip over New York City in the large Ford Tri-Motor. The ship has three engines and two of the country's best-known pilots."

Something was missing, however. Dade himself had never been up in an airplane. Flying was forbidden by his parents because it was too dangerous. Dade didn't disagree that it was dangerous, but he ached to go up anyway. And for almost a year, his secret was that occasionally a pilot would take him up. The first time was May 16, 1928. It was the most important event of the day for him, so he wrote in his diary the initials "W.U." for "Went Up." He repeated the entry a half dozen times before his parents found out.

For the most part, Dade could only stand by and watch while others were learning to fly. One of his good friends was Elinor Smith, a year older than Dade — at age 15 she had become the youngest woman in the world to fly solo. A year later, she had her pilot's license. In April, 1929, Smith took off from Curtiss Field to attempt to break the women's solo endurance record.

From Dade's diary: **April 24, 1929.** *Heard Elinor Smith "buzzing" around all night. It is getting terrible these days, so bad that you can't sleep for these young girls keeping you awake. Anyway she broke the record. Solo endurance for women. Darn nice work I calls it.*

In those heady days, anyone who spent time at

Curtiss Field or the other small local airfields was a witness to the dangers of flying. Photographers for the New York newspapers made a living hanging around the airfields and rushing to take pictures of the latest crash.

Dade had a front-row seat to both the romance as well as the dangers of flying in the 1920s. When he was 14, one of the more spectacular wrecks took place when the French air ace René Fonck, with a crew of three in a Sikorsky S-35 overloaded with gasoline, attempted to take off from adjacent Roosevelt Field. When the biplane ran out of runway, it crashed as it bounded into Curtiss Field and exploded in flames. Two crew members died.

Dade started keeping a diary in 1928 and kept it up for six years, writing down the day's events before going to sleep at night. He once said that he used to keep track of all the pilots who had been killed, but he stopped counting when he got to 100.

July 1, 1929. *This afternoon Bill Stultz was killed. He was flying his tapered wing Waco. With him were two friends of his that were also killed. That makes four crack-ups in the last seven days, and seven fellows killed within a mile of the field.*

"His father was violently opposed," Smith said years later from her home in California. "He told me he had a lot to do with cleaning up after the crack-ups. He saw things that he shouldn't have seen at that age.

"He was caught up in flying in the way everybody was," Smith added. "My family were very supportive. His were not. He wanted very much to fly, and at the same time, he saw a dark side of it I never saw. As much as I grieved over the friends I was losing, I never went over to a cockpit and pulled them out. He did."

Earlier that summer, however, Dade's parents gave in. Perhaps they knew they could hold him back no longer.

June 11, 1929. *Boy! Tonight I consider myself one of the luckiest fellows in the whole United States. Dad has consented to let me fly. I could hardly sleep last night.*

Dade started taking flying lessons on July 9. He soloed 10 days later, and on Nov. 25 Dade was given his pilot's license. Five days earlier, however, he had made the following entry, spelling mistakes and all, in his diary:

November 20, 1929. *Old "Fleet" number 242-H has seen its last ride. It cracked up to-day and the pilot*

was killed. It happened this way.

A fellow by the name of Reid drove out to the field and rented the ship for a little while. He learned to fly some months ago and has a private license. He usually comes out about once a week and does some flying. Today he brought a friend of his with him, a fellow by the name of Baley. They took off about 12 o'clock in the 242-H. They flew in tword the city and when they were over New York the motor konked. Reid told Baily to jump and he did. Baily landed safely a few minutes later. Reid who was still in the ship tried to glide down to Central Park but could not make it and they say he fell into a spin. The ship crashed into some building and he was killed.

With all this in mind I took my final check hop for my private license this afternoon.

Earlier that summer in 1929 Dade had his own brush with danger, but as a passenger, not as a pilot. On June 21, Elinor Smith was flying a Cessna monoplane to Wilkes-Barre, Pa., where she was performing at the opening of a new airport. She invited her friend to go along.

"Looking back now, I can see why my parents were so upset about my wanting to fly," Dade said in his book. "I was only 15 and Ellie only 16. Sure, she was already an excellent pilot, but still, we were just a couple of teenagers. Imagine today, letting a 15-year-old go with a 16-year-old to the Poconos. I don't mean a boy-girl thing, I mean flying."

About 70 miles out of New York City, as they headed into the mountain area, the mist got thicker and the mountaintops closer. Smith decided to set the plane down in the nearest level spot she could find. She chose a farm field that looked fairly level. It wasn't quite what she had hoped for.

Friday, June 21, 1929. *The field looked fairly good so we slipped in and leveled off. The Cessna of course started to float and when she finally did "fall off" it dropped with a bang. There was a row of tall trees ahead so we could not "gun" it and get over them. Just as she hit Elinor kicked a little rudder so as not to dive in and the wheels hit a rut and washed the landing gear completely off. My door opened and I almost fell out. The ship skidded along for a few feet and finally stopped. You'd think the world was at an end for the noise.*

"We were stuck there," Smith said. "Just as we were climbing out, a farmer came running out and said, 'Be very careful. There are snakes there.'

Business boomed for Dade Brothers Inc. during World War II. It packed and shipped aircraft such as these Grumman Avenger TBFs.

George picked me up and leaped over the field. Then we got to the farmer's house. I had to call Kendall Oil, my sponsor. The farmer and his wife got the impression that we were Mr. and Mrs. Lindbergh [Lindbergh had married Anne Morrow in May]. We had the darnedest time convincing them that we weren't."

Any business that had something to do with aviation, Dade was attracted to. For a while in 1930 he worked for a man who owned a huge airplane equipped with loudspeakers that he flew low over heavily populated areas and broadcast advertisements. Strapped into the tail section, Dade would call out: "At your grocer today — a free dish towel for two boxes of Silver Dust — Silver Dust, the housewife's delight." Then they would throw out thousands of paper circulars advertising one product or another.

Then Dade bought his own plane, an Aeronca C-2, from a student at Brown University. A small plane, it weighed only 700 pounds with a top speed of 50 mph. An RKO movie distributor gave him a job plugging films. With his 6-foot-4 frame squeezed into the small airplane, he'd fly low along the beaches and, with a megaphone, announce something like, "Now playing at your local theater: 'Dixieland,' from RKO."

This venture ended quickly in September, 1930, when Dade cracked up the little plane while making a forced landing in a field near Noank, Conn. To soften the blow, he aimed to hit a haystack in the middle of the field, but found that the hay was covering up a large pile of rocks. The plane was a mess, but the crack-up led him into a business that would become hugely profitable during World War II. Dade's younger brother, Bob, drove up with one of their father's old trucks and hauled the wreck back home. The brothers did such a good job of getting the plane back with no further damage that the Dade brothers — later incorporated as Dade Brothers Inc., a general contracting firm located on a 10-acre site at the northwest corner of Glen Cove and Old Country Roads in Carle Place — started getting requests from fliers to pick up their wrecked planes. Packing a wrecked plane — or a disassembled new plane, for that matter — for transport was a tricky business, since the long-distance haul could cause as much damage as the crash. Large parts of the wings and fuselage, if tied up tightly, could not withstand the bumps and twists of travel.

Dade designed what he called a biaxial support system, in which those parts of a plane that are designed to take a pounding — the landing gear and the tail wheels — would be the only parts of the boxed plane that would take any stress while being shipped. By the mid-'30s, Dade Brothers was licensed by the Interstate Commerce Commission to carry wrecks in 17 states. "Sometimes if you made the mistake of getting to a wreck too fast, you had to cut the bodies out yourself."

But all this happened over a period of years, as the Depression deepened into the mid-'30s. Dade graduated from Hempstead High School in 1931, and went on to the School of Commerce at New York University, from which he graduated in 1935. In his senior year he was student council president, and he flew his own plane to a conference in Boston, where the hotshot flier mightily impressed Edith Gorman, a student representative from Winthrop College in Rock Hill, S.C. They were married 11 months later, which Dade later said was "the nicest thing aviation ever did for me."

Packaging wrecked planes and shipping them back to their home airfields was merely a warm-up for what Dade was about to get into. In May, 1937, famous stunt pilot Al Williams had Dade Brothers move his Grumman-made Gulfhawk II biplane to the Lakehurst Naval Air Station in New Jersey to await the arrival of the Hindenburg dirigible, which was to carry Williams' plane on its return trip to an air show in Europe. But in one of the 20th Century's most famous accidents, the hydrogen-filled Hindenburg burst into flames on arrival, leaving the Gulfhawk II stranded.

The liner Queen Mary was leaving New York the next day, however, and Dade Brothers was called to the rescue. Dade and his men packaged the plane and got it to the liner on time, making a name for themselves in the process. By word of mouth, the shipping orders came in. Even before the beginning of World War II, Dade Brothers was shipping planes to France, South America, Iceland, Finland and Sweden. One of those planes was Brewster Aeronautical Corp.'s F-2A Buffalo, manufactured in Long Island City for the Finnish Air Force.

When the war began, Dade Brothers went into high gear. They contracted with major airplane manufacturers, Seversky, Grumman, Douglas, Lockheed, and shipped their planes overseas by the hundreds. Dade Brothers had plants all over the country.

In late spring of 1944, the British Navy invited Dade to England to view firsthand the end result of his packaging skills. "My biggest thrill came the day before D-Day," he later told the Mineola-Garden City Rotary Club. "I saw wave after wave of British bombers passing overhead on their way to the continent. They started about midnight and continued for several hours. The next day, American bombers were seen in the air in what looked like a never-ending stream. At any moment one could have counted literally hundreds of bombers in the air, and these were accompanied by fighter escort." Many of those fighters had arrived in England packaged in large wooden boxes with the large Dade Brothers logo stenciled on the side: a box with wings.

By the end of the war, Dade Brothers reported sales of more than $50 million for its packaging of thousands of planes for overseas shipping. These included Grumman's F-4F Wildcat, Republic's P-47 Thunderbolt, as well as planes from Brewster in Long Island City and Bell Aircraft in Buffalo. In 1945, at age 33, Dade was named one of the U.S. Junior Chamber of Commerce's "Ten Outstanding Young Businessmen of the Year."

As Dade later said, it all started with the wreck of his little Aeronca in a rocky haystack in Connecticut.

For a number of years after the war, Dade had his hand in a number of businesses, including Dade Trucking Inc. and Dade Associates Inc., a business and financial consulting firm formed with some high-powered Nassau County Republicans. But from his office across the street he could see that major changes were coming to Roosevelt Field. He could see that the "cradle of aviation" — an expression coined by Sperry Gyroscope Co. president Preston Bassett in a 1950 book — was about to be grounded.

What Dade could see was that a piece of Long Island's history that he loved was about to be lost. Housing developments were sprouting up all over the Hempstead Plains, and real estate magnate William Zeckendorf was planning to turn the old airfield into a shopping center.

Dade pleaded with them to save Hanger 60 — the oldest hanger on the field, where he used to live — and use it for a museum. Instead, they tore it down, paved it over and made a parking lot.

If there was a point in time that the idea for the Cradle of Aviation Museum was born, that was it.

Dade wanted an air museum that would preserve Long Island's aviation history, and some time later he joined an organization that had the same mission, the Long Island Early Fliers Club. Formed in the late '50s by men and women who had worked in aviation on Long Island, the group originally raised money to buy 25 acres across from what is now Francis Gabreski Airport in Westhampton Beach. The group envisioned building an aviation museum on the property, but the idea never got off the ground, so to speak.

When he became president of the Early Fliers Club in 1973, Dade got a brilliant idea. What if, he speculated with his flier friends, what if the club presented Nassau County with a restored antique airplane. Wouldn't the county then build a museum to house it? The museum emphasis quickly shifted to the old Mitchel Field, where, unlike Roosevelt Field, old hangars still existed.

Then Dade got himself involved in the most publicized airplane restoration event in anyone's memory

on Long Island. Frank Strnad, an Early Flier and an aviation historian who published an aviation history photo book with Dade, located Lindbergh's first Jenny. It was owned by Ernest LeClere, a farmer in Coggin, Iowa, who had bought it as a wreck, missing its engine, in 1927. LeClere, a Jenny flier himself, used some parts for spares and stored the remains in a barn loft until 1973 when Dade bought it from him for an undisclosed sum. When he first saw it, it was quite a mess.

"It was covered with dirt and there had been chickens or doves roosting up there in the pig barn," Dade later told Newsday. "The smell was terrible. You'd touch anything and the dust would fly." The fabric from the wings had been eaten by cows. The fuselage had been taken and turned into a sleigh, and the engine had long since been removed.

The old Jenny, or what remained of it, was shipped

Dade, seen here shortly before his death in 1998, made his basement into an aviation museum of sorts, and filled it with photos and model planes.

to Dade's Glen Head home, whose basement soon would be renamed "The Jenny Works." For the next three years, with Dade supervising, about two dozen Early Fliers, working one night a week, completely restored Lindbergh's plane, which he had purchased for $500 in Americus, Ga., in the spring of 1923. Dade had to rework the entrance to his basement and garage to accommodate the fuselage and wings.

As the Jenny neared completion, someone asked Dade if he was tempted to fly it. His head told him that his pilot's license had long since expired, and that the Federal Aviation Administration would require rigid tests. Then his heart took over.

"But the more I thought about it," he said in "Getting Off the Ground," "I had this insane dream of putting on my aviator goggles and the World War One scarf and the leather coat, and sneaking the plane to a secret grassy field, and just gunning it for the sky. To fly above Long Island in Lindbergh's plane. I thought about it for about 30 seconds before reality hit me. If somebody tried to take it up, he might destroy the plane, and himself, and all the work we had put into it. Jenny will never fly again."

In 1973, Lindbergh traveled to Glen Head to see the remains of his old Jenny, and he later sent Dade a letter putting his seal of approval on its authenticity. Then, in 1977, President-elect Jimmy Carter asked to have the restored Jenny appear on a float in his inaugural parade, since Americus, Ga., is only 10 miles from his own hometown of Plains.

Although the Cradle of Aviation Museum has taken years to get to a point where it can actually open, Dade was appointed its first director in the late '70s, for a salary of a dollar a year. And he once wrote down what he considered one of its most important policies: "If and when the aircraft museum is a reality, it will not be just another collection of aircraft hardware — it must tell a story."

One of Dade's favorite stories — and favorite airplanes — involved a tattered 1929 Kinner Fleet biplane trainer that he had located in 1986 gathering dust and cobwebs in an upstate farmer's barn south of Albany. It bore the license number NC 614-M. It was only after he returned home and looked at his old diary that Dade realized that the biplane was one of a dozen Fleets owned by the Roosevelt Aviation School at the airfield. More important, it was the same plane in which he had done his first loops in 1930, the year after he got his flying license.

Before going to bed that Sunday evening when he was 18 and flying was new and the world was good, Dade got out his diary.

August 31, 1930. *I took off and flew her up to 4,500 feet. At first I was kind of timid, but then I thought I'd try some steep dives and climbs anyway. I stuck the stick forward — and — down we went. When the ship was doing about 125 M.P.H. I pulled back gently — up — she came. When I got in a position where I was perpendicular to the earth, I decided the heck with it, I was going to make a stab at it anyway. I yanked the stick back — and — before I knew it I was on my back — and I'm telling you it is some sensation. I wasn't scared, yet I had a queer feeling. I looked up over the top wing — and darned if I didn't see the ground — it was upside down. Well that was the first time I ever saw that — maybe because I've never been drunk. I cut the "gun" and the ship came out in a dive. I levelled off and went over for a second one. All in all I did six consecutive loops before I finished. I decided I might as well learn how while I was up there.*

Looking at the diary entry 56 years later gave Dade shivers of pleasure; it was like meeting a long-lost friend. "The first airplanes that you fly, you kind of get an affection for them that is hard to describe," he told a reporter. "I just loved that little Fleet."

The story of Long Island as the cradle of aviation was Dade's passion for the last quarter-century of his life. He was part of that story.

In March, 1998, two months before he died, Dade was present at a gathering of high school students with three astronauts who spent their childhoods on Long Island. The occasion was the launch of Newsday's History in Motion traveling museum. The leader of the astronauts was Cmdr. Kevin Kregel of Amityville, who talked about the excitement of viewing his hometown from 170 miles above the surface of the Earth.

Facing Kregel in the front row that day, hanging on to every word, was the 85-year-old George Dade. When the talks had finished, Dade, stooped and ill, asked if he could be introduced to the astronauts. He rose and approached Kregel, who immediately held out his hand.

"You helped pave the way for me," Kregel said.

Dade smiled and appeared to blink back tears. ●

Dade shows off an early map of Roosevelt Field in his "Planes of Fame" collection at home in Glen Head in early 1998. He may not have been a daredevil flier or designer of aircraft, but the boy from Blackduck, Minn., made his own mark on aviation. His company packaged more than 30,000 American fighters for overseas delivery. And later in life, he was the driving force behind the Cradle of Aviation Museum in Garden City.

George C. Dade was a link between Lucky Lindy and the Space Age. Seen here two months before his death at 85 in 1998, Dade chats with NASA astronaut and Amityville native Cmdr. Kevin Kregel. "You helped pave the way for me," Kregel told him.

Long Island's Space Travelers

N ine NASA astronauts spent their formative years stargazing from Long Island's shores.

Ellen S. Baker. Born on April 27, 1953 in Fayetteville, N.C. but raised in Queens. Daughter of Queens Borough President Claire Shulman. A graduate of Bayside High School, she received a bachelor of arts degree in geology from the State University at Buffalo, a doctorate of medicine from Cornell University and a master's in public health from the University of Texas. Joined NASA in 1981 as a medical officer at the Lyndon B. Johnson Space Center. Became an astronaut in 1985, logging more than 686 hours in space on three flights. She flew on the STS-71 Atlantis in 1995, the first shuttle to dock with the Russian space station Mir and exchange crew.

Fernando (Frank) Caldeiro. Born June 12, 1958 in Buenos Aires, Argentina. Graduated from W.C. Bryant High School in Long Island City. Received an associate's degree in applied science in aerospace technology from the State University at Farmingdale, a bachelor of science degree in mechanical engineering from the University of Arizona and a master of science degree in engineering management from the University of Central Florida. Hired by NASA Kennedy Space Center in 1991 as a cryogenics and propulsion systems expert for the safety and mission assurance office. Selected as an astronaut candidate in 1996, he is a mission specialist working on life support systems. Assigned to the Operations Planning Branch.

Charles J. Camarda. Born May 8, 1952, in Queens. Graduated from Archbishop Molloy High School in Jamaica. Received a bachelor of science degree in aerospace engineering from Polytechnic Institute of Brooklyn, a master of science degree in engineering science from George Washington University, and a doctorate in aerospace engineering from Virginia Polytechnic Institute and State University. Selected as an astronaut candidate by NASA in 1996. Qualified for flight assignment as a mission specialist. Asssigned to the Astronaut Office Spacecraft Systems Operations Branch.

Mary Louise Cleave. Born Feb. 5, 1947 in Southampton. Grew up in Great Neck, where she attended Great Neck North High School. Received a bachelor of science degree in biological sciences from Colorado State University. Earned a master of science degree in microbial ecology, and a doctorate in civil and environmental engineering from Utah State. Mission specialist on two space flights. First mission included two space walks and deployment of three communications satellites. Second mission aboard the orbiter Atlantis in 1989. Crew members successfully deployed the Magellan Venus exploration spacecraft, the first U.S. planetary science mission launched since 1978. Magellan arrived at Venus in mid-1990 to map its entire surface. Retired from NASA in May, 1991.

Robert L. (Hoot) Gibson. Born Oct. 30, 1946, in Cooperstown, N. Y. Lived for several years on Long Island, graduating from Huntington High School. Received an associate's degree in engineering science from Suffolk County Community College and a bachelor of science degree in aeronautical engineering from California Polytechnic State University. Made his first solo flight over Long Island at 16 and earned his pilot's license at 17. Became a Navy pilot and was selected by NASA in 1978. Flew five missions. On his last mission, in 1995, Gibson commanded the crew of the first space shuttle mission to dock with the Russian space station Mir to exchange crews. Chief of the Astronaut Office from October, 1993, to September, 1994, he participated in the investigation of the space shuttle Challenger accident. Retired from NASA in November, 1996, currently a pilot with Southwest Airlines.

Kevin R. Kregel. Born Sept. 16, 1956, grew up in Amityville. Graduate of Amityville Memorial High School, where he played varsity baseball and soccer. Received a bachelor of science degree in astronautical engineering from the U.S. Air Force Academy and a master's degree in public administration from Troy State University in 1988. A Navy pilot before joining NASA as an aerospace engineer and instructor pilot. Kregel has been on four space flights and has logged more than 52 days in space. Served as spacecraft commander on third mission, which focused on experiments studying the affect the weightless environment of space has on physical processes. Also served as spacecraft commander on fourth mission, an 11-day mission that orbited the earth 181 times and covered 4 million miles in 268 hours and 38 minutes. Forty seven million miles of the earth's land surface was mapped.

Michael J. Massimino. Born Aug. 19, 1962, in Oceanside and grew up in Franklin Square. Graduate of H. Frank Carey High School in Franklin Square. Received a bachelor of science degree in industrial engineering from Columbia University in 1984 and master of science degrees in mechanical engineering and in technology and policy from the Massachusetts Institute of Technology, where he also earned a doctorate in mechanical engineering. Selected as an astronaut candidate by NASA in 1996 and qualified for flight assignment as a mission specialist. Was assigned to the Astronaut Office Robotics Branch.

William M. Shepherd. Born July 26, 1949, in Tennessee, but considers Babylon his hometown. A graduate of Arcadia High School in Scottsdale, Ariz., he received a bachelor of science degree in aerospace engineering from the U.S. Naval Academy, and the degrees of ocean engineer and master of science in mechanical engineering from the Massachusetts Institute of Technology in 1978. Served with the Navy Seals. Joined NASA in 1984 and served as a mission specialist aboard three space flights, logging 440 hours. Received training in Russia and was scheduled to be on a three-person crew headed for the International Space Station in 2000.

James D. Wetherbee. Born Nov. 27, 1952, in Flushing and grew up in Huntington Station. Graduated from Holy Family Diocesan High School in South Huntington. Bachelor of science degree in aerospace engineering from the University of Notre Dame in 1974. A Navy pilot, he became an astronaut in 1985, logging more than 955 hours on four space flights. Was the mission commander of STS-63 Discovery (1995), the first joint flight of the Russian-American space program. Mission commander for STS-86 Atlantis (1997), the seventh mission to meet and dock with Mir. This mission delivered a control computer, exchanged U.S. crew members, and executed a spacewalk to retrieve experiments previously deployed on Mir. Later was named deputy director of the Johnson Space Center in Houston.

— **Georgina Martorella**

Higher, Faster, Farther

Moments That Shaped Long Island Aviation

1833

June 15. Charles F. Durant, in one of many balloon ascents from Castle Garden at the southern tip of Manhattan, flew over Brooklyn and landed at the Union Course racetrack at Jamaica. This was the introduction of aeronautics to Long Island.

1874

July 21. Washington H. Donaldson, in the Hippodrome balloon, flew from New York City and landed at Lynbrook. From Lynbrook he flew to Hempstead, the first point-to-point flight on Long Island. Later that day, Donaldson made a moonlight ascent of short duration, landing on the Hempstead Plains, four miles west of the village of Hempstead.

1896

In 1896. The first documented flight of a winged aircraft on Long Island occurred when William Randolph Hearst, hoping to create headlines for his New York Journal, purchased a German Lilienthal glider. It was flown several times on a friend's Long Island estate, possibly at Sands Point, by Harry Bodine. This oldest surviving aircraft was put on display at the National Air and Space Museum in Washington.

1909

In June. Under commission from the Aeronautic Society of New York, headquartered at the Morris Park racetrack in the Bronx, Glenn Curtis built and test-flew his Golden Flyer. This was the first commercial sale of an aircraft in the United States. In search of a better airfield, Curtiss and others came to Long Island's Hempstead Plains, where a "nice flat place" east of Mineola was chosen.

July 17. Glenn Curtiss in his Golden Flyer circled the Mineola airfield at tree-top height for about a half hour and qualified for the Scientific American's prize of $10,000, for the first flight of 25 kilometers. (He covered just over 25 *miles*.)

Aug. 13. Charles F. Willard made the first "extensive" cross-country flight, 12 miles from Mineola to Garden City, to Westbury, to Hicksville, where he made a safe forced landing.

Sept. 25. In a Wright biplane, Wilbur Wright took off from Garden City, circled the Statue of Liberty and returned to his take-off field.

Oct. 4. In a Wright Flyer, Wilbur Wright made a round trip from Garden City to Grant's Tomb, Manhattan.

Dec. 9. Henry Walden flew the first monoplane built in the United States at the Washington Avenue field in Garden City.

1910

Aug. 20. Clifford B. Harmon made the first airplane flight across Long Island Sound. He took off from Mineola and landed at Greenwich, Conn. Harmon received the Country Life in America trophy for this achievement.

Sept. 26. At the Hempstead Plains, Bessica Raiche became the first American woman to pilot an airplane. (Although Blanche Stuart Scott flew in an airplane on Sept. 2, circumstances of her flight were ruled questionable. See Page 16.)

Oct. 22-31. The largest aeronautical event held was the International Aviation Tournament at Belmont Park racetrack. England, France and the United States sent contestants. Glenn Curtiss, Orville and Wilbur Wright were present but did not compete. Each day, cash prizes were awarded for events such as highest altitude, greatest distance, longest time aloft and fastest speed. On the last day of the meet, in an aircraft in which he had never flown nicknamed the Baby Wright Roadster, Ralph Johnstone set a world altitude record by climbing to 9,714 feet. Strong winds pushed him from Belmont Park to Middle Island.

1911

In March and April. Moisant Flying School, the nation's first civilian flying school, opened on the Hempstead Plains at Mineola.

Aug. 2. Harriet Quimby earned the first license issued to a woman (No. 37), at the Moisant Flying School, Mineola.

Summer. The American Aeroplane Supply House, the first aircraft manufacturing company on Long Island, opened for business at 266 Main St., Hempstead. This firm, under license, built and sold six Blériot monoplanes.

Sept. 17. Calbraith Rodgers, in a Wright Model B type biplane named the Vin Fiz Flyer (after his soft drink company sponsor), attempted a coast-to-coast flight for the William Randolph Hearst prize of $50,000. To be eligible, this flight had to be completed within 30 days. Rodgers took off from Sheepshead Bay. His flight was accompanied by a three-car private train which carried his mother and wife, mechanics and $4,000 in spare parts. Sixty-five forced landings and 49 days later, he arrived at Pasadena, Calif., on Nov. 5. His plane had been repaired so often, only the rudder and one strut of the original remained. Even though he exceeded the time limit, Rodgers continued the flight knowing he would not be awarded the prize.

Sept. 23. At an international air meet, Earle Ovington in a Blériot monoplane, made the first U.S. airmail flight, flying from Nassau Boulevard Aerodrome to Mineola. Ovington carried 640 letters and 1,280 postcards.

1912

July 1. Harriet Quimby died when her airplane crashed into Dorchester Bay, Mass., at an aviation meet.

1914

In 1914. At Bezons, France, the French government awarded 50,000 francs to Long Island inventors Elmer A. Sperry and son Lawrence Sperry for developing a gyro-stabilizer (automatic pilot).

1915

In December. Organized by Edward Lowe Jr., Charles Willard and Robert Fowler, the L.W.F. Co. was created in Long Island City to build aircraft with wooden fuselages.

Most events cited on Pages 199-207 are reprinted with permission from "The Development of the Aerospace Industry on Long Island," by Raymond V. DiScala, edited by William K. Kaiser, and published in 1968 by Hofstra University in Hempstead, N.Y. Others are based on Newsday research.

In 1915. The New York National Guard became the first flying guard unit in the country, training at the Hempstead Plains Airfield.

1916

April 11. In a Sloane-Day biplane, with 120-hp. Hall-Scott engine, Lloyd Thompson established a new altitude record of 13,950 feet over Garden City.

June 1. The Wright Co. announced that it had acquired acreage on the Hempstead Plains for an aviation center.

Sept. 2. Lawrence Sperry, in a Sperry Messenger, flew 50 miles from Moriches to Amityville at night.

Sept. 12. Guided missile equipment — an amphibious airplane equipped with automatic stabilization and direction gear developed by the Sperry Co. and P.C. Hewitt — was demonstrated at Amityville. Still in experimental stages, the equipment was flown by a pilot for the demonstration.

1917

May 3. Under provisions of the National Defense Act, the Army's First Reserve Aero Squadron was formed at Mineola. The field's name was changed to Hazelhurst Field, in honor of Lt. Leighton W. Hazelhurst, a deceased Army flier.

June 14. Naval air patrol stations were created at Montauk, Rockaway and Bay Shore.

Aug. 14. The Navy began experimenting with launching torpedoes from aircraft. At Huntington Bay, a dummy torpedo was launched from a seaplane, but struck the water at an angle and ricocheted, nearly striking the plane.

In August. Glenn Curtiss established a new factory at Garden City. One of several "Curtiss companies," the firm was known as the Curtiss Aeroplane and Motor Corp.

Oct. 18. Caleb S. Bragg established a new altitude record of 21,500 feet at Mineola Field.

1918

Jan. 1. The First U.S. Marine Corps aviation squadron was transferred from Hazelhurst Field to Lake Charles, La., because of the severe winter flying conditions on Long Island.

March 6. An unmanned "flying bomb" was successfully launched and flown for 1,000 yards at the Sperry Flying Field, Copiague. The launching device was a falling weight catapult.

May 15. The Post Office Department's first airplanes, four Curtiss JN4H Jennies, were test-flown at Belmont Park. At Belmont Park and Washington, D.C., with Army pilots and planes, the first New York-to-Washington and Washington-to-New York air deliveries (with stops in Philadelphia) were inaugurated. This was the first regularly scheduled U.S. airmail flight. From Washington, the "first" flight, piloted by Lt. George Boyle in a Curtiss JN-4, became lost and snapped a propeller in a forced landing in a Maryland cornfield.

July 16. The Army dedicated a large plot south of Roosevelt Field as Mitchel Field in honor of John Purroy Mitchel, an Army pilot and ex-New York mayor who died in a plane crash.

Aug. 6. The Post Office Department assumed control of airmail from the Army, which had supplied pilots and planes.

Sept. 24. Hazelhurst Field was renamed Roosevelt Field in honor of Theodore Roosevelt's son, Lt. Quentin Roosevelt, an Army aviatior who was shot down and killed in France on July 14, 1918.

Nov. 25. The Curtiss NC-1 set passenger-carrying records by taking 50 men on a test flight. Actually, 51 men were aboard for a count after landing revealed that a machinist mate had stowed away. The flight lasted less than a minute.

In 1918. Off Port Washington and in the Great South Bay off Amityville, Lawrence Sperry tested the first "guided missiles," then called aerial torpedoes. These were unmanned aircraft, usually launched from a catapult-track.

Also, the Curtiss Aircraft Co. opened a factory in Garden City for the aircraft research and development, the first factory of its kind in the country. By the end of World War I, it had 3,000 employees.

1919

March 7. Maj. Reuben F. Fleet and Capt. Earl F. White set a record for long-distance flight in the United States by flying from Dayton, Ohio, to Roosevelt Field. They flew the 664 miles in 4 hours and 33 minutes.

May 3. The first passenger air service in the United States began as two women were carried in a Flying Boat from Long Island to Atlantic City and back by Pilot Robert Hewitt.

May 8. Three Curtiss-built, Garden City-assembled, flying boats — the NC-1, NC-3 and NC-4 — took off from Rockaway for Chatham and Cape Cod, Mass, and then Trepassey Bay, Newfoundland, the first leg of a transatlantic flight. All reached Newfoundland safely, but the NC-4 was the only one (after stops at Horta in the Azores, and Lisbon, Portugal) that reached the final destination, Plymouth, England, on May 31.

May 14. The Navy nonrigid airship C-5, Lt. Commander E.W. Coil, pilot, made a record flight from Montauk Point to St. Johns Newfoundland, covering 1,050 nautical miles in 2 hours and 50 minutes. (The C-5 blew out to sea while at St. Johns when no one was aboard.)

July 6. In the first east-to-west transatlantic crossing by air, the British dirigible R-34 landed at Roosevelt Field 108 hours and 12 minutes after leaving East Fortune, Scotland.

July 9. The R-34 took off from Roosevelt Field and landed at Pulham, England, after a flight of 75 hours, 3 minutes, completing the first transatlantic round trip flight.

July 27. From Port Washington, Maj. S.E. Parker and Capt. G.T. Wilcox, in a Curtiss Seagull, began the longest commercial flight to date. Carrying paying passengers, they flew up the Hudson River to the St. Lawrence River to the Great Lakes, then down the Mississippi River to New Orleans, to Tampa, Fla. They arrived Feb. 12, 1920.

Oct. 8-19. Sponsored by the American Flying Club, the first U.S. Trans-Continental Air Race was held. Forty-eight planes left Roosevelt Field on the 5,400-mile race — from Roosevelt Field to San Francisco, and back. Lt. Belvin W. Maynard, in a four-engine DeHavilland, won. Maynard's times: westward, 3 days, 6 hours, 4 minutes; eastward, 3 days, 21 hours, 31 minutes. (Winner was chosen on basis of elapsed time. Three other participants bettered Maynard's flying time.)

Dec. 3. The first Army Aeroplane Coast Patrol began when two airplanes left Mitchel Field en route to Langley Field, Va.

1920

April 20. Roland Rholfs, flying a Curtiss Wasp equipped with floats, set a seaplane speed record of 138 mph at the Naval Air Station, Rockaway Beach.

May 7. The first U.S. Intercollegiate Air Meet, with 11 U.S. universities participating, was held at Mitchel Field.

June 12. Col. W.K. Wilson defeated Col. W.E. Gilmore in an air race from Washington, D.C., to Central Park in Bethpage, 248 miles. Each flew all-metal Junkers-Larsen monoplanes. Winning time was 2 hours, 25 minutes.

July 16. The Curtiss Aeroplane and Motor Corp. purchased a part of the old Hazelhurst airfield.

Aug. 8. Two Junkers-Larsen monoplanes, which took off from Central Park in Bethpage, arrived in San Francisco carrying the first coast-to-coast airmail.

Sept. 18. William C. Hopson, a Post Office pilot, set a speed record of 3 hours, 1 minute, from Cleveland to Roosevelt Field, Mineola. He piloted a DeHavilland 4 over the 425 miles. By Dec. 3, the record would be down to 2 hours, 48 minutes.

Oct. 6. Paul Collins demonstrated a system of fire-proof illumination consisting of torches and reflecting mirrors. This feat, performed at Roosevelt Field, made night landings safer.

In November. Army pilot Corliss Mosely won the first Pulitzer trophy race at Mitchel Field. Mosely covered a 29.02-mile tri-angular course four times at 156.6 mph in a Verville-Packard. Thirty-seven planes began the race and 25 finished. Second place went to Harold Hartney and third to Bert Acosta.

1921

July 9. What were said to be the world's largest and the smallest airplanes were successfully tested over Curtiss Field. The Baby Vamp, piloted by Bert Acosta, was a biplane that weighed 350 pounds and had a wing span of 18 feet. The Giant Hippo was a 30-passenger airliner that weighed 8,600 pounds and had a 74-foot wing span.

Aug. 16. At Port Washington, a Loening-made monoplane, the Flying Yacht, set an altitude record for hydro airplanes of 19,500 feet. It carried four passengers.

Nov. 22. Bert Acosta, in a Curtiss-Navy racer, attained a speed of 197.8 mph at Curtiss Field.

Dec. 10-14. Clifford L. Webster, with mechanic Horace Wilson in a Curtiss Seagulls flying boat, set a distance record. They flew from Port Washington to Palm Beach, Fla. (1,257 miles) in 21 hours, 32 minutes.

In 1921. The Lawrence Sperry Aircraft Co. at Farmingdale built six Sperry M-1 Messengers for the Army. This small bi-plane, with a 20-foot wingspan, was made to carry dispatches. Gen. William Mitchell, chief of the Air Service, called this plane "the motorcycle of the air." Sperry used one to commute from his Hempstead home to his plant in Farmingdale.

1922

March 22. Lawrence Sperry landed his 500-pound Sperry Mes-senger on the steps of the Capitol in Washington, D.C.

May 15. New York City's first aerial lighthouse was installed at the American Airways Seaplane Base, College Point.

Aug. 27. The L.W.F. Owl, a biplane with three 400-hp. Liberty engines, the largest bomber ever constructed in the United States, was tested at Mineola. This aircraft was designed for night flying, hence the name. Only one model was built and it was purchased by the Army for test purposes.

Sept. 3. Bessie Coleman, the first licensed black pilot in the world, performed takeoffs and sweeps in a Curtiss JN-4 for a crowd of thousands at an air show at Curtiss Field. It was her first flight over American soil since she returned from Europe, where she learned to fly. Aviation schools in the United States, inhospitable to blacks and women, had rejected her.

Oct. 2. Lt. Russell Maughan piloted an Army Curtiss racer bi-plane, powered by a 375-hp. Curtiss D-12 engine, to set a world record of 220 mph at Curtiss Field.

1923

May 2-3. Army Lts. John A. Macready and Oakley Kelly, in a Fokker T-2 monoplane, flew from Roosevelt Field to San Diego, 2,516 miles, in 26 hours and 50 minutes. This was the first nonstop transcontinental flight.

Oct. 12. T. Schleuming won the first parachute jumping con-test ever held when four contestants jumped from 4,500 feet at Mitchel Field.

Nov. 2. Lt. Harold J. Brow flew an RC-1 airplane, with a Curtiss D-12 engine, to a world record of 259.47 mph over the three-kilo-meter course at Mitchel Field. On Nov. 4, A.J. Williams, in an R2C-1 with a D-12 engine, improved the record to 266.59 mph, also at Mitchel Field.

Dec. 13. Lawrence Sperry drowned when his Messenger plane went down in the English Channel during a flight from En-gland to Holland.

1924

Feb. 16. From Mitchel Field, two squadrons of Army planes flew to Brookville and dropped flowers over the grave of Lawrence Sperry during funeral services.

March 1. The first instrument flight was made from McCook Field, Ohio, to Mitchel Field, 575 miles.

May 11. A twin-engine cabin model, the Sikorsky S-29, de-signed to carry 14 passengers, crashed on a test flight at Roosevelt Field. The very same airplane was rebuilt and used (and destroyed) as a German bomber in the 1930 film classic "Hell's Angels."

June 23. Lt. Russell Maughan, piloting an Army Curtiss PW-8, took off from Mitchel Field to "race the sun" across the conti-nent. Maughan landed in San Francisco after flying 21 hours and 44 minutes. It was the first transcontinental flight within 24 hours.

July 1. The first scheduled transcontinental airmail service was inaugurated. The route, from Roosevelt Field to San Francisco, was via Chicago, Omaha and Salt Lake City.

In 1924. At Mitchel Field, Army officers devised a method of broadcasting from aircraft. Broadcasts from 4,000 feet, under favorable conditions, would carry 200 miles.

1925

March 4. The first of 10 Curtiss Carrier Pigeons, built specifical-ly for airmail delivery with a Liberty 12 400-hp. engine, was tested by Charles S. (Casey) Jones at Garden City. The landing gear collapsed and the engine overheated.

1926

March 27. In preparation for his proposed flight over the North Pole, Lt. Commander Richard E. Byrd, on a test of his new three-engine Fokker monoplane, took off from Curtiss Field and landed at Mitchel Field next door.

May 10. At Roosevelt Field, 15-year-old Elinor Smith of Free-port had her first solo flight.

Sept. 21. In an effort to capture the $25,000 Orteig Prize for the first aircraft to fly from New York to Paris, Capt. René Fonck, a French aviator, piloting an S-35 Sikorsky, tri-engine biplane, crashed on take-off from Roosevelt Field. Two crew members, Jacob Islamoff and Charles Clavier, burned to death. Fonck and his navigator, Navy Lt. Lawrence Curtin, were uninjured.

In 1926. R.J. Reynolds, tobacco heir, formed the Ireland Amphibian Co. of Mineola and Reynolds Airways Inc. He also owned Curtiss Field until 1929.

Also, Fairchild Aviation Corp. built the FC-1A as a picture-tak-ing aircraft.

1927

April 12-14. To test the endurance of the Wright-powered Bellan-ca monoplane Miss Columbia, Clarence Chamberlin and Bert Acosta, in preparation for a transatlantic flight, took off from Roosevelt Field and for 51 hours and 11 minutes flew back and forth the length of Long Island. This flight established a world endurance record.

April 20. Anthony Fokker, with explorer Richard E. Byrd, Floyd Bennett and Lt. George O. Noville, in a test flight of the three-engine Fokker America, made a crash, nose-over landing at Roosevelt Field. Floyd Bennett, with a broken leg and inter-nal injuries, was the most seriously hurt. He was forced to leave the crew.

May 20. At 7:52 a.m., Charles A. Lindbergh took off from Roosevelt Field in the Spirit of St. Louis. After 33 hours and 30 minutes, he landed at Le Bourget Field, Paris. This was the first successful, nonstop, solo transatlantic flight.

June 4. Clarence Chamberlin and passenger Charles Levine took off from Roosevelt Field in the Miss Columbia. After 42 hours and 45 minutes, they landed at Eisleben, near Berlin, Germany, setting a world distance record of 3,911 miles.

June 29. Richard E. Byrd, Lt. George O. Noville, Bert Acosta and Bernt Balchen took off from Roosevelt Field in the Ameri-ca. They reached Paris, which was covered with fog, and land-ed just off the beach at Ver-sur-Mer, France.

July 19. Charles A. Lindbergh, in the Spirit of St. Louis, took off from Mitchel Field on a Guggenheim Fund-sponsored tour of the United States. He returned to Mitchel Field after completing a tour of 48 states and 82 cities on Oct. 23.

Oct. 11. Ruth Elder and George Haldeman took off from Roosevelt Field in the American Girl, a Stinson monoplane with a Wright 220-hp. engine, on a New York-to-Paris attempt. The plane was forced down at sea 325 miles northeast of the Azores. The crew was rescued by the S.S. Barendrecht Oct. 13. This flight set a new over-water distance record of 2,623 miles.

In 1927. Sherman Fairchild took over the Fulton Motor Truck building at Farmingdale and incorporated the Fairchild Aviation Corp. This company was formed to take over five other companies engaged in aerial photography, map-making, aircraft production, aerial cameras and aircraft engines.

1928

April 1-9. Air Corps Lt. B.R. Dallas and Beckwith Havens, flying in a Loening Amphibian, made the first amphibian flight across the continent, traveling from Long Island to San Diego, 3,300 miles, in 32 hours and 45 minutes.

April 15. Col. Arthur Goebel and Harry J. Tucker, in the Lockheed Vega Yankee Doodle, set an east-west record flying from Roosevelt Field to Los Angeles in 23 hours and 20 minutes. They refueled at Phoenix, Ariz. On Aug. 20, they set a nonstop record of 18 hours, 58 minutes, from the same coastal fields.

May 2-3. Lt. Royal V. Thomas, in the Bellanca monoplane Reliance, made a record solo flight at Mitchel Field of 35 hours, 25 minutes and 8 seconds.

Aug. 22. Elinor Smith set a women's altitude record at Roosevelt Field of 11,663 feet. She flew a Waco biplane, Curtiss OX-5 90-hp. engine.

Oct. 21. Elinor Smith became the first pilot to fly under four East River bridges.

1929

Jan. 30-31. Elinor Smith set a women's world solo endurance record at Roosevelt Field of 14 hours, 30 minutes. She flew a Bird biplane, OX-10 110-hp. engine. On April 24-25, she increased the mark to 26 hours, 20 minutes, at Roosevelt Field. She flew a Bellanca Pacemaker, Wright 225-hp. engine.

Feb. 4-5. Capt. Frank M. Hawks and mechanic Oscar E. Grubb flew a Lockheed nonstop from Los Angeles to Roosevelt Field, setting a west-east record of 18 hours, 21 minutes.

March 27-28. At Roosevelt Field, in a Wright J-5 Bellanca, Martin Jensen set a world record for a solo duration flight of 35 hours, 33 minutes, 20 seconds.

June 27-29. Capt. Frank M. Hawks, in the Lockheed monoplane Air Express, set an east-west record by flying from Roosevelt Field to Los Angeles in 19 hours, 10 minutes, 32 seconds. He returned in 17 hours, 38 minutes.

Sept. 24. Financed by the Guggenheim Fund for the Promotion of Aeronautics, Army pilot James Doolittle, after two years of experimentation, made the first "blind" flight — testing an artificial horizon, a Sperry automatic pilot, a new altimeter, and a new radio direction finder, at Mitchel Field.

Nov. 2. At Curtiss Field, Valley Stream, alumnae of the First Women's Air Derby (1928), held the first meeting of the International Women Pilots Association known as the Ninety-Nines, so named because there were 99 charter members.

Dec. 6. Grumman Aircraft Engineering Corp. was incorporated. During December, Leroy Grumman and Leon (Jake) Swirbul rented a garage in Baldwin to produce floats and other parts for amphibious aircraft. The company recognized Jan. 2, 1930, as its official birthday.

In 1929. Roosevelt Field, Garden City, was incorporated and assumed control of the "old" Curtiss and Roosevelt flying fields.

1930

March 3. Capt. Boris Sergievsky set an altitude record of more than 20,000 feet at North Beach, Queens. He flew a Sikorsky

seaplane powered by two 525-hp. Hornet engines.

March 10. From Roosevelt Field in a Bellanca monoplane, Elinor Smith set a women's altitude record of 27,418 feet.

March 15. At Port Washington, Capt. Frank M. Hawks piloted the first glider released from a seaplane.

April 6. Capt. Frank M. Hawks, piloting a towed glider, The Texaco Eaglet, flew from San Diego to Roosevelt Field, 2,860 miles, in 36 hours, 47 minutes flying time.

May 19. A world record for mass parachute jumping was set at Roosevelt Field when 20 men jumped from a twin-engine Curtiss Condor biplane.

May 27. Col. Roscoe Turner, in a-Wasp powered Lockheed Vega, set an east-west flight record, Long Island to Los Angeles, in 18 hours 43 minutes.

Aug. 6. From Curtiss Field, Capt. Frank M. Hawks flew his Travelair, a low-wing monoplane, to Los Angeles in 14 hours, 50 minutes, 43 seconds, to set an east-west record. On Aug. 13, he set a west-east record, flying from Los Angeles to Curtiss Field in 12 hours, 25 minutes, 3 seconds.

Oct. 8. Laura Ingalls piloted a DeHavilland Moth biplane, powered by a four-cylinder Wright Gypsy engine, to a women's east-west record when she flew from Roosevelt Field to Grand Central Airport in California in 30 hours and 27 minutes.

1931

March 28: The Navy issued a contract for the Grumman Aircraft fighter XFF-1, the company's first fighter.

April 10. Elinor Smith, in a Bellanca Skyrocket, from Roosevelt Field, reached an unofficial women's altitude record of 32,500 feet over New York City.

June 23-July 1. Wiley Post and Harold Gatty left Roosevelt Field in a Lockheed Vega monoplane, the Winnie Mae. After 8 days, 15 hours and 51 minutes, including several stops, they circled the world, covering 15,128 miles.

In 1931. Alexander P. de Seversky founded the Seversky Aircraft Co. at Farmingdale. It was incorporated and produced the XPBS-1, a four-engine patrol boat, for the Navy. The company announced that it would design the fastest fighter in the world for the Army Air Corps.

Also, Floyd Bennett Field, New York's first municipal airport, opened on the south shore of Brooklyn. Its proximity to Manhattan drew activity from Roosevelt Field. Within a decade, however, the Brooklyn airport's importance was diminished when LaGuardia Field opened to commercial traffic in 1939.

1932

July 5. James Mattern and Lt. Bennett Griffin left Floyd Bennett Field in the Lockheed Vega monoplane Century of Progress. After 29 hours and 31 minutes over 4,106 miles, they landed in Berlin. This was the first successful nonstop flight from New York to Berlin.

Sept. 19-30. Pilots James Herman Banning and Thomas C. Allen flew a 4-year-old plane powered by a 14-year-old Army surplus engine from Los Angeles to Curtiss Field in Valley Stream, becoming the first black pilots to fly coast to coast. They said their flight had no scientific aim, but was done to achieve a milestone for black Americans. Calling themselves "hobo pilots," they left with less than $100 between them but stopped in cities where friends donated food and fuel.

Nov. 14. Col. Roscoe Turner, flying a Wedell-Williams aircraft, set an east-west record by flying from Floyd Bennett Field to Burbank, Calif., in 12 hours, 17 minutes, including two stops.

1933

June 2. Capt. Frank M. Hawks established a west-east nonstop record of 13 hours, 26 minutes, from Los Angeles to Floyd Bennett Field.

July 22. Wiley Post in the Winnie Mae landed at Floyd Bennett Field after circling the world in 7 days, 18 hours, 49 minutes.

Sept. 25. Col. Roscoe Turner, in a Wasp-powered Wedell-Williams plane, set a west-east record of 10 hours, 5 minutes, 30 seconds in a flight from Burbank, Calif. to Floyd Bennett Field.

Oct. 8-9. Two hundred thousand people attended the Charity Air Pageant held at Roosevelt Field. Edna Marvel Gardner, in a Waco airplane, won the women's open race; Cecil (Teddy) Kenyon won the women's amateur contest, William Zelar won the men's division. A delayed parachute jump from 11,000 feet was made by Clem Sohn.

Oct. 9. Maj. Alexander P. de Seversky, in his SV-1 amphibian, powered by a Wright engine, set a world speed record for the aircraft of 180.3 mph at Roosevelt Field.

Oct. 13. At Roosevelt Field, 200,000 people watched James R. Wedell capture a $2,500 prize for piloting his Wedell-Williams monoplane at an average speed of 302 mph.

Nov. 19. James R. Wedell, in his Wedell-Williams monoplane powered by an 800-hp. Pratt & Whitney Wasp engine, set a speed record of 5 hours, 1 minute, 39 seconds between Floyd Bennett Field and Miami, Fla.

1934

Aug. 1. The Sikorsky S-42 Flying Boat (Clipper), while flying over Long Island, broke eight world records. Capt. Boris Sergievsky piloted the S-42. The plane averaged 160.4, 155.2, 156.1 and 158.1 mph on its four laps over a 311-mile course. Crew members were Edwin Musick and Charles A. Lindbergh.

Sept. 1. Col. Roscoe Turner set a west-east record and won the Bendix Trophy Race by flying from Burbank, Calif. to Floyd Bennett Field in 10 hours and 3 minutes.

1935

In 1935. During early winter, many Long Island aviators dropped food to birds marooned by heavy snows in the wild fowl sanctuary at Jones Beach State Park.

1936

April 21. Howard R. Hughes, in a Northrop Gamma monoplane, Wright Cyclone engine, flew from Miami, Fla., to Floyd Bennett Field, 1,087 miles, in 4 hours, 21 minutes.

1937

Aug. 25. New York Mayor Fiorello LaGuardia announced the $1.3 million purchase of North Beach Municipal Airport in Flushing from the Curtiss-Wright Corp. The site would be used for construction of a large modern airport.

Dec. 4. A small low-wing monoplane ran wild for 30 minutes at Floyd Bennett Field. The pilotless plane taxied, uncontrolled, up and down runways and aprons at 35 mph. The plane was lassoed by police and field attendants.

Dec. 7. Jane Shattuck Topping piloted a Barkley-Grow twin-engine, low-wing metal monoplane on a record 2-hour, 20-minute flight from Detroit to Roosevelt Field, a 500-mile distance. The flight averaged 230 mph.

1938

May 12. To demonstrate the range of Boeing B-17 bombers, three of these aircraft took off from Mitchel Field to intercept the Italian Liner Rex 700 miles at sea. The pilots were Maj. Vincent Meloy (carrying the lead navigator, then 1st Lt. Curtiss LeMay), Capt. C. Cousland and Capt. A. Y. Smith.

May 15. Rear Adm. Richard E. Byrd dedicated the newly built Babylon Seaplane Base.

July 11-14. Howard Hughes and four companions set an around-the-world record of 3 days, 19 hours, 8 minutes, 10 seconds in a twin-engine Lockheed No. 14 monoplane called the New York World's Fair 1939. They flew from Floyd Bennett Field, via Paris, Moscow, Omsk, Yakutsk, Fairbanks and Minneapolis, 15,432 miles.

July 17-18. Douglas (Wrong-Way) Corrigan, in his eight-year-old $900 Curtiss Robin, a J-6 monoplane, flew non-stop from Floyd Bennett Field to Dublin, Ireland in 28 hours

and 13 minutes. He had filed a flight plan for California, though he was known to have wanted to make a transatlantic flight. He maintained he had misread his instruments.

In 1938. Seversky Aircraft Corp. was reorganized under the name of the Republic Aviation Corp. at Farmingdale.

1939

Feb. 11. Lt. Ben S. Kelsey of the Army Air Corps made a non-stop flight in a Lockheed XP-38 pursuit plane, from March Field, Calif., to Mitchel Field in 7 hours, 45 minutes, 36 seconds. The 2,424 miles were flown at an average speed of 312.5 mph. Kelsey crash-landed at Mitchel. While Kelsey was slightly injured, the aircraft was demolished. Gen. H. Arnold, chief of the Army Air Corps, directed that henceforth all experimental models must be made in pairs.

May 20. On the 12th anniversary of the Lindbergh flight, a Pan American Airways Boeing flying boat took off from Manhasset Bay to launch transatlantic commercial flying. Arthur E. LaPorte was the pilot. (There were no paying passengers aboard. Requirements specified that five mail-carrying flights be completed before passengers could be carried.)

July 10. Howard Hughes, in a specially built Lockheed monoplane, two 1100-hp. Wright Cyclone engines, left Floyd Bennett Field on an around-the-world flight. He landed at Floyd Bennett Field on July 14, 3 days and 19 hours later.

Aug. 1. Maj. S. M. Umstead, Capt. L. F. Harman, with Mark Koogler and L.S. Sibisky as passengers, in a B-17B, established international speed records by flying from Los Angeles to Mitchel Field with average speed of 265.382 mph.

Sept. 1. With the German invasion of Poland, Nassau County police placed a 24-hour guard around Port Washington harbor because British aircraft were using facilities there.

Dec. 2. The new municipal airport at North Beach, Flushing, was opened by New York City. Soon it would be named LaGuardia Field.

1940

Feb. 26. The U.S. War Department established the Air Defense Command at Mitchel Field to integrate U.S. defenses against an enemy air attack.

June 21. With World War II taking shape, the first air delivery of fighting planes from America to British territory was made when 55 Northrop A-17A attack bombers were flown from Mitchel Field to Halifax, Nova Scotia.

1941

In 1941. Grumman Aircraft completed the construction of its new plant in Bethpage and produced 426 planes for the Navy, including models of the JRF Goose, the folding-wing F4F Wildcat, the J4F Widgeon, and the J2F Duck.

The Republic Aviation Corp. produced 50 AT-12s, a 1,050-hp. R-1830-45 engine, advance-trainer, low-wing monoplane, which was known as the Guardsman. This airplane had been built for Sweden as the 2PA fighter bomber. Early in World War II, exports were not permitted and these were acquired by the U.S. Army.

Republic received an initial order for 773 P-47B (and P-47C with improved engine mount), fighters. The P-47 was in continual production throughout World War II.

1942

In 1942. Grumman Aircraft built F-4F Wildcat, TBF Avenger, J-4F Widgeon, J-2F Duck, J-RF Goose, F-6F Hellcat military airplanes. It also operated sub-assembly plants in Amityville, Babylon, Lindenhurst, Port Washington and Syosset.

Also, the federal government established an airfield (later MacArthur Airport) as a "defense landing area," in Ronkonkoma. After World War II, the Town of Islip took over the facility; airline service began in the 1960s.

1943

Feb. 22. From Port Washington, the Pan American Airways' Yankee Clipper, after a transatlantic crossing, made a crash landing at Lisbon, Portugal. Twenty-five persons were killed.

April 6. Fifty women were to complete the eight-week engineering course for training as aides for Grumman Aircraft at the Freeport State Aviation School.

April 8. A tuition-free course in aeronautical engineering, principally designed to train women as aides at Grumman Aircraft, began at Columbia Uniterity.

Sept. 11. Suffolk County's Board of Supervisors added 45 acres to the Army's defense landing field, then under construction (later MacArthur Airport).

Dec. 2. The New York City Planning Commission increased the construction budget for Idlewild Airport at Jamaica Bay by $5.5 million to $12.6 million.

Dec. 20. At Floyd Bennett Field, the Coast Guard reported experiments using a helicopter as an ambulance. In demonstrations in 1944, a stretcher was attached to the side of the fuselage and landings were made at the steps of the dispensary.

In 1943. Grumman Aircraft developed the F-7F Tigercat as the latest of its Navy fighters.

1944

Aug. 11. An electric powered rescue hoist was installed on a helicopter at the Coast Guard station at Floyd Bennett Field. In a test over Jamaica Bay, the guard demonstrated the feasibility of rescuing people from the water. As a result, the guard installed hoists in helicopters for such situations.

In 1944. Grumman Aircraft produced 6,139 Hellcats, 65 F-7F Tigercats, 77 Goose amphibians, and 44 J-4F Widgeons for the Navy and Coast Guard.

Republic continued production on orders for 3,743 P-47D-RE's. The firm also built 130 P-47M models, a fighter-bomber. Republic also received an order for 1,667 P-47N-RE models.

Brewster Aeronautical Corp., Long Island City, built 599 F-3A Vought Corsair fighters and 35 Sb-2A Bermuda dive bombers.

1945

July 28. A B-25 medium bomber took off from LaGuardia Field and crashed into the Empire State Building. The pilot, Lt. Col. William F. Smith Jr., and his crew were killed.

In 1945. Republic Aviation fulfilled its final contract for P-47 fighters with the delivery of the 15,329th Thunderbolt. The company announced that it would begin work on two commercial aircraft, the Rainbow transport and the amphibian Seabee. Republic had orders to build 100 P-72-RE "buzz-bomb-interceptors," and six were under construction when the order was cancelled. After the Japanese surrender, orders for 5,934 P-47 models canceled. Republic received an order for three XP-84 fighters. The XP-84 was a straight-wing, jet-powered successor to the P-47. This aircraft, the prototype, was powered with a General Electric J-35 engine and three were built. It would be known as the Thunderjet.

Also, Grumman Aircraft also had many unfilled orders cancelled. Too late for the war, Grumman unveiled the F-8F Bearcat Navy fighter, powered with a 2,500-hp. Pratt & Whitney engine. The firm said it had produced 4,038 military aircraft during the war. Grumman also began postwar production of the Widgeon amphibian.

1946

In 1946. The Brewster Aeronautical Corp., which made WWII warplanes at Long Island City, was closed.

Fairchild Engine and Aeroplane Corp., Farmingdale, received a preliminary contract for the development of a new engine utilizing atomic power.

1947

In 1947. Under a lease with New York City extending to 1997, the Port Authority of New York began to develop and operate LaGuardia Airport and New York International Airport, also known as Idlewild.

1948

July 1. New York International Airport officially opened at Jamaica Bay. On July 31, it was dedicated by President Harry Truman and Gov. Thomas Dewey. Its initial size of 1,100 acres later grew to 4,930.

1949

Feb. 5. An Eastern Airlines' Lockheed constellation set an airliner transcontinental record by flying from Los Angeles to LaGuardia Field in 6 hours, 17 minutes, 39 seconds.

Oct. 8. Marking the 50th anniversary of Nassau County, officials presented a plaque at Roosevelt Field that said, in part, "To these, Long Island's pioneers of aviation, the people of Nassau County pay tribute during this Golden Jubilee celebration for having given so much of their time and their efforts toward making Long Island the Cradle of American Aviation in a very real sense."

In 1949. Mitchel Field was relieved of responsibility of the air defense of New York City because of the danger involved in operating tactical aircraft over the growing residential areas nearby. Its mission became training.

1950

Jan. 22. Paul Mantz piloted a North American F-51 Mustang to a transcontinental record of 4 hours, 52 minutes, 58 seconds from Burbank, Calif., to LaGuardia Field.

In August. Roosevelt Field, the scene of many historic flights, was acquired by the firm of Webb and Knapp for development as a real estate subdivision.

In 1950. New York International Airport served 394,344 passengers, and LaGuardia Airport served 3.6 million, the Port Authority said.

1951

May 31. A white "X" — 20 inches wide, 20 feet long — was painted on the main runway at Roosevelt Field, signifying that the field was closed to aircraft. J. Nelson Kelly, Roosevelt Field's first operations manager, made the last official takeoff from the field. On Oct. 10, a "Flying Bloodmobile," made a landing and takeoff to publicize the need for blood donors for Korean War wounded.

In 1951. Republic Aviation, in an effort to alleviate skilled manpower shortages, established training centers at Farmingdale, Freeport, Huntington and Hempstead. To accommodate the Korean War effort, additional manufacturing facilities were established at Port Washington, Greenlawn and Montauk Point. Republic received orders for 2,711 of the F-84F (235 of these were manufactured by General Motors). Production continued through 1952, 1953 and 1954. Republic also produced the F-84G, fitted with nuclear weapons capability, automatic pilot and in-flight refueling. A total of 3,025 (including 1952, 1953 and 1954) were ordered.

1952

May 2. From New York International, Pan American Airways flew 95 people to Shannon, Ireland — the most commercial passengers ever to fly the Atlantic Ocean in one plane.

1953

In March. Republic Aviation Corp., Farmingdale, delivered the 4,000th F-84 Thunderjet to the Air Force.

In 1953. The Navy built a $22 million plant and test field for Grumman Aircraft on a 4,500-acre site on the Peconic River, Calverton.

1954

March 29. Capt. Joseph B. Glass piloted an American Airlines

DC-7, powered by four 3,250-hp. Wright Turbo Compound engines, on a record nonstop flight of 6 hours, 10 minutes, from Los Angeles to New York International Airport, 2,469 miles. The plane carried 39 passengers and averaged 405 mph.

March 31. Joe De Bona piloted a North American F-51C pistol aircraft on a record 4-hour, 24-minute, 17-second flight from Los Angeles to New York International Airport, 2,469 miles. The average speed was 560 mph.

In 1954. Republic Aviation opened a 31,500-square-foot plant in Hicksville to accommodate the firm's guided missile and plastics activities. Also, Republic won a contract to develop the F-105 Thunderchief for the Air Force; 833 were produced from 1959 through 1965.

1955

June 29. Fairchild Engine Division announced it planned to shut down its Mineola plant in July upon completion of a $40 million contract with the Atomic Energy Commission.

In July. Grumman Aircraft marked its silver anniversary. In 1955, the company turned out its 23,000th aircraft, its 2,500th jet fighter, and its 400th amphibian. Production continued on the F-11F-1 Tiger and the F-9F-8 Cougar jet fighters, the SA-16A Albatross, and the S2F-2 antisubmarine aircraft.

1956

June 28. Republic Aviation disclosed it was working on two guided-missile systems, including one "that can be considered more advanced than the Earth satellite."

Sept. 21. A Grumman F-11F-1 Tiger, piloted by Grumman test pilot Tom Attridge, shot itself down while conducting test firings off eastern Long Island by running into 20-mm. projectiles it had fired only seconds before.

1957

Feb. 1. A Northeast Airlines DC-6A crashed on Rikers Island within a minute after takeoff from LaGuardia Airport. Twenty people died.

July 16. An F-8U-1P Crusader, piloted by Marine Maj. John H. Glenn Jr., set a transcontinental speed record with a crossing from Los Alamitos, Calif., to Floyd Bennett Field, 2,456 miles, in 3 hours, 23 minutes, 8 seconds at an average speed of 725 mph. This was the first upper-atmosphere supersonic flight from the West Coast to the East Coast.

Nov. 27. A new transcontinental military speed record of 2,445 miles in 3 hours, 5 minutes and 39 seconds was set by an RF-101C Voodoo from Los Angeles to Floyd Bennett Field.

In 1957. The International Arrivals Building and airline wing buildings opened at New York International Airport.

1958

January. Grumman Aircraft won an eight-company competition to build the A-6A Intruder aircraft.

June 3. Sperry Gyroscope Co., Lake Success, developed a new, advanced, flight instrument that enabled this country's first manned space plane, the X-15, to return to the Earth's atmosphere without burning up.

Sept. 8. A Pan American Boeing 707 took off from New York International Airport and landed in London, completing the first flight of a U.S. civil jetliner across the Atlantic. Flying time was 7 hours, 28 minutes.

In 1958. Republic Aviation began research on an outer-space orbital re-entry vehicle.

1959

Feb. 3. An American Airlines Electra turboprop airplane carrying 72 passengers crashed into the East River near LaGuardia Airport, killing 65.

March 2. Fairchild Engine and Aerorplane Corp. announced the closing of its Deer Park plant. The plant produced the J-83 engine, no longer required by the Air Force.

Dec. 6. To reduce congestion at LaGuardia Airport, 90 daily flights were diverted to Newark, Boston or New York International Airports. The Port Authority planned a $56 million rehabilitation program for the airport.

1960

Dec. 16. In the worst air disaster in U.S. history, 127 persons aboard planes and six on the ground died when a United DC-8 jet en route to New York International Airport collided with a TWA Super-Constellation over Staten Island.

In 1960. New York International Airport served 8.8 million passengers, and LaGuardia Airport served 4.2 million, the Port Authority said.

1961

April 15. Mitchel Air Force Base closed as an airport.

May 24. Lt. Richard L. Gordon Jr. and Lt. Bobby R. Young flew a McDonald Phantom II, twin-jet fighter from Ontario, Calif., to Floyd Bennett Field, 2,445 miles, in a record 2 hours, 47 minutes. They won the Bendix Cup.

Aug. 12. Ground was broken at MacArthur Airport, Ronkonkoma, for a 60,000-square-foot Federal Aviation Agency air-traffic control center for the New York area.

1962

March 1. An American Airlines 707 jet crashed in Jamaica Bay seconds after takeoff from New York International Airport. All 95 persons aboard were killed, then the highest toll in U.S. history in the crash of a single airplane.

Oct. 5. Sperry Gyroscope Co., Lake Success, announced it was patenting a new gyroscope using liquid instead of a wheel as the spinning element. Sperry said this was the first such gyroscope to operate successfully and to go into production.

Nov. 7. NASA announced that Grumman Aircraft had been selected as the prime contractor for the lunar excursion module.

1963

Sept. 7. As part of Long Island Aviation Day, the $15 million air-traffic control center for the New York area was dedicated at MacArthur Airport, Ronkonkoma.

Dec. 18. New York City Mayor Robert Wagner announced that New York International Airport would be renamed John F. Kennedy International Airport to honor the slain president.

1964

May 15. The Air Force grounded its fleet of more than 500 F-105 Thunderjet warplanes because of recent crashes. Republic Aviation Corp., Farmingdale, halted testing of F-105's.

Sept. 23. Oscar Bakke, regional director of the Federal Aviation Agency, announced that Zahns Airport, Amityville, and the Deer Park Airport, Bay Shore, were in danger of being closed because they were needed for real estate development.

In 1964. A new passenger terminal and control tower opened at LaGuardia Airport, completing a major part of the airport's rehabilitation program. The Port Authority rejected a $4.3 million federal grant to extend LaGuardia's runways.

1965

Feb. 8. An Eastern Airline DC-7B with 84 persons aboard crashed into the ocean off Jones Beach. All 84 persons were killed.

Oct. 18. The Ninety-Nines organization of women fliers organized a Long Island chapter at MacArthur Airport.

In 1965. Republic Aviation was acquired by Fairchild Hiller Corp.

Also, the lease between New York City and the Port Authority for operation of LaGuardia and JFK Airports was extended to 2015.

1966

Aug. 22. An Air Force captain, his wife and their four children were killed when their rented twin-engine Piper Comanche crashed near Lake Ronkonkoma after takeoff from MacArthur Airport.

Dec. 7. Republic Airport, Farmingdale, opened to general aviation after three decades as a test field for warplanes.

In 1966. JFK Airport grew. National Airlines planned a $15 million passenger terminal, Pan Am planned a new freight terminal, and $21 million in airport improvements were announced.

1967

March 16. Gov. Nelson Rockefeller announced a plan to establish a fourth metropolitan area jetport at Calverton. The plan fell apart months later after opposition from the Navy, which owned the field, and its occupant, the Grumman Corp., as well as by some local officials.

1968

Feb. 28. Gov. Nelson Rockefeller announced a sweeping $2.9 billion plan to link the New York area's transportation centers by rail and bus. His proposals included a 20-minute train between Manhattan and JFK Airport, and a merger of Republic and Zahns Airports.

July 15. Aeroflot and Pan Am each began once-a-week, round-trip service between Moscow and JFK Airport. It was the first direct service between Moscow and New York City.

1969

In January. Grumman Aircraft was awarded a contract to build F-14 Tomcat fighters for the Navy.

March. The Metropolitan Transportation Authority acquired Republic Airport, Farmingdale.

July 20. The lunar module built by Grumman Aircraft carried astronauts Neil Armstrong and Edwin Aldrin to a smooth landing on the moon at 4:17 p.m. EDT. At 1:54 p.m. July 21, the module ascended to return them safely to their main capsule.

In 1969. Port Authority commissioners authorized work to begin on a major redevelopment program at JFK Airport.

1970

Jan. 5. American Airlines and TWA delayed the start of non-stop service to Chicago from Islip MacArthur Airport because the airport's runways needed strengthening.

Jan. 21-22. Pan Am began commercial service on the Boeing 747 jumbo jet between JFK Airport and London.

April 13. An explosion aboard Apollo 13 forced the three-man crew to occupy Grumman's lunar module, using it as a "life boat" for a short period so that oxygen could be conserved in the main space capsule that would later return them to Earth.

Dec. 30. Grumman's F-14 crashed short of the runway during its second test flight at Calverton. Two crewmen ejected safely. A flight-control-system problem was cited.

In 1970. In the preceding decade, demand for commercial flights surged. JFK Airport served 19 million passengers, double that in 1960, and LaGuardia Airport served 11.8 million, almost three times the number in 1960, the Port Authority said.

1971

Jan. 15. The Grumman E-2C Hawkeye, an airborne electronic warfare and communications aircraft, had its first flight.

In February. Nassau County Executive Ralph Caso suggested building the metropolitan area's fourth jetport — a "wetport" — on an offshore landfill of solid waste.

In August. The Metropolitan Transportation Authority proposed converting Republic Airport into a transportation hub serving mostly corporate aircraft, with a new railroad terminal, office buildings, parking for 6,000 cars, an electrified rail line to Manhattan and local express bus service.

1972

April 30. After taking heavy financial losses on the F-14, Grumman Corp. lost its bank credit. It regained credit in 1974 from a group of nine U.S. banks.

1974

In July. New tracking equipment was installed at the air traffic control center at Islip, serving JFK, LaGuardia and Newark Airports.

In 1974. Fairchild Republic Corp. produced the first A-10 tank killer. A total of 713 were built from 1975 to 1984.

1975

June 24. 113 persons died when an Eastern Airlines Boeing 727 crashed at the edge of JFK Airport during a thunderstorm. It was New York City's second-worst air disaster.

1976

May 2. A Pan American Airways 747 completed the longest non-stop flight for a commercial aircraft, carrying more than 100 passengers from JFK Airport to New Delhi, India. The flight covered 8,088 miles in 13 hours, 31 minutes, Pan Am said.

1977

Nov. 22. British Airways and Air France Concordes began regular service between Europe and JFK Airports. The Port Authority had tried to block the supersonic planes because of noise concerns. The planes each carried 100 people from London and Paris, respectively, in 3½ hours.

1978

Sept. 7. After 10 years, Pan Am ended its passenger service between Moscow and JFK Airport, and service to nine other European cities as well, to concentrate on higher-demand routes. Aeroflot continued to fly from JFK to Moscow.

1979

May 19. A Cessna 182 crashed into a house in Massapequa, killing the four people aboard and two people asleep in the house.

1980

Feb. 27. The Town of Babylon committed itself to buying the 121-acre Zahns Airport in North Amityville for $2.6 million to make way for the New Horizons Business Center.

In 1980. JFK Airport served 26 million passengers, up 41 percent from 1970, and LaGuardia Airport served 17.4 million, a 48 percent increase, the Port Authority said.

1981

In 1981. Grumman faced a hostile takeover bid from LTV Corp. A U.S. court later rejected LTV's bid.

1982

In 1982. Republic Aviation won a $3 billion contract to build 650 T-46A trainers for the Air Force.

1983

March 31. Lockheed Air Terminal Inc. signed a 5-year deal to manage Republic Airport. The airport had been run at a loss for a decade by the Metropolitan Transportation Authority.

1984

Dec. 14. Grumman's X-29 was successfully tested by test pilot Chuck Sewell of Setauket. The plane was characterized by its forward-swept wings, a 40-year-old concept that could not be put into practice until strong materials were developed to prevent the wings from being torn off at high speed. The X-29 was used by NASA flight research until 1992.

1985

Feb. 11. Republic Aviation rolled out its T-46A trainer.

1986

March 27. The Air Force canceled the T-46A program. Only a handful were built. It was the last aircraft built by Fairchild

Republic. On Oct. 17, Congress cut funds for the jet.

In 1986. Long Island defense employment, chiefly concentrated on aircraft production, hit a peak of 64,400. Although Grumman would employ a recent peak of 23,000 people in 1987, that year saw the start of a sure decline in the area's defense industry jobs.

1987

March 13. Fairchild Republic, a major Long Island defense contractor, announced it would close, leaving 2,800 workers without jobs.

March 27. Newsday reported that the Navy planned to buy only 127 of a planned 304 F-14 Tomcat jets in the 1990s, signaling problems for Grumman.

1988

In 1988. A Long Island Regional Planning Board study projected the loss of 21,600 defense jobs on Long Island in the next 10 years.

Also, the number of commercial passengers at Long Island MacArthur Airport was 1.22 million, a record, and more than double the 546,996 passengers counted in 1983.

1990

Jan. 25. Avianca flight 52, a Boeing 707 bound for JFK Airport, ran out of fuel and crashed at Cove Neck; 73 people died and 85 survived.

May 12. Four people were killed when a four-seat Coast Guard Auxiliary Bellanca Viking aircraft from Republic Airport crashed into the Great South Bay.

In 1990. JFK Airport served 29.7 million passengers, up 11 percent from 1980, and LaGuardia Airport served 22.7 million, a 30 percent increase, the Port Authority said.

1992

March 22. While attempting takeoff at LaGuardia Airport, a USAir twin-engine Fokker F28-4000 plunged into frigid Flushing Bay, killing 27 of 51 people aboard. Investigators said the plane had too much ice on its wings to fly.

1993

Oct. 2. Northwest Airlink made its last flights from Republic Airport, Farmingdale, ending Republic's only regularly scheduled air service at the time.

1994

Jan. 17. With defense spending on the decline, Grumman Corp. said it would close its Calverton aircraft manufacturing plant and eliminate 800 Long Island jobs.

Feb. 28. EDO Corp. of College Point, a maker of aircraft and other defense parts, said it would sell two-thirds of its manufacturing space and eliminate about 100 jobs in Queens.

April 4. Grumman Corp., Long Island's major aircraft maker, agreed to be bought for $2.17 billion by the Northrop Corp.

April 9. A Piper Comanche and a Cessna 152 collided over East Farmingdale, killing all four on board. A federal agency said a Republic Airport traffic controller did not provide proper information to one of the pilots.

Sept. 22. Northrop Grumman Corp. said it would cut 2,500 jobs on Long Island in 1994 and 1,000 in 1995, reducing its Long Island work force to 3,800.

In 1994. The Federal Aviation Administration began operating a new 321-foot-high control tower at JFK Airport.

Also, although people filled planes at Long Island MacArthur Airport, national fare wars caused some carriers to cut service (and costs). Service was uneven in 1994; daily departures fell from 150 to 130 from May to July. After 1988's record 1.22 million passenger count, these sums were reported: 1.08 million in 1989, 1.16 million in 1990, 1.19 million in 1991, 1.2 million in 1992, 1.17 million in 1993, 1.23 million in 1994.

1995

June 26. An E-2C Hawkeye advance-warning and control plane, the last military airplane built on Long Island, took off from the Northrop Grumman Corp. field at Calverton.

July 27. Mayor Rudolph Giuliani said New York City would explore the sale of JFK and LaGuardia Airports to the private sector. By 1999, on a different tack, the city took applications from firms willing to monitor the airports, and then take them over, after the Port Authority's leases expire in 2015.

1996

July 17. TWA Flight 800, a 747 jetliner bound from JFK Airport to Paris, blew up in midair and crashed into the ocean off Long Island, killing all 230 people aboard.

In December. Defense contractor EDO Corp. said it would close its College Point, Queens, plant after 72 years and move operations and 130 employees to the New Horizons Business Center, once site of Zahns Airport in North Amityville.

1997

June 22. Many of 20,000 people at an air show at Gabreski Airport in Westhampton saw two Formula V planes clip wings and crash during a four-plane race. One of the pilots died.

Sept. 3. To cut costs, USAir, the largest carrier at Long Island MacArthur Airport, ended its big-jet service after 37 years at the field. It said it would operate six daily small-plane commuter flights. The same day, the lesser-known AirTran Airways began service from MacArthur to Boston and to Orlando, Fla.

1999

March 14. Southwest Airlines, a major national carrier, began 12 daily flights from Long Island MacArthur Airport. Southwest reinvigorated the airport: In 1999, MacArthur served 1.9 million passengers, up from 905,313 in 1998.

In Fall. Construction began on an 8-mile, $1.9 billion AirTrain elevated rail line along the Van Wyck Expressway to link JFK and LaGuardia Airports. Completion was expected in 2003.

Dec. 3. A charter plane with 138 passengers left JFK Airport for Cuba, the first direct passenger flight leaving New York for Havana since diplomatic ties were severed in 1961. The event was part of the easing of some U.S. sanctions against Cuba.

In 1999. JFK Airport served 31.7 million passengers, up about 7 percent from 1990, and LaGuardia Airport served 23.9 million, up about 6 percent, the Port Authority said.

2000

April 5. President Bill Clinton signed a law to give regional jets with 70 or fewer seats unrestricted access to LaGuardia Airport. The move meant the possible addition of 300 flights a day, raising environmental concerns. The airport already saw an average of 1,000 plans landing and taking off each day.

Aug. 15. Southwest Airlines announced plans to build four new gates at MacArthur Airport by 2001. The airline said using only three of MacArthur's 19 gates for its 19 daily flights made operations difficult. The Town of Islip projected that 2.5 million passengers would use the airport in 2000.

Aug. 23. The National Transportation Safety Board closed its investigation into the 1996 explosion of TWA Flight 800, the most comprehensive probe in U.S. aviation history. The board found that the 747 crash was caused by "an explosion of the center wing tank resulting from ignition of the flammable fuel / air mixture in the tank." The board did not name an ignition source. Damaged wiring was a suspected source of a spark. Investigators ruled out theories involving a missile, bomb or structural failure.

In 2000. Looking ahead, the Port Authority projected that 42.5 million passengers would use JFK Airport in the year 2010, and 28 million would use LaGuardia. •

PHOTO CREDITS

Foreword: Page ii: Henry A. Liese Collection; Page v: Photo by Ginny DeMille

Chapter 1: Page x: Culver Pictures Inc.; Page 2: Cradle of Aviation Museum; Page 3: Cradle of Aviation Museum; Page 4: Cradle of Aviation Museum; Page 5: National Archives; Page 6: Culver Pictures Inc.; Page 9: Culver Pictures Inc.; Page 10: Henry A. Liese Collection.

Chapter 2: Page 12: Henry A. Liese Collection; Page 14: (Quimby) Brown Brothers, (Quimby and Moisant) Smithsonian Institution Aerospace Museum; Page 15: Brown Brothers; Page 16: (Blériot) Henry A. Liese Collection, (Raiche) Smithsonian Institution; Page 17: (Quimby) Brown Brothers, (Airplane) Bettmann / CORBIS; Page 19: Cradle of Aviation Museum; Page 20: Brown Brothers; Page 21: Brown Brothers; Page 22: Cradle of Aviation Museum; Page 25: both, Brown Brothers

Gallery 1: Page 26: Nassau County Division of Museum Services, Long Island Studies Institute at Hofstra University; Page 27: (Rubber Cow) Cradle of Aviation Museum photo by Frederick T. Weber, (Pusher) Nassau County Division of Museum Services, Long Island Studies Institute at Hofstra University; Page 28: (Takeoff) N.Y. Daily News, (Chamberlin) AP Photo, (Havens) Newsday Archive; Page 29: both, Nassau County Division of Museum Services, Long Island Studies Institute at Hofstra University; Page 30: Frank Strnad Collection; Page 31: (Ninety-Nines) Cradle of Aviation Museum, (Gillies) Ninety-Nines Museum of Women Pilots, Oklahoma City, Okla.; Page 32: (Stuart) Frank Strnad Collection, (Bellanca) Cradle of Aviation Museum; Page 33: both, Cradle of Aviation Museum; Page 34: both, Cradle of Aviation Museum; Page 35: (Matilda Moisant) Smithsonian Institution Aerospace Museum, (John Moisant) Nassau County Division of Museum Services, Long Island Studies Institute at Hofstra University, (Jerwan) Henry A. Liese Collection; Page 36: (Turner) Cradle of Aviation Museum, (Coleman) Nassau County Division of Museum Services, Long Island Studies Institute at Hofstra University; Page 37: National Archives; Page 38: (DeSeversky) Newsday Archives, (Patterson) Cradle of Aviation Museum; Page 39: (Newkirke) Cradle of Aviation Museum, (Gabreski) National Archives

Chapter 3: Page 40: Cradle of Aviation Museum; Page 42: Cradle of Aviation Museum, Page 43: Cradle of Aviation Museum; Page 45: Cradle of Aviation Museum; Page 47: (Walden) Cradle of Aviation Museum, (License) Cradle of Aviation Museum; Page 49: Cradle of Aviation Museum

Chapter 4: Page 52: Underwood Photo Archives, SF; Page 54: Nassau County Division of Museum Services, Long Island Studies Institute at Hofstra University; Page 55: Underwood Photo Archives, SF; Page 56: Cradle of Aviation Museum; Page 59: Underwood Photo Archives, SF; Page 61: Underwood Photo Archives, SF; Page 62: Culver Pictures Inc., Inc.; Page 63: Frank Strnad Collection; Page 64: Underwood Photo Archives, SF

Gallery 2: Page 66: Henry A. Liese Collection; Page 67: (Burnelli) Cradle of Aviation Museum, (Boland) Nassau County Division of Museum Services, Long Island Studies Institute at Hofstra University; Page 68: (Kaplan) Frank Strnad Collection, (Marchetti) Cradle of Aviation Museum; Page 69: (Cootie) Frank Strnad Collection, (Geary) Henry A. Liese Collection; Page 70: (Spencer) Culver Pictures Inc., (Huntington) Frank Strnad Collection; Page 71: (Fairchild) The Daniel Pflug Collection, (paraplane) Frank Strnad Collection; Page 72: (Dixie Clipper) Pan American Airways, (Bermuda Clipper) Frank Strnad Collection; Page 73: (Curtiss) Cradle of Aviation Museum, (amphibian) Frank Strnad Collection; Page 74: (Fity) Nassau County Division of Museum Services, Long Island Studies Institute at Hofstra University; Page 75: both, Henry A. Liese Collection

Chapter 5: Page 76: Underwood & Underwood/CORBIS; Page 78: Henry A. Liese Collection; Page 81: Underwood & Underwood/CORBIS; Page 82: Underwood & Underwood/CORBIS; Page 83: Underwood & Underwood / CORBIS; Page 84: Newsday Photo by Bill Davis

Chapter 6: Page 86: Rizzo Family Photo; Page 89: Newsday Photo by Michael Ach; Page 91: Cradle of Aviation Museum; Page 92: Rizzo Family Photo; Page 94: Rizzo Family Photos; Page 96: Rizzo Family Photos; Page 98: Photo by Dick Milligan

Gallery 3: Page 100: Henry A. Liese Collection; Page 101: both, Cradle of Aviation Museum; Page 102: (Hilliard) Henry A. Liese Collection, (Jenny) Cradle of Aviation Museum; Page 103: both, Cradle of Aviation Museum; Page 104: (S-35) United Press International, (crash) Nassau County Division of Museum Services, Long Island Studies Institute at Hofstra University; Page 105: both, Cradle of Aviation Museum; Page 106: (Thunderjet) Newsday Photo by Cliff DeBear, (Mustang) Newsday Photo by Harvey Weber; Page 107: (C-123) Cradle of Aviation Museum, (DC-3) Newsday Photo by Ike Eichorn

Chapter 7: Page 108: Northrop Grumman; Page 110: Northrop Grumman; Page 111: Northrop Grumman; Page 112: all, Northrop Grumman; Page 113: Northrop Grumman; Page 115: Northrop Grumman; Page 116: Northrop Grumman; Page 117: Northrop Grumman; Page 118: all Northrop Grumman; Page 119: Northrop Grumman

Chapter 8: Page 120: Northrop Grumman; Page 122: Newsday Archive; Page 123: Northrop Grumman; Page 125: Frank Strnad Collection; Page 126: Northrop Grumman; Page 127: Northrop Grumman photo by Allen Gould

Gallery 4: Page 130: Cradle of Aviation Museum; Page 131: (balloon) Cradle of Aviation Museum, (R-34) United Press International; Page 132: (airship) Cradle of Aviation Museum, (Elder) Bettmann; Page 133: (Sheepshead Bay) Cradle of Aviation Museum, (poster) Frank Strnad Collection; Page 134: both, Brown Brothers; Page 135: both, Cradle of Aviation Museum; Page 136: Henry A. Liese Collection; Page 137: both, Henry A. Liese Collection; Page 138: Newsday Archive; Page 139: (Byrd, Chamberlin) Cradle of Aviation Museum; (plane) Newsday Archive; Page 140: (Paris) AP Photo; (Roosevelt Field) UPI/Bettmann; Page 141: (police) Nassau County Division of Museum Services, Long Island Studies Institute at Hofstra University; (Broadway) Newsday Archive

Chapter 9: Page 142: Cynde Goodwin Collection; Page 144: Northrop Grumman; Page 145: Northrop Grumman; Page 146: (Sewell) Cynde Goodwin Collection, (landing gear) Northrop Grumman; Page 147: The Northrop Grumman; Page 149: Northrop Grumman; Page 150: Newsday Photo by Ken Spencer; Page 151: Cynde Goodwin Collection; Page 152: Northrop Grumman; Page 153: (crash) Bettmann/CORBIS, (Avenger) Cynde Goodwin Collection, (F-14) Cynde Goodwin Collection

Chapter 10: Page 154: Newsday Photo by Bill Davis; Page 156: The Tom Kelly Collection; Page 157: Northrop Grumman; Page 158: Northrop Grumman; Page 160: (Kelly) Newsday Photo by Bill Davis, (module) Cradle of Aviation Museum; Page 163: NASA; Page 164: Newsday Photo by Bill Senft; Page 167: (module) Newsday Photo by Daniel Goodrich, (Kelly) Newsday Photo by Don Jacobsen

Gallery 5: Page 168: Henry A. Liese Collection; Page 169: (Belmont Park) Nassau County Division of Museum Services, Long Island Studies Institute at Hofstra University, (Garros) Newsday Archive; Page 170: (Antoinette) Culver Pictures Inc., (racetrack) Frank Strnad Collection; Page 171: (Johnston) Nassau County Division of Museum Services, Long Island Studies Institute at Hofstra University, (Wrights) Henry A. Liese Collection; Page 172: both, Henry A. Liese Collection; Page 173: both, Bay Shore Historical Society; Page 174: (squadron) Nassau County Division of Museum Services, Long Island Studies Institute at Hofstra University, (Sperry) Frank Strnad Collection; Page 175: both, Newsday Archive; Page 176: (Wright) Frank Strnad Collection, (engine) Nassau County Division of Museum Services, Long Island Studies Institute at Hofstra University, (Dart) Nassau County Division of Museum Services, Long Island Studies Institute at Hofstra University; Page 177: (Bushmeyer) Cradle of Aviation Museum, (bombers) Nassau County Division of Museum Services, Long Island Studies Institute at Hofstra University; Page 178: (Condor) Cradle of Aviation Museum, (Lear and Hughes) Frank Strnad Collection; Page 179: both, Cradle of Aviation Museum; Page 180: (Curtiss Field) Frank Strnad Collection, (cars) Culver Pictures Inc.; Page 181: (aerial view) Newsday Archive, (airport) Cradle of Aviation Museum; Page 182: (B-25) Cradle of Aviation Museum, (soldiers) Newsday Archive; Page 183: (country club) Frank Strnad Collection, (women) Cradle of Aviation Museum; Page 184: both, Cradle of Aviation Museum; Page 185: (Terminal City) Port Authority of New York and New Jersey, (Republic) Frank Strnad Collection

Chapter 11: Page 186: George Dade Collection; Page 189: George Dade Collection; Page 190: George Dade Collection; Page 193: George Dade Collection; Page 195: Newsday Photo by Bill Davis; Page 197: (with map) Newsday Photo by Bill Davis, (with Kregel) Photo by Anthony Lopez

CONTRIBUTORS

David Behrens, a Newsday feature writer, is co-author of "The Child in Crisis" and was a member of a Newsday team that won a Pulitzer Prize in 1974 for a series called "The Heroin Trail."

George DeWan is Newsday's Long Island history writer and was a lead reporter for the newspaper's "Long Island: Our Story" series.

Philip Dionisio is Newsday's graphics director and a private pilot.

Michael Dorman, a Newsday editor, is the author of 17 books.

Drew Fetherston is a Newsday writer and the author of "The Chunnel" and "Greed."

James Kindall, a former Newsday feature writer, is working on a novel.

Laura Muha is a free-lance writer and a contributing editor of Biography magazine.

Lauren Terrazzano, a Newsday writer, was a member of the paper's Pulitzer Prize-winning team that covered the crash of TWA Flight 800 in 1996.

ACKNOWLEDGMENTS

Newsday wishes to thank the librarians and historians whose dedication to preserving Long Island's past made this book possible. In addition, we express special thanks to these people and organizations for their assistance: the Cradle of Aviation Museum in Garden City, N.Y., curator Joshua Stoff and assistant curator Rebecca Looney; the Museum Services Division of the Nassau County Department of Recreation and Parks, director Dale Bennett, Mildred Murphy DeRiggi, Nassau County site director of the Long Island Studies Institute, and Gary R. Hammond, assistant site director and a research consultant on this book; Henry A. Liese, collector, for access to his photo collection; Helen Strnad, for access to the photo collection of her late husband, Frank Strnad; Mike Hlinko, a Northrop Grumman history center volunteer, for his photo research; Richard Milligan, a retired Grumman employee, for his assistance in securing photos.

STAFF

Harvey Aronson, editor; Phyllis Singer, executive editor; Lawrence Striegel, news editor; Jeffrey Schamberry, photo editor; Robert Eisner, cover and book design; James Stephen Smith, layout editor; Kevin Amorim, Robert Kahn, Richard L. Wiltamuth, copy editors; Andreas Constantinou, Lorina Capitulo, photo staff; Marcia Ratcliff, James Bernstein, Georgina Martorella, Laura Mann, historical research; Kathryn Sweeney, photo research; Marilyn Sacrestano, Mary Wyman, marketing; Julian Stein, production; James Leo, Kim DeManuel, Nicholas Guidice, Elizabeth Williams, photo preparation; Ina Gravitz, indexer.

BIBLIOGRAPHY

Works that were helpful in compiling photo galleries and moments in Long Island aviation included:

Dade, George C., and Strnad, Frank, "Picture History of Aviation on Long Island, 1908-1938," Dover Publications Inc., 1989.

DiScala, Raymond V., and Kaiser, William K., "The Development of the Aerospace Industry on Long Island: A Chronology, 1833-1965," Hofstra University Yearbook of Business, 1968.

Lindbergh, Charles A., "The Spirit of St. Louis," Charles Scribner's Sons, 1953.

Stoff, Joshua, "The Aerospace Heritage of Long Island," Long Island Studies Institute, Heart of the Lakes Publishing, 1989.

Stoff, Joshua, "Picture History of Early Aviation, 1903-1913," Dover Publications Inc., 1996.

Thruelsen, Richard, "The Grumman Story," the Grumman Corp., Praeger Publishers, 1976.

Reaching for the Stars

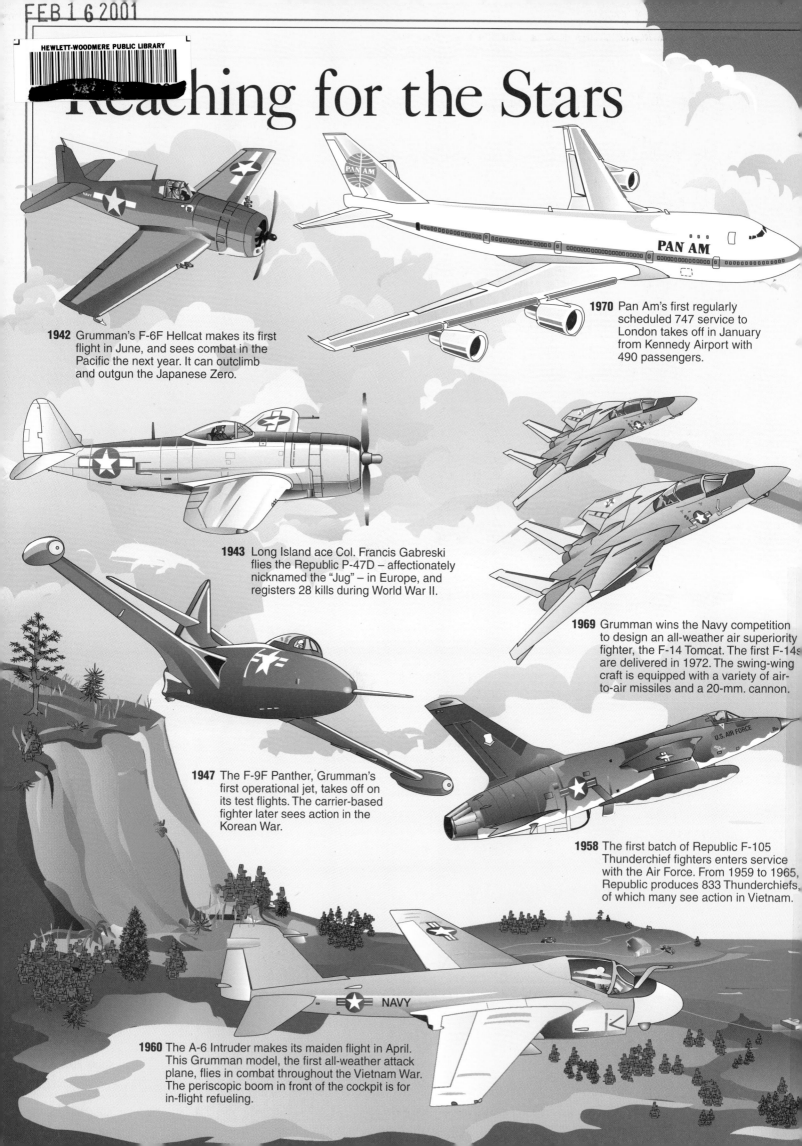

1942 Grumman's F-6F Hellcat makes its first flight in June, and sees combat in the Pacific the next year. It can outclimb and outgun the Japanese Zero.

1970 Pan Am's first regularly scheduled 747 service to London takes off in January from Kennedy Airport with 490 passengers.

1943 Long Island ace Col. Francis Gabreski flies the Republic P-47D – affectionately nicknamed the "Jug" – in Europe, and registers 28 kills during World War II.

1969 Grumman wins the Navy competition to design an all-weather air superiority fighter, the F-14 Tomcat. The first F-14s are delivered in 1972. The swing-wing craft is equipped with a variety of air-to-air missiles and a 20-mm. cannon.

1947 The F-9F Panther, Grumman's first operational jet, takes off on its test flights. The carrier-based fighter later sees action in the Korean War.

1958 The first batch of Republic F-105 Thunderchief fighters enters service with the Air Force. From 1959 to 1965, Republic produces 833 Thunderchiefs, of which many see action in Vietnam.

1960 The A-6 Intruder makes its maiden flight in April. This Grumman model, the first all-weather attack plane, flies in combat throughout the Vietnam War. The periscopic boom in front of the cockpit is for in-flight refueling.